CURRICULUM OPPORTUNITIES IN A MULTICULTURAL SOCIETY

Alma Craft and *Geoff Bardell*
(Editors)

Harper & Row, Publishers
London

Cambridge
Hagerstown
Philadelphia
New York

San Francisco
Mexico City
Sao Paulo
Sydney

First published 1984
All rights reserved
Harper & Row Ltd
28 Tavistock Street
London WC2E 7PN

British Library Cataloguing in Publication Data

Curriculum opportunities in a multicultural society.
  1. Education—Great Britain—Curricula
  2. Children of minorities—Education—Great Britain
  1. Craft, Alma   II. Bardell, Geoff
  375′.0082′0941   LB1564.G7

ISBN 0–06–318285–8

Typeset by Inforum Ltd, Portsmouth
Printed and bound by
Butler & Tanner Ltd, Frome and London

CONTENTS

ACKNOWLEDGEMENTS

This book has grown out of our involvement in the Schools Council programme of work in multicultural education, and in particular from the project on 'Assessment in a Multicultural Society'. Seven of our contributors had already written discussion documents for the assessment project which considered ways in which subject-specific examinations at 16+ might develop a multicultural perspective. These are published for the Schools Council by Longman, York in the Council's Programme Pamphlet Series. For this book, they have each extended their ideas to write more generally about multicultural curriculum development in their respective subjects. We are most grateful to the Schools Council for allowing the authors to draw upon their assessment project reports.

We would also like to thank all fourteen contributors for their patience and courtesy in responding to our comments and suggestions. We feel sure that their commitment and concern to make a practical contribution to the multicultural education of all pupils will prove helpful to the many teachers now seeking to respond to cultural diversity.

Finally, we would like to thank Marianne Lagrange of Harper and Row who first initiated the idea of a book of this kind, Audrey Honeyman for her tireless and conscientious typing of a complex manuscript, and Maurice Craft and Ewa Bardell for continuous support, advice and encouragement.

Schools Council
November 1983

Alma Craft
Geoff Bardell

CONTRIBUTORS

GEOFF BARDELL, Principal Research Officer at the Schools Council, has worked as a teacher and for the Welsh Joint Education Committee. He is co-author of *Examining in a Multicultural Society*, and Lead Officer for the Council's *Assessment in a Multicultural Society* project.

JEAN BLEACH, Director of the ILEA project, *Second Language Learners in the Mainstream Curriculum*, was previously Coordinator of the Schools Council *Language for Learning* project. She taught English in London inner-city schools for fourteen years, the last five as Head of English at Langdon Park School, Poplar.

JOHN BROADBENT, who has experience in teaching French, German, Urdu and English at secondary school level, now works for the Language Service in the London Borough of Brent. He has contributed a chapter to *Minority Community Languages in School* (NCLE/CILT).

ALMA CRAFT, Coordinator for Multicultural Education at the Schools Council, has undertaken research into the education of ethnic minority pupils in London and Melbourne. Her publications include the review of multicultural education in *Educational Research and Development in Britain, 1970–80* (NFER–Nelson).

JACK DOBBS is Director of Musical Studies at Dartington College of Arts in Devon. He has worked as a school teacher, county music adviser, university lecturer and research fellow, and was Director of Music at a Malayan Teachers' College.

NIGEL FILE is Head of History at Tulse Hill School, South London, where he has developed ideas for teaching and assessing history in a multi-cultural society. He is co-author, with Chris Power, of *Black Settlers in Britain, 1555–1958* (Heinemann).

RAY HEMMINGS has taught in a variety of schools, and was until recently Senior Lecturer in Mathematical Education at the University School of Education, Leicester. He is a founder-member of the Leapfrogs Group, and is currently co-editor of the ATM journal, *Mathematics Teaching*.

DAVID HICKS is Director of the Centre for Peace Studies at St Martin's College, Lancaster. His extensive publications on geography, multicultural education, world studies and education for peace include *Minorities: a Teacher's Resource Book for the Multiethnic Curriculum* (Heinemann).

OLIVER LEAMAN is a lecturer in education at the I.M. Marsh campus of Liverpool Polytechnic. His research interests are in equal opportunities and the secondary school movement curriculum, with particular reference to gender and ethnicity.

ALLAN LEARY taught ceramics in Nigeria for ten years and is now Head of Art at Josiah Mason Sixth Form College in Birmingham. He is an honorary Research Associate of the Centre of West African Studies at Birmingham University.

ANGELA MUKHOPADHYAY, a sociology graduate from Exeter University, has worked as a social worker and taught for five years in the International School in Calcutta. She is now Head of Social Science in a large comprehensive school in the West Midlands.

SUE OLIVER has taught home economics in ILEA comprehensive schools and in St Lucia in the Eastern Caribbean. She has also lectured in Home Economics and Teaching Studies at Bath College of Higher Education.

FRANCES SHEPHERD, an ethnomusicologist, is at present Lecturer in Indian Music at Dartington College of Arts, and is much involved in working with several organizations in the UK promoting the teaching of Indian music.

MICHAEL VANCE is a biology teacher working in a Haringey multiethnic comprehensive school with large numbers of pupils of Cypriot (Greek and Turkish) and West Indian origin. He is also active in community groups combating racism within education.

IOLO WYN WILLIAMS is Professor and Head of the School of Education, University College of North Wales, Bangor. He has worked in the West Indies, is active in the Royal Society of Chemistry's Education Division and directs the *Third World Science* project.

ANGELA WOOD is Head of Religious Education in North Westminster

School, London, and is currently organizer for the Standing Conference on Interfaith Dialogue in Education. She has written several school textbooks and has worked as an examiner in Religious Studies.

Editors' Introduction

Alma Craft and Geoff Bardell

Cultural diversity in Britain is no new phenomenon. Religious, regional, class and gender differences have always been undeniable aspects of the social structure. However, the twentieth century has witnessed a marked increase in cultural heterogeneity, with the settlement here of individuals and groups with many distinctive languages, belief systems and physical characteristics. Persecution drove many Jews here from Eastern Europe and later from Nazi Germany, employment opportunities attracted people from the Commonwealth, many of whom were 'black' or 'brown'; the free population movement of the EEC has brought a range of ethnic minority communities.

This plural composition of British society is increasingly recognized; national and local statements now welcome this reality, and are beginning to set out the implications for legal, social and educational practice. For their part, teachers and teacher educators have been analysing the nature of their task in preparing young people for life in and for a multicultural society.

There has been a flood of publications concerned with multicultural education, a great many exploring definitions and approaches (e.g. James and Jeffcoate 1981),[1] others developing an agenda for curriculum and assessment development (e.g. Rampton Report 1981;[2] Little and Willey 1981).[3] Many teachers have now been persuaded by classroom experience or national debate that multicultural education is a vital part of their professional responsibility, whether they teach in a multicultural school or in a locality with few or no pupils of ethnic minority origin. However, there are plenty of teachers who have yet to be persuaded that multicultural education is relevant to their subject specialism, and many others who are unsure what it might mean in practice for their particular subject.

Translating multicultural education into practical classroom terms is challenging and demanding, and has led to some exciting subject-based curriculum developments.[4] The purpose of this book is to disseminate these ideas and to illuminate the multicultural possibilities of some of the traditional school subjects. Our authors are all teachers or teacher educators whose work is classroom based. They have each explored the implications of multicultural education for their own subject and wherever possible have illustrated their suggestions with examples of course content, teaching strategies and project work; in many cases they have also indicated useful and easily available resources. A number of general guidelines for selecting multicultural curricula have already been published (e.g. Schools Council 1982);[5] this book is intended to help teachers visualize multicultural education in terms of their own teaching.

There has been much discussion about the proper focus of multicultural education: whether it should concentrate on the particular needs of ethnic minority pupils; whether it should proceed by stressing the positive contribution of cultural diversity in the education of all children; or whether its main concern should be the study and elimination of individual or institutional racism. In writing for this book, we asked our authors to use a chapter framework which considered all three aspects:

- We asked them to discuss whether ethnic minority pupils might have particular contributions to make or particular classroom needs in relation to individual curriculum subjects. Building on pupils' cultural experience can enhance pupil self-esteem and performance, as well as enriching the curriculum for all; responding to diversity includes encouraging pupils to study their own culture, particularly their language or religion, and involves being aware that certain topics must be treated extremely sensitively or may even be taboo for some pupils.
- We also asked our authors to analyse how their subject could contribute to *all* pupils' understanding and acceptance of cultural diversity, through using examples from a variety of cultures and avoiding solely Anglocentric emphases or interpretations. Ignorance and prejudice about other cultures and lifestyles can easily lead to racism – discrimination against and persecution of minority groups. It is our view that multicultural curriculum permeation, which presents cultural diversity as natural and valuable, can provide an essential framework for the reduction of indivi-

dual and institutional racism; it reflects an acceptance of cultural pluralism and may gradually lead pupils into an open and positive attitude
towards those who look, speak or behave differently from themselves.
  – Finally we asked our authors to consider ways in which their subject
could make a more specific and direct contribution towards the combating of racism, through the content of the syllabus. History and geography,
for example, have ample opportunities to help pupils understand the
phenomenon of population movements as both cause and effect of discrimination and exploitation today in Britain as well as in other times and
places. Literature can help explore the emotional and psychological
facets of intercultural relations. Social science can develop the tools for a
rational discussion of culture and race. Biology lessons can provide
important facts concerning the interplay of inheritance and environment
in racial characteristics.

The 13 chapters which follow cover perhaps the most commonly taught
subjects in the secondary school curriculum. A key aim was to go beyond
those subjects which tend to be associated with multicultural education (i.e.
usually those in the social sciences and arts) although we are well aware that
the coverage is still incomplete. There are no chapters, for example, on
crafts, economics, physics or technology, or on any interdisciplinary areas,
but it is hoped that others will be encouraged to write about the opportunities for multicultural curriculum development for areas not covered here.
  Although this book concentrates on issues related to the formal school
curriculum, multicultural education will only be effective if there is a whole
school ethos which is positive in outlook towards cultural diversity. Visuals
in corridors and classrooms, library resources, relations with local communities, attitudes towards other languages and cultures, expectations of
pupils of ethnic minority origin, recruitment of staff, and firm policy
guidelines to deal with racist behaviour and attitudes are at least as important in providing an appropriate context for developing a multicultural and
anti-racist perspective.
  Part One includes four subjects from the humanities. Nigel File advocates that local and national history should be related to a wider international context. He argues that an understanding of the multicultural history
of Britain, including an insight into the history of ethnic minority groups in
our society, would help all pupils appreciate multicultural issues in the
contemporary world. In a chapter on geography, David Hicks writes that
'geography is not just about places, it is also inevitably and essentially about

people'. He describes the opportunities for multicultural geography arising from recent developments within geography itself, and within the related fields of development education, world studies and peace education.

The social sciences can inform pupils about cultural diversity and can equip them to analyse their own experiences and the world around them. Angela Mukhopadhyay outlines ways in which social science subjects can develop young people's critical evaluation of 'facts' and can help with the classroom study of racism and ethnocentrism. Teachers of religion have a particular responsibility to make explicit to their pupils that racism is immoral. Angela Wood's chapter on Religious Education illustrates the rich potential of a pluralistic approach to the subject, where Christianity is treated alongside the other main faiths represented in the classroom.

The two chapters in Part Two are concerned with language and litera-ture. English is a crucial subject in multicultural education; mastery of standard English is an essential step towards educational and vocational success, but we are now increasingly conscious of the validity of dialects (e.g. West Indian or cockney) and aware of the need for sensitivity towards the speech forms of pupils whose home language is not English. Oral work provides many opportunities for open discussion of intercultural relations and tensions; careful choice of prose and poetry to be studied can enlarge pupils' experience of cultures and lifestyles. Jean Bleach's chapter locates the discussion of these multicultural issues firmly within recent develop-ments in the teaching of English.

To study another language is to begin to study another culture. John Broadbent explains how this can best be achieved, and suggests that it may often be appropriate for secondary schools to teach the home language of ethnic minority pupils as an alternative to the traditional modern languages, such as French and German.

Part Three focuses on mathematics and science. As Gillian Klein has commented (1983)[6] there are now some textbooks which illustrate mathe-matical concepts or scientific experiments with pictures or drawings of boys and girls from a range of backgrounds; and yet the content remains largely monocultural. Ray Hemmings' chapter presents one of the few detailed accounts of the multicultural history of mathematics, and of the ways in which the study of counting and games and art in other cultures can illustrate fundamental mathematical rules and concepts. He also suggests the use of examples from other cultures in statistical work. The chapter by Iolo Williams begins to examine the multicultural possibilities of chemistry teaching, drawing on his experience with the *Third World Science* project.

Michael Vance gives detailed examples of the potential contribution of biology, with particular reference to the discussion of genetic differences and 'race'. In her chapter, Sue Oliver reminds us that the close association of home economics with home and family makes an ethnocentric curriculum particularly insensitive and inappropriate. She shows by focusing on food and nutrition how the content of the subject can be enriched by culturally diverse examples, and she explains how relatively informal teaching can provide a fruitful context for combating racism.

The last part of the book reviews the arts and physical education. Jack Dobbs and Frances Shepherd portray vividly the rich possibilities of music when non-European sources are also included in the curriculum; they discuss how creating, performing or listening to music can help all pupils value cultural diversity. Similarly, Allan Leary, writing about art and design, shows the greater opportunities afforded by a less Eurocentric approach to the subject.

Finally, Oliver Leaman's chapter looks at physical education, dance and outdoor pursuits. He examines some of the stereotypes (particularly those concerning pupils of Afro-Caribbean and Asian origin) associated with this area of the curriculum, and he suggests some strategies which would enable all pupils to participate in and benefit from physical education activities, regardless of their abilities. He concludes with a strong plea that any such multicultural strategies in this subject should be a part of a whole school policy.

In a society which believes in cultural pluralism, a major task for teachers is to prepare all their pupils for a world which is culturally diverse. We hope that the curriculum opportunities explored in this book will be a positive contribution to professional activity concerned with putting multicultural ideals into practice.

Notes and references

1 James, A. and Jeffcoate, R. (1981) *The School in the Multicultural Society, a Reader*. London: Harper and Row with the Open University Press.
2 DES (1981) *West Indian Children in Our Schools: Interim Report of the Committee of Inquiry into the Education of Children from Ethnic Minority Groups* (Rampton Report). London: HMSO.
3 Little, A. and Willey, R. (1981) *Multi-Ethnic Education: The Way Forward*. Schools Council.
4 Teachers are beginning to share locally developed materials through a computer-based information service. Further details are available from Access to Information on Multicultural Education Resources (AIMER), Bulmershe College of Higher Education, Reading RG6 1HY.
   A book edited by James Lynch, *Teaching in the Multicultural School* (Ward Lock 1981),

includes chapters which describe some of the ways in which subject teachers can respond to the particular needs of pupils in schools which are multicultural in composition.

A new journal, *Multicultural Teaching*, has articles and reviews of new ideas and materials which can support and inform subject teachers.

5 Schools Council (1982) *Multicultural Education*. This includes guidelines on curriculum, materials and assessment drawn from previous Schools Council publications.

6 Klein, G. (1983) Multicultural teaching materials in mathematics and science, *Multicultural Teaching*, Vol 1, No 3.

PART ONE

HUMANITIES

CHAPTER 1*

HISTORY

Nigel File

The early 1970s saw a vogue for European studies which went beyond foreign language teaching into the realms of culture and history, the driving forces of which, it might be argued, were the attempt to cement Britain's membership of the EEC and to bind more closely those countries of North-Western and Mediterranean Europe which are part of the loosely knit Council of Europe. They were 60 years too late. As the Council of Europe and other groups in Britain tried to gell a pan-European culture, Europe was already frozen by the bi-polar glacis of the USA and the USSR, a situation which was itself being changed by emergent China and which has more recently led to a new world split into North–South.

How can the history curriculum respond to calls for relevance in trying to resource such issues without constantly appearing to be chasing some shadow of yesterday's concern? One answer is to ignore the present and celebrate history for its own sake. Another is to reject content and find or even invent historical situations which flesh out so-called historical skills. The former is a valuable activity but seems to command no more claim to curriculum time than chess or any other pastime. The latter seems to ignore the human aspects of the subject; school history provides opportunities for both analytical skills *and* a story of the past, and thus 'whose past?' or 'what past?' become just concerns. In any case many teachers see the search for relevance, though not necessarily through contemporary history, as a stimulating and essential part of their pedagogic practice.

---

* Some of the ideas in this chapter are an extension of those in *Assessment in a Multicultural Society: History at 16+* by Nigel File. Schools Council Programme 5 Pamphlet Series. Longman, York, 1983.

Reassessing the curriculum rationale for all students

In this last quarter of the twentieth century, the idea that a monocultural society, one where there is a single ethnic group and social class, or a multiclass monoethnic society, should study only its own history seems unbelievably inward looking. Perhaps it was relevant for eighteenth-century Britain, nineteenth-century Germany and Italy, and the twentieth-century emerging nations as part of the process of nation building. National history alone is neither necessary in a country as mature as Britain nor, because of Britain's imperial past, is it remotely possible to tell 'the story of Britain' without including Britain's world links; equally it is misleading to present any analysis of the ethnic composition of the British people without showing the great cultural diversity from the Roman era onwards. The need to go beyond national history was recognized as early as 1967 by Her Majesty's Inspectorate of Schools in its education pamphlet *Towards World History*:

> . . . this principle [of the evident significance of contemporary history] has always lain near the root of historical study in schools, and . . . our pre-occupation, in the past, first with British social history bears witness to it. The question today is whether, now that we have so evidently become 'one world', the study of our own constitutional and social history in isolation is sufficient. If we have become part of one world (a twentieth-century development) must we not concern ourselves with the history of that world, as the only proper approach to understanding it? (1967)[1]

Towards World History was concerned with promoting what is commonly understood to have become global studies or education in global under-standing. Its outstanding advocate, in the field of history, remains E.H. Dance, whose *History for a United World* (1971) goes far beyond the view that global understanding can only be located in contemporary history.[2] Although the title is rather idealistic, the content provides an unparalleled introduction to the diversity of world history and to how recurrent themes normally associated with European history can be interpreted through the experiences of many peoples. If, in the years after these two publications, there had been a significant reassessment of the curriculum away from ethnocentric history and towards world history, then it is likely that any concerns about history education for and in a multicultural society would have been matters of style and degree.

The quest for relevance

Towards World History put forward a view that we should think most carefully about the concerns of history, and that history teaching should be instrumental in helping students appreciate problems and issues in the contemporary world. Ten years later the DES advocated: '. . . the curriculum should reflect a sympathetic understanding of the different cultures and races that now make up our society' (DES, 1977).[3] This is different from education for global understanding. It implies that understanding Britain's own multicultural society should be a concern of history teaching. The Rampton Report hoped that a multicultural curriculum would have as its aim that: '. . . the knowledge and values transmitted by the school [should] seek to remove the ignorance upon which much racial prejudice and discrimination is based' (1981).[4]

Thus, history teaching has the potential to promote global understanding and to reduce racist misunderstanding within a society which is culturally diverse. The history of racism in Britain is dealt with by F. Shyllon (1974 and 1977),[5] E. Scobie (1972),[6] and J. Walvin (1971 and 1973),[7] and illustrated by File and Power (1981).[8] The relationship of British historians to racism is analysed by E. Williams (1966)[9] and a more up-to-date survey is provided by the Runnymede Trust (1980).[10] Misunderstanding exists at the national level linked to ideas of settlement and belonging, but myths and stereotypes are even more common at the international level in views of, for example, Africa, Asia, the Caribbean and Latin America. The varied historical experience in and beyond Britain can challenge stereotypes and in some cases put the record straight.

The pattern for curriculum construction

Three domains exist for the pupil which can be built up through the dimension of time. These are the locality (including individual family histories), the nation and the wider world. HMI comments:

> . . . so local and national history must be related to a wider context, not only in Europe but in America, Africa and Asia. So within five years of compulsory secondary education, some balance must be established between local, national and world history . . . This does not mean that it is sufficient for these three elements merely to be presented at some time during a five year syllabus. Local history and its rich sources emphasised in the first year and abandoned thereafter, or an awareness of the world beyond Europe, studied in the final year and unrelated to the national history in the middle part of a

syllabus is not a balance. It also imposes too sharp a distinction between the three elements . . . (1978).[11]

These three reference points in a pupil's historical understanding can each encompass a multicultural perspective; the historical roots of this society have a wealth of evidence to illustrate the multicultural dimension of all localities; the nation is multicultural as is the world.

Special needs?

So far the assumption has been made that a world perspective is important for all pupils, and that education for life in a multicultural society could be an important aim in history teaching. The ethnic minorities, frequently the objects of racism, do not need this education in the same sense: their parents and/or grandparents are likely to have experienced colonialism; or they may be refugees from Europe or Latin America, or from anti-semitism or totalitarianism of one sort or another.

Britain has provided a haven for many – Aliens Acts, Commonwealth Immigration Acts and revised Nationality status notwithstanding – but the racism experienced by many of the settlers (see Hinds 1966)[12] has led to an increased sense of cultural exclusiveness and the maintenance of traditions and links with areas of origin. The earliest thrust of multiracial education aimed at integration by giving people a sense of what it was to be British. This ignored the fact that most colonial education systems were based totally around British history, geography and literature. Indeed, it was only when people from these colonies, particularly those of Afro-Caribbean and Asian origin, came to Britain that they discovered that they were not regarded by the rest of the population as British. It was difficult to reconcile an education system which might be stressing the Whig interpretation of history, where Britain was the land of an ever extending freedom and tolerance, with the colour bar and the Nottingham and Notting Hill race riots. Integration as the goal of education then gave way to the 'deficit theory'. It was argued that immigrants and particularly those of Afro-Caribbean descent had negative self-images and that educators could somehow give them back, in the best colonial or missionary tradition, what they lacked. I would suggest that this identity crisis was more the creation of white and black people who had become upwardly mobile through education, losing their roots but rejecting their place in middle class society. Such people projected their dilemma onto a hapless group who were certainly experiencing no success in society but who, because of rejection, certainly had a strong sense of identity and who were using historical reference points to a much greater extent than the population at large.

The third attempt to provide for the needs of ethnic minorities is in terms of educating for pluralism. Pupils are seen as having a bicultural status whereby they relate both to the country of their birth (i.e. Britain) and to the country or continent(s) of their parents and grandparents. This view, which is not the same as the tragedy of people 'between two cultures', stresses the active and dynamic nature of culture where people choose how they define themselves to be, and participate in society from a position of cultural strength. The education service, in this view, should respond to individual and group needs. It should look at what is common in our humanity and how far cultural and racial divisions are useful. HMI (1978) suggest that a pupil's search for her/his own identity is related to a curiosity about the past.[13] It is essential, therefore, that history teachers make it possible for pupils to investigate what they see as their past from the viewpoint of their cultural needs. These are not fixed and should not be stereotyped. As has been stated earlier, pupils enjoying a bicultural status, are likely to have bicultural interests, and their view of themselves is likely to be modified throughout their lives.

The Rampton Report formulated a broad aim that 'all children should learn about their own cultures and histories and those of other groups and see them treated with equal seriousness and respect' (1981).[14] This is a slightly different emphasis to the above as it suggests fairly tightly knit groupings, presumably Afro-Caribbean peoples, West Asian peoples, East Asian peoples, African peoples and so on. In this sense it is defining cultural groups in advance. This is realistic but not without its dangers. The practicalities of this suggestion will be investigated later in the chapter but it is consistent with the broad idea of Britain as a plural society.

The final factor to be considered is whether the history teacher should make a particular response to minority groups who are often the objects of racial intolerance. Rampton identifies two particular issues with regard to pupils of West Indian origin. First: 'A West Indian child in a predominantly white society needs to see that people like himself are accepted in society generally and that it is recognised that ethnic minority groups have made, and are making, important contributions in all walks of life.' Secondly, the Report comments that the difficulties faced by West Indian children in schools might wrongly be associated with language problems rather than linked to 'more subtle factors such as a feeling of alienation, inappropriate subject matter where the child feels he has no significance . . .'[15] These views stress the importance of a curricular response which incorporates the historical experience of cultural origins as well as the contribution of ethnic groups to society now and in the past.

Targets for action

The history curriculum should reflect the desire to reinforce ideas of locality, nation and world throughout a five-year secondary course, and somehow has to cater for those who tend to take a history component for the first three years only. A prime aim will be to educate all pupils to better understand the cultures and races which form part of British society and to remove the ignorance on which racism is partly founded. A local or national focus on the historical dimension of settlement and the achievements of the many groups who have grown to make up British society would serve the twin aims of promoting understanding and helping to prevent the alienation of minority groups. The quest for appropriate subject matter is of direct concern for pupils from minority groups and can be catered for within the world approaches. A focus on perceived culture and its historical roots would mean allowing a much more personal approach to the study of history, and this might be possible through project-type activities. Concern with culture and roots, although raised because of the effects of racism in society and as a response to it, also means that some working class and female students, for example, will scrutinize more closely the assumptions about 'their' history and how far the history curriculum has represented what they see as important parts of their culture, and which achievements have previously been selected to typify the British nation.

In practice

How can teachers possibly do justice to the histories of the many cultural groups within present day Britain? How can teachers resource the needs of individual pupils? How can a reasonable balance of local, national and world history be achieved? Solutions to these questions will vary according to whether the aim is to infuse a preexisting curriculum with some elements which will make it more multicultural or to build up again from the beginning; whether it is an individual teacher trying to change or a whole department; what the ethnic composition of the school is; what individual interests the teachers or students might have and what scope the public examination syllabuses offer. The most fundamental division is probably between world history approaches which deal in themes and then select from literally a world of experiences, and those which are chronological or geographically centred. The theme approach has much to commend it as it reinforces concepts and can show different societies facing common issues, or having similar underlying structures, or producing different but comparable examples of material objects. A skills-based curriculum would similarly draw from many societies rather than from a Eurocentric base.

However, the disadvantage of a world history approach might be that it leaves pupils with no underlying sense of a whole society and certainly no idea of a chronology, or of change within a society. Area studies raise the questions of how many and for how long? Superficiality and even larger-scale stereotyping could easily emerge. Similarly, unwise comparisons between societies could be encouraged involving false evaluations of what is advanced or civilized. To reflect on China's civilization at the time of Britain's barbarity probably serves no more useful purpose than the present oft-quoted divisions into advanced and primitive societies. In making suggestions for practice I will not rule out the possibility of their being fitted into either approach.

While it is obviously possible to study cultural diversity by reference to Britain's present population, the historical roots of that diversity are to be found worldwide. In terms of highlighting some of the history of ethnic minorities for the enlightenment of all pupils, we can look particularly at the Indian subcontinent, the Caribbean and Africa, although other groups of course, for example from the Mediterranean and Southern Asia, would claim representation. Britain's multicultural population is not merely an ex-colonial one, as many groups, including those from Eastern and Mediterranean Europe, Latin America, the Arab world and other parts of Asia, have also settled here. Such diversity could allow for individuals and groups to present aspects of their history to others, where the ethos of the school encouraged the necessary confidence for this to take place.

Study of the history of one (or more) non-European society on its own terms can help to implement a non-Eurocentric approach. In schools with few or no ethnic minority children the area(s) chosen would enable the serious challenging of stereotypes and other misconceptions. In multicultural schools selection of areas would be related to representation within the schools. Those wishing to use published materials in class or small group sets will find that there is much available. Many history books for secondary and junior pupils prepared by teachers from Africa, Asia and the

Caribbean for their own schools are still published in Britain. Several British publishers have world history lists for the home market, too.

Africa

Africa has suffered more than any other continent from being ignored within our history curriculum. Reference to African peoples has largely been limited to the unparalleled invective during the debates on slavery in the nineteenth century, and the intelligence and genetics debates of the twentieth. The only real difficulty with incorporating a fuller view of African history into the curriculum is how to do justice to its longevity and variety.

The Nile valley will provide many starting points, including the wealth of material on Egypt, which does not always stress that it is an African country with an Afro-Asian population, and the later kingdoms of Kush, with its iron-working capital of Meroe, and the kingdom of Axum. East and Central Africa provide several self-contained areas of study. Ethiopia holds a special affection in the eyes of many, as the main country to resist European colonization, as an ancient seat of Christianity and as a modern symbol for the survivors of the African Diaspora. The east coast provides examples of City States which developed as part of the Swahili culture, and interesting groups with different ideas of social organization like the Waklimi. Central Africa provides a rich source in Great Zimbabwe and a classic lesson in the prejudices of European scholars and the racist mentality of the Smith regime. Much teaching about Southern Africa will focus on apartheid, or the liberation movements in Mozambique and Angola. Scholarship on earlier periods of Southern Africa's history will filter down gradually, but much material is available on the interesting period of the Mfecane and particularly on the activities of the Zulu king, Shaka.

The west coast provides a variety of kingdoms illustrating rich and mature periods of African history. They include Ghana, Mali, Songhai, Kanem-Bornu, Oyo, Benin and the Kongo. These kingdoms have had interesting written observations made about them, have surviving examples of their material culture (much of it residing in the basement of the British Museum), and have some interesting contributions related to women's history. Political independence has seen new school curricula in many African countries which can resource both a world history approach and a regional African history focus, as the associated textbooks are nearly all available in Britain and there are some printed source collections and packs available. Within Britain, Basil Davidson's writing is still a wonderful starting point for teachers, as is his school textbook (1978).[16] A film, 'The Ancient Africans', provides a sparkling overview.[17]

Asia

All periods of Asian history can be used effectively, as there is a wealth of visual materials and much surviving material culture. Ancient India has the Indus civilizations and the Mauryan Empire, with much attention possible for the key reign of Asoka. Corresponding to the Middle Ages, an interesting study can be made of the Hindu Vijayanagara Empire of Southern India and finally the great Moslem Mughal Empire. Information and original written sources for all these subjects are good (see Bharee 1982),[18] but audiovisual material is dated or unavailable. China presents a similar time spread of important dynasties and empires. Ancient China of the Shang, Chou, Ch'in and Han periods has inspired many good students' information books. Tand, Sung and Ming China provide much for concrete study, especially urban life in K'ai-feng, good illustrations of farming methods, inventions and technology, and medicine. More abstract subjects such as government and administration are shown clearly in the Ming dynasty, as they are also for the Mughals in India. The Moslem world straddles the continents although it has its roots in Asia. The impact of Mohammed and the spread of Islam has been a fruitful area for books relevant to religious studies and history teaching. Japan's twentieth-century history has given added relevance to detailed study of the roots of that society. The Heian period provides an understanding of the culture of Japan, whilst the Shogunate (and particularly the D Edo) period has rich visual sources, can flesh out the concepts of feudalism and, as the recent 'Shogun' television series showed, has much action and excitement along the way.

Caribbean

The pre-Columbian peoples known as the Arawaks and Caribs have an interesting pre-literate history that might not have received its due attention were it not for the later central interest that Britain had in that area, and the widespread settlement of people from the Caribbean in Britain. The two pre-Columbian societies provide interesting contrasts in human organization, attitudes to violence, trade and technology, law and order. They usually appear as a chapter in school textbooks on Caribbean history, but other resources for their study have yet to be created. The rest of Caribbean history is dominated by the activity of European contact and its consequences, virtually all the Carib and Arawaks suffering genocide in what was truly a fatal impact.

South America

The Aztec and Incan civilizations were cut down while still at their peak. Not for them the gradual decline associated with Mughal India or Ch'ing China. This leaves us with a clearer picture of what were also non-literate societies. Social organization, engineering, urban life, military methods, religious belief and architecture are some facets which make both cultures fascinating study. Each has been well resourced and has been regarded as 'civilized' from the beginning. It is still a fact, however, that artefacts from these two groups are to be found in London's Museum of Man as an ethnographic collection; indeed most world history is located there rather than displayed in the British Museum proper alongside the 'real' history, (i.e. the history of the ancient river valley civilizations, the Mediterranean world and Europe).

North America

This is an area more widely taught, with an emphasis on 'the west' which has suffered from stereotyping by Hollywood if not in educational courses. It would seem to lend itself to an examination of keywords such as 'civilized' and 'savage' in a context more neutral than would be possible with Africa. Although the Plains' Indians (the latter word itself being a lesson in dominant values), are often a subject of study, much of their history was changed as a result of the introduction of horses and guns by the Europeans. Other interesting groups that could be studied would be the Pueblo as an example of a settled, urban society; the Hopewellians and Mississipians, often referred to as the Moundbuilders, who like the creators of Great Zimbabwe, confounded nineteenth- and twentieth-century historians who believed that local people could not have been responsible for such great achievements. An interesting contrast can then be made with some north-west coast groups such as the Tlingits or Kwakiutl whose hunting society produced material wealth and social customs of universal interest.

Contact

Engaging students in the study of aspects of European world domination from a non-Eurocentric viewpoint requires some originality. There are twin dangers either of stressing the European experience at the expense of the dominated or of oversimplifying and stereotyping all Europeans as simply exploiters.

The theme of settlement should have wider application. It should be applied equally to people who move to set up a new life, whether they are Europeans in Africa or North America, or Turkish people in Germany, or Japanese in North America. The Atlantic slave trade brought about amazing population transformations in North and South America and the Caribbean and, although hardly matched for inhumanity at any other time, slavery did exist in other forms. For this reason, the concept of 'forced movement' may be more effective in helping people understand this phenomenon. It would then be possible to compare other forced movements of people such as the Highland clearances or even convict transportation.

Religion has also played a big part in contact through missionary activity by Christians and Muslims, with enduring results. 'Refuge' provides a theme capable of much empathetic development, in considering the experience of people having to move because of conscience or religion, or as runaway slaves. This theme of contact could be applied to any part of the world, Europe and Africa, Europe and Asia, Europe and the Caribbean or the peopling of North America. It can also be applied to non-Europeans in examples such as the Arab world and Africa, the Mughal invaders and Hindu India, China and Japan, the Ottoman Empire and Europe. Many materials can be adapted to fit this approach. It was exemplified by Killingray (1974)[19] and taken up by Catchpole (1981).[20] Film material is better on this topic, an outstanding example being 'White Man's Country' which looks at European settlement of Kenya, with African resistance told by eyewitnesses and the added implication of the importation of Asian peoples, initially as railway navvies.[21]

The theme of contact offers a way of establishing motive and consequence whilst rooting it in a variety of experiences. Cooperation was the vehicle for much contact between Europeans and non-Europeans in the early period of European expansion. Power relationships tended to be equal or overwhelmingly stronger on the side of the 'contacted'. Mutual respect was the order of the day and trading appeared to be beneficial to both sides. This applied to West Africa, India and Japan, as it did to the traditional trade patterns of the Indian Ocean. Occasionally societies in certain periods of their history were able to reject all contact, as was the case of Japan rejecting Chinese and European imperialism and the successful Maori rejection of British colonialists.

Resistance is a more general theme. It stresses the actions groups took in trying to reject contact. This is seen in terms, for example, of the African colonial wars, the North American Indian wars and such epics as the contest between Atahualpa and Pizarro. It can also relate to cultural resistance as in the preservation of language and customs by the victims of the Atlantic slave trade.

Central to the theme is exploitation. Examples of this account for the transformation of Africa, the Americas and Asia into a worldwide colonial system and the enriching of Europe. The effect on the people being exploited, whether in Africa, Asia, North or South America, is as important in terms of multicultural history as the enriching of Europe; both aspects need to be studied, for it is not sufficient for colonial areas only to be mentioned in the context of political disputes between European powers.

Issues of twentieth-century world history

Although not Eurocentric, many students could complete a course in world history which mentions only the superpowers and European involvement in two world wars. The variety of colonial freedom movements and neo-colonialism should have their rightful place, as should the effects of interference by the great powers in the affairs of the 'South'.

Britain as a multicultural society

Some implicit study of this topic seems to be necessary at the moment when the view of many is that Britain became a multiracial society only in the early 1950s with the beginning of postwar West Indian settlement. It is possible to trace the motives for settlement, and the experience and contribution of the many groups that together now make up British society. These include the Celts, Romans, Anglo-Saxons, Vikings, Normans, Huguenots, Jews, North Europeans, Mediterranean peoples, Afro-Caribbeans, Asians, Irish and Scots, Eastern Europeans and South Americans. Africans have been present in Britain since Roman times, Afro-Caribbeans from the time of the sugar trade, and Asians, known then as lascars, from the period of East India trade. Europeans have come as refugees at all times. Some schools already look at the 'problem' of race by studying contact between Celts and Romans, Anglo-Saxons and Vikings, or by consideration of the treatment of Britain's medieval Jewish population whose experience was very similar to that of those who were victims of the Nazi holocaust. Similarly anti-semitism in the early part of the century and the 1930s can be compared with the present treatment of ethnic minority groups.

The negative history of Henry II's Jewish Law, Elizabethan resettlement, the Sierra Leone resettlement and twentieth-century alien and commonwealth immigration legislation, can be contrasted with the positive achievements individuals and groups have made to the common culture (see File and Power 1981).[22]

Racism

A course in this subject certainly lends itself to historical analysis. Extremes which chillingly illustrate its effects are Nazi Germany and present day South Africa. The Institute of Race Relations (1982) has produced materials which are suitable for secondary school pupils and link the theme of racism with a study of colonialism and imperialism.[23] Recent videos such as Thames Television's 'Our People'[24] and the independently produced 'Divide and Rule, Never'[25] are also useful; ILEA's excellent 'Marches: from Jarrow to Cable Street' relates British responses to fascism with a studio-classroom discussion of the film, in the context of movements such as the National Front and the British Movement.[26] Finally, a study of racism, civil rights and black power in the United States could provide a way of dealing with important issues without having to bring in personal positions on the British situation. The US experience of black oppression is severely underresourced, with little available other than monographs on the life of Martin Luther King or dated surveys of the history of black people in general without too much mention of black power. One exception is Roxy Harris' *Being Black*, (1981) which gives a refreshing treatment to documentary testimony.[27]

Personalities

Those who favour the 'heroes/heroines' school of history will find much in *Round the World Histories* produced by Hulton Press, Heinemann's series *African History Makers* and Harrap's *World History Programme*. Some random names would include Harriet Tubman, Marcus Garvey, Mary Seacole, Simon Bolivar, Oladaugh Equiano, Pokohontas, Akbar Khan, and Cheng Ho.

Reorienting British history

There are points at which a typical British history school curriculum could be extended or revised to bring in elements of multicultural history, even though a radical or time-consuming change cannot be contemplated. Agriculture could be extended by looking at food supply to Britain and the development of plantation systems in Ireland, the West Indies, India, Australia, New Zealand, Africa and South America; Britain's interdependence in relation to issues like imperial preference and debates over the Commonwealth and the EEC are also relevant. Labour supply for plantations can be studied and comparisons between the conditions of British and Asian indentured labourers and West African slaves could be made.

Industrial development in Britain should look at sources of finance and the later development of markets within the British Empire for British goods. Comparative working conditions could be studied comparing wage slavery with black slavery. Some appreciation could be given of the contribution of former colonial peoples to the development of the British economy within Britain.

Transport is a popular theme which could be developed to look at Britain as a route focus serving the Empire, the influence of mass communications in the English-speaking world, the development of strategic sites of value to Britain – Gibraltar, Malta, Cyprus, Suez Canal, Aden, Singapore, Hong Kong and some of their subsequent history. Also railway building in Britain could be developed to include the importance of British-made railways throughout the world.

Economic history could easily include the functioning of the triangular trade and its importance in the development of Bristol, Liverpool and London. Much more needs to be produced on Britain's changing trade patterns and the history of the 'North–South' in the evolution of development and underdevelopment. The history of education could include the impact of the British education system on the colonies and the role of missionary societies. Any study of the democratic system could look at the struggle for democracy in the colonies, at the Morant Bay rebellion and at independence movements and the problems of the British model.

Social change seems to receive very limited attention. At a stroke, more could be done on emancipation and the abolition of slavery. Population movement could become an important theme incorporating internal population movements, immigration and emigration, and involving, for example, the Irish, Jews, West and East Europeans, Africans, Asians, South Americans, Australians and West Indians. The working of the Poor Law could be supplemented with further examples of mendacity, vagrancy, convict transportation to Africa, the West Indies, North America and Australia, and the details of the Sierra Leone resettlement.

The scope of working class movements could be extended to include all the effects of the depression, hunger marches, the development of British fascism and opposition to it. The depression could include its effects on the colonies and especially the details of the 1938 Caribbean riots. The effect of former colonial peoples on the trade union movements since 1945 is a dimension which should be explored. A further neglected area in an otherwise popular topic – world wars – is the role of colonial peoples in the two world wars and in Britain's colonial wars as well. Finally, it would seem that a new area of British history could be opened up: the development of civil rights for majority and minority groups. This could examine legislation and conditions relating to women, Roman Catholics, the Irish, the Jews and other ethnic groups. It could consider the development of anti-semitism and other forms of racialism, and opposition to these practices by political, social and religious groups, and it could consider the development of religious emancipation and racial equality.

Reorienting British and European history

Popular themes such as the 'voyages of discovery' could be reinterpreted as 'voyages of encounter' and there are enough examples of non-European explorers to change the concept from exploration to one of world travellers. A good teaching point can be made from textbooks which give the impression that there was nothing in a region before Europeans 'discovered' it. Whatever name it is called, there has been too much emphasis on the activities of the 'explorers' and, as in the idea of contact, some consideration must be given to the circumstances of those contacted.

It should hardly need stating that a topic such as the Crusades is impossible to study from the European viewpoint alone, and should feature equal treatment of the Islamic viewpoint. Similarly studies of the Renaissance or the development of medicine could easily include reference to developments in the Middle East, India and China.

Population movements as part of a European theme could be developed much further by looking at European settlement worldwide, at the settlement in Europe of former colonial peoples and 'guest workers' and at the resettlement of Europeans following civil or religious disturbances. The importance of colonization in the development of Europe is an important theme, as is the need to take some account of the results of contact. Multicultural societies in France, Holland, Portugal and Britain can be explored as a legacy of colonial Europe. The Muslim occupation in Spain and the Ottoman Empire in Europe add historical depth to Europe as a multicultural society.

Accounts of the French revolution should include its effect on Haiti and the revolutionary leadership of Toussaint L'Ouverture. Another term, 'the scramble for Africa', should more clearly be labelled the 'conquest of Africa' and greater account should be taken of its effect on the Africans themselves. Finally, the rise of fascism should be extended to include all its European variants including Britain, Spain, France, Belgium and Eastern Europe.

Skills

It is possible to develop a set of skills to deal with history from anywhere in the world. In more advanced courses the ways of investigating history in non-literate societies or in societies which built in wood in tropical conditions would make an interesting extension study. A key message of the Schools Council *History 13–16* project is that it is just as feasible to have materials relating to the archaeology of Kilwa as to ancient Greece, or to cast the net wider in terms of depth studies where written evidence is important. Using the materials, it ought to be possible to look at stereotyping and the part the study of history can play in questioning false assumptions. The project's topic 'History Around Us' is ideally suited to a multicultural approach anyway. Early attempts to emphasize skills were made by the ILEA *World History* project and it is still worth considering for that reason, particularly the last unit on the Caribbean where this approach was most marked. In addition to this Caribbean unit, which was developed for a mixed-ability situation, the Caribbean Extra pack, developed for less able pupils, also deserves attention.[28]

The cultural legacy

Much can be done. The best starting points are Dance's book[29] and probably the *Times Atlas of World History* (Barraclough 1978).[30] Once individuals or groups give serious consideration to the implications of history servicing the needs of a multicultural society their historical perspective will be changed for good.

Notes and references

1 HMI (1967) *Towards World History* Education Pamphlet No 52. DES.
2 Dance, E.H. (1971) *History for a United World*. London: Harrap.
3 DES (1977) *Education in Schools*, a Consultative Document. London: HMSO.
4 DES (1981) *West Indian Children in Our Schools* Interim Report of the (Rampton) Committee of Inquiry into the Education of Children from Ethnic Minority Groups, Cmnd 8273, p. 34. London: HMSO.
5 Shyllon, F. (1974) *Black Slaves in Britain*. Oxford: Oxford University Press.
   Shyllon, F. (1977) *Black People in Britain, 1555–1833*. Oxford: Oxford University Press.
6 Scobie, E. (1972) *Black Britannia*, Chicago.
7 Walvin, J. (1971) *The Black Presence*. London: Orbach and Chambers.
   Walvin, J. (1973) *Black and White, The Negro and English Society, 1555–1945*. London: Allen Lane.
8 File, N. and Power, C. (1981) *Black Settlers in Britain, 1555–1958*. London: Heinemann.
9 Williams, E. (1966) *British Historians and the West Indies*. London: André Deutsch.
10 Runnymede Trust (1980) *Britain's Black Population*. London.
11 HMI (1978) *11–16 Document* (Red Book), History Revised Version. DES.
12 Hinds (1966) *Journey to an Illusion*. London: Heinemann.
13 HMI (1978) *op. cit.*
14 DES (1981) *op. cit.* p. 34.
15 DES (1981) *op. cit.* pp. 13 and 24.
16 Davidson, B. (1978) *Discovering Africa's Past*. London: Longman.
17 Patterson, E. (1978) *The Ancient Africans*.
18 Bharee, P. (1982) *South Asia: Handbook for Teachers*. London.
19 Killingray, D. (1974) *A Plague of Europeans*. London: Penguin.
20 Catchpole, B. (1981) *The Clash of Cultures*. London: Heinemann.
21 'White Man's Country' (1971) London Contemporary Films.
22 File, N. and Power, C. (1981) *op.cit.*
23 Institute of Race Relations (1982) *The Roots of Racism* and *Patterns of Racism*.
24 'Our People' (1979) Thames TV, London. Available as series of 6 videotapes from Guild Learning, Guild House, Oundle Road, Peterborough.
25 'Divide and Rule, Never' (1978) Concord Film Council.
26 'Marches: from Jarrow to Cable Street' (1979) Central Film Library, Central Office of Information.
27 Harris, R. (1981) *Being Black*. London: New Beacon Books.
28 ILEA World History Project (1978) *Caribbean Extra*.
29 Dance, E.H. (1971) *op.cit.*
30 Barraclough, S. (ed.) (1978) *Times Atlas of World History*. London: Times Books.

CHAPTER 2

GEOGRAPHY

David Hicks

A multicultural world

Young people in our schools now will spend most of their lives in the twenty-first century. The future that they will inherit, whether fulfilling or alienating, depends largely on how we resolve a range of dilemmas, both national and global, that face us today. Central amongst these is the question of how one should educate children if they are to live peacefully and responsibly in a multicultural world.

A multicultural society requires us to promote equality of opportunity, equality of rights and tolerance for cultural diversity. Although there are some signs of positive change, such a society has yet to be created in Britain. It still requires the removal of social inequality, prejudice and discrimination and in particular it requires that the majority *listen* to the voices of various minority groups.

What part then does geography have to play in education for a multicultural society? Indeed should it have a part at all? For some geographers would argue that it should not.

Geography is not just about places, it is also inevitably and essentially about people. The New Collins Concise English Dictionary (1982) defines geography as 'the study of the natural features of the earth's surface, including topography, climate, soil, vegetation etc., and man's responses to them'. There is now within the school curriculum an increasing focus on 'man's response' to his environment, including social, economic, political and urban geography. Indeed it has been argued strongly that geography should focus on the human condition, not just in Britain and Europe, or even the northern hemisphere, but across the globe. Geography should therefore, by definition, be multicultural rather than monocultural. It should reflect the plural nature both of our own society and of the world.

In particular this will require that geography should explore a diversity of perspectives and viewpoints which are indeed significant 'geographical factors'. Geography should acknowledge that:

1. There are many different viewpoints and perspectives on issues such as the environment, resources, political ideas, development and being human.
2. Such viewpoints and perspectives differ both between and within countries and cultures.
3. Such viewpoints and perspectives will also differ according to gender, age and economic condition as well as cultural circumstances.
4. Young people need to be helped towards an understanding of such differences, and the conflicts which may arise from them, since they often relate to an inequitable distribution of power and therefore access to a society's, and the world's, resources.
5. The nature of racism needs to be fully discussed and understood, involving as it does not only prejudice but also explicit or implicit discrimination against groups considered to be 'inferior'.
6. Racism is, therefore, not merely a personal aberration but an institutionalized part of British society arising in some degree out of the colonial heritage.
7. There is a need to explore, also, issues of justice and injustice as an integral part of improving the human condition.

Certainly both adults and young people urgently need social, political, economic and ethical understanding. The skills needed to combat violence, intolerance and prejudice, on local, national and global scales, are no longer a luxury but a necessity.

School geography thus has an important role to play in these matters, and a good deal can be learned from recent trends within geography itself and in closely related fields, such as development education, world studies and education for peace. Developments in geography and in these interrelated disciplines are outlined below.

Some significant developments

Geography

The most important trend in geography over the last decade has been the growth of what is called a 'geography of concern', that is, the realization that unless geography is concerned about real people, their health and happiness, then it fails to make any worthwhile contribution. Three constituent parts of this trend are welfare geography, radical geography and humanistic geography.

It was Smith (1977) who argued that: 'the well-being of society as a spatially variable condition should be *the* focal point of geographical enquiry . . . It simply requires recognition of what is surely the self-evident truth that if human beings are the object of our curiosity . . . then the quality of their lives is of paramount importance.' Essentially a welfare approach focuses on who gets what where. Three complementary approaches can be identified (Bale 1983). These are: describing geographical patterns of welfare at a variety of scales; interpreting and understanding the patterns shown by the mapping; and predicting what more just patterns of welfare would look like. In terms of a multicultural geography this could mean mapping the distribution of global wealth, looking at a range of explanations for the inequalities, and calculating the implications of a more just distribution. Similar principles can be applied on a local scale, as Huckle (1983a) has done in examining the disadvantaged position of minority groups over housing.

Radical geography broadens still further the critique that needs to be made of society (Peet 1978). It had its origins in the United States during the civil rights movement and the Vietnam War, when academics began to question their own role in reproducing such a violent society, and became disillusioned with mainstream geography as it then was. This led to a new interest in both activism and critical theoretical analysis, the latter involving a new appreciation of both Marxist and anarchist philosophy. To take capitalism as an unquestioned 'given' may be to ignore the very blind spot which lies at the root of many social, political and economic problems today.

If a democratic society requires informed and educated citizens then it also requires the ability to exercise critical judgement, to ask fundamental questions about the ethics of the status quo. A truly multicultural geography needs to ask such questions.

Humanistic geography is particularly interested in the taken-for-granted geography of everyday life, people's feelings, perceptions, fears and experiences within their environment. Our personal or private geographies often exist at the unconscious level but they are nevertheless crucially important in establishing our orientation to life.

According to Fien (1983) humanistic geography focuses on 'the subjectivity of human responses to people, places and events. Thus, like the historian or the novelist, the humanistic geographer seeks to provide people-orientated insights into the experiences, character and purpose of human occupation on the earth.' This approach enables students to become more conscious and aware in everyday life. Heightening consciousness of one's own private geographies can also pave the way to increased empathy for the beliefs and experiences of people in other countries and cultures.

Humanistic geography also lays stress on a learner-centred approach to education and the bringing together of both thinking and feeling, experience and knowledge. One of the examples of this sketched out by Fien is based on the disturbances in St Pauls, Bristol in 1980 (Figure 2.1).

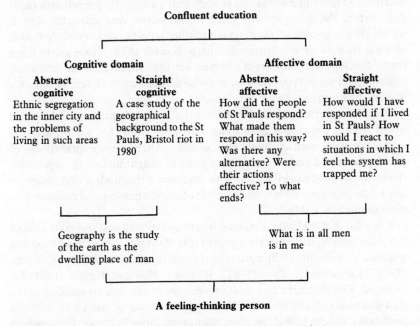

Confluent education

Cognitive domain		Affective domain	
Abstract cognitive	**Straight cognitive**	**Abstract affective**	**Straight affective**
Ethnic segregation in the inner city and the problems of living in such areas	A case study of the geographical background to the St Pauls, Bristol riot in 1980	How did the people of St Pauls respond? What made them respond in this way? Was there any alternative? Were their actions effective? To what ends?	How would I have responded if I lived in St Pauls? How would I react to situations in which I feel the system has trapped me?

Geography is the study of the earth as the dwelling place of man

What is in all men is in me

A feeling-thinking person

Figure 2.1 Multicultural geography: a humanistic approach
Source: Huckle, 1983b

Students are thus asked not only how they might have *felt* in this situation, but also to clarify their own personal position having studied the events at the time. Such case studies can be used most effectively to explore the conflicts that can arise in a multicultural society.

It should be noted that the concerns of welfare, radical and humanistic geography frequently overlap, and are not mutually exclusive. Most importantly they provide, from within the discipline itself, all the ingredients for a dynamic and multicultural geography.

Development education

Whilst development education may have had as its initial focus 'third world' problems, the best work in this field is concerned much more broadly with differing interpretations of underdevelopment, development and over-development. The focus is thus on problems of 'too much' as well as 'too little', on the rich North as well as the poor South.

Much geography teaching has unfortunately tended to concentrate narrowly on the 'third world' per se and often unwittingly perpetuates racist stereotypes. Pupils' images of 'third world' people may affect the way in which they see some of their ethnic minority peers, and certainly public opinion surveys show a correlation here (Bowles 1978). If we are to learn from development education's stress on the importance of attitudes, opinions and stereotypes then we must look much more closely at our own in-built assumptions about development.

Thus Hicks (1980, 1981) has shown that textbook images of the 'third world' reflect colonial attitudes and European priorities, a monocultural rather than a multicultural perspective. Alternative explanations of development and underdevelopment must be taught including, especially, the views of 'third world' writers who often stress that underdevelopment is not a state, but a *process* begun as a result of colonialization and continued by neo-colonialism today.

It is vital that traditional arguments are questioned and the myths about too many people, difficult climates, the role of women, not enough food and uneducated peasants challenged. Good work here has been done by George (1976), Lappé and Collins (1982), Rogers (1980) and Hayter (1981) for example. Development and underdevelopment can also be studied in the rich countries of the world, whether the struggle of native peoples for landrights (Hicks 1981) or case studies of cities such as Birmingham (Birmingham DEC 1982).

World studies

Many developments in world studies are of interest to geographers (Hicks and Townley 1982). World studies can be a subject in its own right but is more often seen as a dimension in the curriculum. The term refers to studying countries and cultures other than one's own; issues to do with peace and conflict, trade and development, human rights and the environment; and the way in which everyday life is influenced by events in the wider world.

The global context is a crucial one in multicultural education. Issues to do with race and cultural diversity in Britain cannot be fully understood unless they are set in their broader context, whether the war in southern Africa or the availability of oil from the Middle East. Geography has an important part to play in helping children understand such contemporary issues.

In writing about the Schools Council/Rowntree project *World Studies 8–13*, Hall (1982) described teachers handling 'unteachable' ideas with younger children. He was referring to the project's emphasis on activities which promote debate and discussion, which are participatory and experiential, thus promoting an exciting and stimulating climate of enquiry (Fisher and Hicks). Such activities fit well with geography's rich experience of role-play and simulation.

World studies teaching also takes a particular interest in the future. Children are asked to consider not only what they think the world *will* be like, but what it *should* be like in the future. If we are concerned about equality and justice in Britain, as well as the wider world, we must explore a range of possible futures (Robertson 1983). What sort of future do different people envisage for our multicultural society? Should we be plotting future geographies?

Education for peace

The overall aim of peace education is to develop the skills, attitudes and knowledge necessary to resolve conflict peacefully in order to work towards a more just and less violent world. The concerns of peace education are broad. They relate to issues of war, violence and conflict, justice and injustice, equality and inequality and environmental concern. They thus overlap considerably with the interests of both welfare and radical geography. Certainly geographers are making contributions to the nuclear debate (Openshaw and Steadman 1982) the outcomes of which clearly have national and global implications.

Geography and multicultural education can draw from peace education in three main ways. Learning to analyse conflicts, whether over resources, boundaries or rights, to ask who is likely to gain what and how, are important prerequisites for understanding the modern world. An appreciation of conflict resolution is also invaluable in our everyday lives. Secondly peace education can provide useful case studies of struggles for justice including those based on non-violence as a strategy for change. Thirdly peace education emphasizes the need for a match between means and ends in the classroom. Thus the *way* we teach is as important as what we teach. Young people should not be seen as empty vessels to be filled, since real education occurs via cooperation and participation, an engagement between pupil and teacher as real people. Learning becomes a shared responsibility, undertaken in a non-authoritarian fashion. In particular peace education challenges us to look at our own classrooms and what goes on in them, since this is where tolerance and empathy must begin.

In briefly reviewing significant developments in geography and allied fields several key ideas have been identified which are particularly relevant to a multicultural geography. These are the need to:

– focus on human well-being
– ask fundamental questions about the status quo
– emphasize private geographies
– counteract popular myths
– look at underdevelopment in the UK
– include a global dimension
– help make sense of contemporary events
– use experiential teaching styles
– explore future geographies
– look at conflict analysis and resolution
– look at struggles for justice
– reconsider classroom climate.

Multicultural geography – current initiatives

Geography has long been interested in pupils' perceptions of, and attitudes towards, other places. Mental maps are an important stock in trade. Geographers have also claimed an interest in the development of pupils' attitudes as an important contribution to education for international understanding.

The work of people such as Carnie (1972) has illustrated the early age at which young children develop such attitudes. Negative stereotypes based on images received from the media, parents and peer groups play a large part in the creation of prejudices and often well *before* children have any real knowledge of the groups concerned. Geographers can thus play an important role at all levels of education in fostering positive images – of the Russians and the Irish as well as non-Europeans.

Public opinion surveys show that many people in Britain suffer from 'national introversion', are uninterested in the wider world and parochial in their attitudes (Bowles 1978). Attitudes towards 'third world' peoples and members of minority groups within Britain are generally prejudiced and often racist. Only recently, however, have geographers really begun to face up to their responsibility over pupils' attitudes towards people from countries and cultures other than their own.

The multicultural debate has prompted geographers to reexamine the curriculum opportunities their subject offers. Three positive ways forward that any teacher can use are now described. They are not mutually exclusive, neither are they enough in themselves. They offer starting points, however, points of reinforcement, ideas to use and develop more widely.

Resources

Various detailed studies have been made of geography textbooks currently in use, many of which appear to support colonial views of the world. Such views are not only outdated and therefore incorrect, they are also insulting and unjust. Anyone concerned about multicultural geography should consult the research in question, for example Hicks (1980) on images of the 'third world', the papers edited by Kent (1982), Wright (1983a) on Africa and Gill (1983) on examinations, to name but a few. From images of 'third world' peoples' attention has begun to shift specifically towards the treatment of race in geography textbooks (Wright 1983b) and much of the writing here seems to reinforce existing misperceptions.

We need to continue checking and rechecking the materials and resources that we use. A lot of progress has been made in this field but we need to engage in a process of critical appraisal in our own classrooms, with our own colleagues and in our local teacher groups. We need to consider both what we teach and what we teach with. When choosing books a non- or anti-racist stance must be as important a criterion as readability, illustrations and cost. And there is no reason why the books we already have should not be studied by the pupils themselves for bias. In that case we may well also need to offer alternative viewpoints and perspectives to offset the existing messages being received.

The checklist of questions (Hicks 1981) contained in the Teacher's Guide for the new *Geography for the Young School Leaver* (GYSL) books on development offers some useful examples:

  – Is it assumed or suggested that there is only one cause of poverty? Is
    underdevelopment seen as a condition which mainly arises out of over-

population or environmental restraints, without due consideration being given to historical or economic factors?
- Is it pointed out that underdevelopment can also be explained as an historical process which arises out of the unequal relationship between rich and poor countries and which continues to hinder development today?
- Is it shown that the colonial period had a profound impact on the present day geography of 'third world' countries?
- Is it shown how values affect the way people perceive an issue in the first place and how they analyse the causes of conflict? Are differing value positions explored and does the author acknowledge her/his own biases?

Questions such as these should prompt others, for example: Is it assumed or suggested that everyone is equally happy and satisfied in a multicultural society? Is any attention given to the socio-economic position of minority groups vis-à-vis society as a whole? Checklists such as these can be used to highlight strengths and weaknesses and indicate where further information may be required.

Teaching and learning methods

The issues facing a multicultural society often arouse controversy, and are subject to debate in the media and in everyday life. If pupils do not have the opportunity to discuss issues such as cultural similarities and differences, values and beliefs, the nature of bias in the media, the growth of racist attacks, then they are being ill-equipped to deal with life in Britain in the 1980s. Richardson (1982a) has suggested that effective discussion can be promoted by using several simple techniques. For example, when pupils work in small groups, no larger than six, they are liable to feel more secure and able to talk. A precise task needs to be given and it also helps if pupils have something concrete to handle. This may be a series of photographs, quotations or facts on slips of paper, or some of the cards referred to below. It is helpful if the task involves cooperation, such as: 'Agree as a group on which two photographs you think are most typical/untypical of Brazil. Write down two questions you would like to ask about each photograph.'
Tasks which involve comparing, contrasting, selecting and reporting back create opportunities for pupils to explore their own thoughts and feelings about things and to test them out with others. Such development of discussion skills should be an essential part of creative geography teaching.

Practice

There are now a variety of resources which can be used in the classroom to

Figure 2.2 Examples from a pack of 100 cards 'The Rich and the Poor' published by and available from EARO, The Resource Centre, Back Hill, Ely, Cambridgeshire, CB7 4DA.

explore issues relating to living in a multicultural society and an inter-dependent world. One example is the pack of cards (Starkey 1979) called *The Rich and the Poor*. The set contains 100 cards, each with a photograph, fact or quotation on it relating to the rich world/poor world divide. There are detailed instructions on how they may be used; they could be well backed up with a book such as Kidron and Segal's *The State of the World Atlas* (1981).

The nine cards shown in Figure 2.2 have been chosen to highlight particular issues to do with development. Working in pairs pupils have to rank the cards in answer to a question such as 'Which cards most strikingly highlight problems of development?' Pupils then rank them in a diamond formation thus:

Their first choice is at the top and the last at the bottom. This pattern often makes ranking easier to carry out than if cards had to be in an exact sequence. Two pairs then come together to explain their choices to each other. A master chart can be filled in by the teacher to show pupils' first choices. How did pupils make their choices? Do any patterns emerge? There will be plenty of scope for discussion and ideas for future work after an activity such as this.

Improving multicultural geography – five proposals

The following proposals are in no way exhaustive. They do, however, indicate five steps toward improving what goes on in the geography classroom. They are starting points for taking action.

1. Innovation

Successful geography teaching depends on innovation, not just for the sake of change but because we live in a rapidly changing world that is in many ways becoming increasingly inequitable and unjust. This should constantly raise questions about what and how we teach. For many people, as Ford Prefect well knew, innovation is an SEP (Adams 1982):

> 'An SEP', he said, 'is something that we can't see, or don't see, or our brain doesn't let us see, because we think that it's somebody else's problem. That's what SEP means. Somebody Else's Problem. The brain just edits it out, it's like a blind spot. If you look at it directly you won't see it unless you know precisely what it is. Your only hope is to catch it by surprise out of the corner of your eye.'

Both innovation and other issues raised in this book may be seen as SEPs. We need to identify our own such blind spots and also help each other do the same.

2. Ideology

One of the clearest discussions of the role of ideology in geography teaching is that by Walford (1981). He reminds us that every educational document and statement arises out of a particular ideological position which is more likely to be implicit than explicit. He identifies four broad traditions and the styles of geography teaching which relate to them. Being clear about these traditions will not only help teachers be clear about where they individually stand, but also clearer about what they and others are doing.

The four traditions are the liberal–humanitarian, the child-centred, the utilitarian and the reconstructionist. The main elements of the liberal–humanitarian tradition are a concern with passing on that which is considered best in one's cultural heritage and with the continuity of worthwhile ideas. In the child-centred tradition the stress is on self-development and autonomy. Subjective experience is valued as an important learning focus in education and the process of teaching and learning duly emphasized. The concern of the utilitarian tradition is to prepare pupils to go well-equipped into society, to earn their living. In this view subjects with a strong vocational stress are valued most. The reconstructionist tradition sees education as a potential lever for creating change in society. It asks questions about the status quo and in geography prompts questions about spatial injustice and environmental concern. Action and participation skills are encouraged.

3. Images

Much of this chapter has discussed, or referred to, popular images of non-Europeans. The point cannot be made too strongly that much geography is monocultural geography, seeing the world from a white, male perspective. Richardson (1982b) suggests seven guidelines for teaching and learning about other countries, which he states as a series of questions:

1. Are we helping students to differentiate, so that they do not speak of all Russians, all Muslims, all Europeans, all Blacks?
2. Are we helping students to perceive foreigners as human beings similar to themselves, with hopes, anxieties, intentions, will-power?
3. Are we helping students to perceive foreigners therefore as morally various, not wholly evil? Do they avoid the equation us/them = good/bad?
4. Are we helping students to interact with and learn from other cultures? Are we helping them therefore to cope with culture shock?
5. Are we helping students to understand the concept of interdependence – the notion that there are close cultural and economic connections between their own country and other countries?
6. Are we helping students to understand that us/them stereotypes have their roots in economic and political structures, not in individual personality alone?
7. Are we helping students to understand the concept of justice in its two main aspects, politics and morality?

Similarly we need to ask what girls learn about themselves in geography. We need to explore the parallels between racism and sexism, and ways in which geography fails to acknowledge the contribution of women to the economy and in fact frequently renders them invisible (Larsen 1983).

4. Methods

Geography has a long tradition of using varied teaching methods and a wide range of resources: maps, filmstrips, slides, films, visits and fieldwork as well as role-play and simulation games. This tradition provides a firm foundation for further developments. In particular geography can learn from world studies and development education and their interest in activities and techniques that promote active learning (Fisher and Hicks). Examples have already been given in this chapter of discussion exercises and the use of ranking activities.

5. Policy

A geography department which takes multicultural matters seriously will have a stated policy on these issues. One of the stated curriculum aims will need to refer to combating prejudice and working towards equality. Departmental policy needs, in turn, to be an integral part of school and LEA policy. A good example of the latter is provided by Berkshire's document

Education for Racial Equality (1983) which focuses particularly on peoples of Asian and Afro-Caribbean origin, and which sets out its policy, the implications of this and the support required. It argues that there will be racial equality in Britain when ethnic minorities

. . . participate fully in society and the economy, and are therefore proportionately involved in management and government at all levels, and are not disproportionately involved in menial work, or in unemployment or underemployment . . . [and when they are] proportionately involved in teaching and administration at all levels, in higher and further education, and in streams, sets, classes and schools leading to higher and further education.

The document goes on to stress that there will be racial justice when

. . . the practices, procedures and customs determining the allocation of resources do not discriminate, directly or indirectly against ethnic minority people . . . [and] when the factors determining successful learning in schools do not discriminate, directly or indirectly, against ethnic minority children.

Let us make sure that geography is not found wanting in these matters.

References

Adams, D. (1982) *Life, the Universe and Everything*. London: Pan.

Bale, J. (1983) Welfare approaches to geography. *In* J. Huckle (ed.) 1983a.

Berkshire Education Committee (1983) *Education for Racial Equality*.

Birmingham Development Education Centre (1982) *The World in Birmingham: Development as a Local Case Study*, a handbook and photopack.

Bowles, T.S. (1978) *Survey of Attitudes Towards Overseas Development*. London: HMSO.

Carnie, J. (1972) Children's attitudes to other nationalities. *In* Norman Graves (ed.) *New Movements in the Study and Teaching of Geography*. London: Temple Smith.

Fien, J. (1983) Humanistic geography. *In* J. Huckle (ed.) 1983a.

Fisher, S. and Hicks, D.W. (forthcoming) *World Studies 8–13*, A Teacher's Handbook. Edinburgh: Oliver and Boyd.

George, S. (1976) *How the Other Half Dies: The Real Reasons for World Hunger*. Harmondsworth: Pelican.

Gill, D. (1983) Education for a multicultural society: the constraints of existing O level and CSE geography syllabuses. *In* Association for Curriculum Development in Geography and the Commission for Racial Equality *Racist Society: Geography Curriculum*.

Hall, D. (1982) World Studies: their place and emphasis, *Times Educational Supplement* 3rd December, Geography extra.

Hayter, T. (1981) *The Creation of World Poverty: An Alternative View to the Brandt Report*. London: Pluto Press.

Hicks, D.W. (1980) *Images of the World: An Introduction to Bias in Teaching*

Materials. Centre for Multicultural Education, University of London Institute of Education.

Hicks, D.W. (1981) Geography and development education. In *Geography and Change* Teacher's Guide, GYSL Development Education Project. London: Nelson/Schools Council.

Hicks, D.W. (1982) *Minorities: A Teacher's Resource Book for the Multi-ethnic Curriculum*. London: Heinemann.

Hicks, D.W. and Townley, C. (eds.) (1982) *Teaching World Studies: An Introduction to Global Perspectives in the Curriculum*. Harlow: Longman.

Huckle, J. (ed.) (1983a) *Geographical Education: Reflection and Action*. Oxford: Oxford University Press.

Huckle, J. (1983b) Anti-racist teaching through geography, some principles for curriculum change: an introduction to a workshop on housing. *In* Association for Curriculum Development in Geography and the Commission for Racial Equality *Racist Society: Geography Curriculum*.

Kent, A. (ed.) (1982) *Bias in Geographical Education*. Department of Geography, University of London Institute of Education.

Kidron, M. and Segal, R. (1981) *The State of the World Atlas*. London: Pan.

Lappé, F.M. and Collins, J. (1982) *Food First: The Myth of Scarcity*. Tunbridge Wells: Abacus.

Larsen, B. (1983) *In* J. Whyld (ed.) *Sexism in the Secondary Curriculum*. London: Harper and Row.

New Collins Concise English Dictionary (1982) Glasgow: Collins.

Openshaw, S. and Steadman, P. (1982) On the geography of a worst case nuclear attack on the population of Britain, *Political Geography Quarterly* 1(3).

Peet, R. (ed.) (1978) *Radical Geography: Alternative Viewpoints on Contemporary Social Issues*. London: Methuen.

Richardson, R. (1982a) Talking about equality: the use and importance of discussion in multicultural education, *Cambridge Journal of Education* 12(2).

Richardson, R. (1982b) Culture and justice: key concepts in world studies and multicultural education. In D.W. Hicks and C. Townley (eds.) 1982.

Robertson, J. (1983) *The Sane Alternative: A Choice of Futures* (available from 9 New Road, Ironbridge, Shropshire TF8 7AU).

Rogers, B. (1980) *The Domestication of Women*. London: Tavistock.

Smith, D.M. (1977) *Human Geography: A Welfare Approach*. London: Edward Arnold.

Starkey, H. (1979) *The Rich and the Poor*, a pack of 100 cards available from EARO, The Resource Centre, Back Hill, Ely, Cambridgeshire.

Walford, R. (1981) Language, ideologies and geography teaching. *In* R. Walford (ed.) *Signposts for Geography Teaching*. Harlow: Longman.

Wright, D. (1983a) 'They have no need of transport. . . ' a study of attitudes to Black people in some geographical texts. *In* Association for Curriculum Development in Geography and the Commission for Racial Equality *Racist Society: Geography Curriculum*.

Wright, D. (1983b) The geography of race, *Times Educational Supplement* 15th July.

Wright, D. (1983c) A priority for the eighties, *Times Educational Supplement* 1st April, Geography Extra.

CHAPTER 3*

SOCIAL SCIENCES

Angela Mukhopadhyay

The recent, rapid growth of social science teaching in the secondary school, particularly in the 14–16 year age group, should provide the opportunity to develop a sound basis for a multicultural curriculum.[1] The content and approach of the social sciences provides great potential for the development of knowledge, concepts and skills which can deepen students' understanding of the multicultural and multiracial nature of societies in an increasingly interdependent world.

The social sciences curriculum can provide pupils with knowledge and information about cultural diversity in Britain and in the world, and about the global nature of social, political and economic issues. It can also equip students with a conceptual framework which can serve to analyse their own experiences and the world around them. Key concepts for multicultural education include culture, ethnicity, ethnocentrism, power and race.† The methodology of social science teaches students the skills for careful collection, analysis, and interpretation of data, and can develop their capacity for critical evaluation of 'facts'.

---

* Some of the ideas in this chapter are an extension of those in *Assessment in a Multicultural Society: Social Sciences at 16+* by Angela Mukhopadhyay. Schools Council Programme 5 Pamphlet Series. Longman, York, 1984.

** The author is grateful to Chris Brown of West Midlands College for his comments on this chapter.

† The term race is problematic. As Michael Vance has argued in Chapter 9 on Biology, it has little genetic basis and leads to misleading categorization of people into 'racial groups'. Nevertheless, myths about racial differences between 'white' and 'black' people persist and have shaped attitudes and social structure. In this chapter the term race is used for ethnic groups who are distinguishable by the colour of their skin.

In addition, the social sciences are uniquely placed to investigate and 'deconstruct' attitudes and ideologies.[2] Multicultural education is inextricably concerned with attitudes. Students' attitudes are firmly acquired by the time they reach secondary school and inevitably contain conscious or unconscious elements of racism and ethnocentrism. Such attitudes have a pervasive effect on the way in which pupils interpret and evaluate cultural phenomena which may be introduced, in social science and in other curriculum areas. In many cases the introduction of these examples will be interpreted or evaluated to confirm negative stereotypes of strangeness and inferiority. Social science possesses the structures and procedures to facilitate a cognitive study of racism and ethnocentrism, which may go some way to reveal the basic assumptions from which such negative stereotyping derives. While such a study would not be directly designed to change attitudes, it engages students' attitudes and sensitizes them to the social, economic and political processes involved in their origin and perpetuation.

The content and approach of current teaching syllabuses

Social sciences are rarely taught below the fourth year in secondary schools and therefore teaching is even more highly dominated by GCE O level and CSE syllabuses than other subject areas. A recent review of current syllabuses revealed the confusion and controversy which exists over the content and approach of secondary school social science.[3] The review showed that very few courses are utilizing the potential of social science to develop a multicultural approach. Syllabus content is more commonly structured by themes and topics than by concepts. Acquisition of content dominates over acquisition of concepts and skills. Much of what is being taught and examined would probably be better termed social education as it consists largely of information designed to guide pupils through the complexity of life in an industrial society. Thus teaching about the family sometimes involves discussions on methods of contraception; teaching on work involves techniques for filling in job applications and interviews; discussion of housing involved investigation of dry rot and condensation problems. Valuable though this information is, it does little to further the development of the more conceptual and analytical approach of social science. Even in syllabuses exhibiting a more social scientific approach, topics are often presented in an Anglocentric way, portraying a consensus view of British society rather than attempting to penetrate the diversity which is a normal and acceptable part of a plural society. The use of terminology such as 'immigrant' or 'Asian' in many syllabuses and examination questions itself reveals a fair degree of stereotyping. When diversity is discussed it is frequently associated with social problems and deviance and located in discrete topics separate from other areas of the syllabus which discuss British society. Such an approach has the effect of confirming the experience of ethnic minority groups as separate and problematic and does little to enhance the validity of such experience as a legitimate part of British society.

Despite rich sources of anthropological data or resources developed by the World Studies Project or in development education, very few courses make any attempt to develop a more global approach either through reference to cross-cultural comparison or by investigating global, social, economic and political interdependence. Questions on racism and ethnocentrism tend to focus on questions of standards of morality or individual causation rather than developing other social scientific explanations. Little reference is made either to explanations which show that ideologies and attitudes evolve as a response to economic, social and political processes, or to the contributions of interactionist sociologists which illustrate the detrimental effects of stereotyping and labelling in human interaction.

There are a few syllabuses which exemplify the valuable contribution which social science can make to a multicultural curriculum. These syllabuses tend to take different approaches. One course relies heavily on the pupil's own experience in a multiethnic community using the individual, school and community as a resource with which to develop students' understanding of social science. Another course utilizes a conceptual framework which enables illustration from diverse cultures, while another penetrates other sociological explanations such as phenomenology, conflict and interaction and uses cross-cultural comparison to make these approaches accessible to secondary school students. Other syllabuses follow a more traditional topic-based approach but use race and culture along with sex and class as dimensions which infuse each and every topic. It is interesting to see how in these syllabuses the multicultural approach enriches a very high standard of interesting and imaginative social science. Particularly effective is the way multicultural data are used to develop greater conceptual understanding and to sharpen critical and analytical skills to facilitate a more objective approach to factors which may be taken for granted in the context of the student's own culture. Students often regard their own behaviour as so normal and meaningful that it is difficult for them to distance themselves from their own commonsense assumptions and understanding. This often hinders social scientific analysis. Studying other cultures both within and beyond their own society can often be a reflexive process, because in appreciating other cultural conceptions of 'normal' we question our own. Thus, quite apart from any moral or educational philosophies which may justify the development of a multicultural approach in social science, it can also lead to a better grasp of social science and a higher quality of teaching.

Developing a multicultural perspective in social sciences

Some teachers complain that examination syllabuses act as a constraint to curriculum innovation. Obviously in social sciences, where so much teaching is dominated by examinations, this claim may have some validity. Examinations set the agenda for discussion by structuring and delineating topics and deciding on the mode of assessment, but the transmission and interpretation of the syllabus is the responsibility of classroom teachers. As social scientists we should be aware that learning outcomes of students are determined as much by the method and approach of the teacher and the ethos and interaction of the classroom and school or college, as by the content of the syllabus. Thus multicultural education may require teachers to examine their classroom methods and the values and attitudes which underpin the ethos and organization of the classroom and school as much as the content of what they teach.

Examining boards and their subject committees are not entirely outside teachers' influence, and they may be prepared to take the lead and revise present syllabuses, especially since the introduction of a multicultural approach can offer such positive advantages for the grasp of the concepts and ideas of social science. It would appear that some current syllabuses already leave scope for the interpretation and development of a multicultural perspective. However, even when this is so there is some evidence to suggest that some teachers may not respond. For example, it is clearly intended that the conceptual approach taken by the Joint Matriculation Board's GCE O level Social Science should encourage the introduction of a broad selection of information and examples from world cultures. If such an approach were taken it might be expected that students would recognize the validity of other cultures. Nevertheless, the examiner's report of 1981 stated: 'The ethnocentric view demonstrated suggested that a case study of another culture might form a valuable part of the course.'[4]

Similarly, syllabus outlines, question setting and continuous assessment of project and course work often exhibit a fair degree of flexibility in content choice. The following section suggests some ways teachers can utilize this flexibility.

Permeation of existing syllabuses

Teachers need to develop ways of permeating already existing syllabuses so as to provide all pupils with knowledge, attitudes and skills to foster understanding of a multicultural society. Essential to such an approach is the need to provide greater space for ethnic minority students to utilize what should be the considerable academic advantages of being bicultural and bilingual, rather than treating them as peripheral and problematic.

Permeation of syllabuses is probably easier and more effective if the syllabus is framed by concepts rather than topics. Concepts are enabling rather than restrictive and give the teacher flexibility to choose illustrations from a diversity of cultures and situations which may be appropriate to the environment of the school, composition of the class or to the teacher's own interest, knowledge and experience. Concepts provide a framework of thought which once grasped can be used by students themselves to analyse and explain their own experience. This is clearly important in multiethnic classes where it is impossible for teachers to catalogue the details of each and every culture represented in their class, even if they had the knowledge. Concepts can be helpful in providing a unifying force for the analysis of all cultures, since they illustrate that cultures may be composed of similar elements. An institutional or topic-based approach often creates an us/them division because students have preferred meanings for topics such as family and education. Whereas when social science concepts are introduced, they are generally new to students, do not carry such meanings, and can therefore be used to compare cultures on a more equal basis.

The topic-based approach can actually create difficulties for teachers who are interested in exploring cultural diversity. Examination questions are less flexible and encourage prescriptive content. Usually this prescriptive content is related to an Anglocentric approach, underpinned by the notion that students should learn information about their nation as if that nation were ethnically homogeneous, and ignoring the differences which are a central feature of an interdependent multicultural society.

Nevertheless, there is still some potential for a multicultural approach. Figure 3.1 is designed to illustrate how race and culture along with sex and class could permeate a topic-based approach.

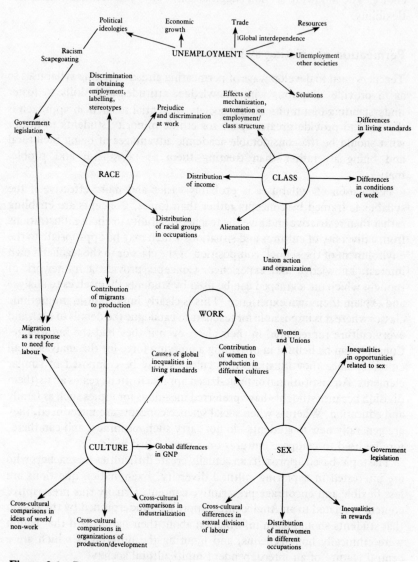

Figure 3.1 Permeating topic 'work' with dimensions of diversity

Teaching about cultures and combating ethnocentrism

Permeation in itself may not be sufficient to overcome ethnocentrism. The introduction of anthropological data needs sensitive and careful handling if it is to avoid confirming notions of the strangeness and inferiority of other cultures. Sometimes introducing examples of other cultures in isolation may lead to their being regarded as bizarre customs or cultural exotica. The teacher's intention may be to illustrate the diversity of human experience, but in practice students may interpret information to confirm ethnocentric attitudes. This can be exaggerated when pupils find it difficult to appreciate the validity of third world cultures which are, in their eyes, surrounded by poverty or lack of technological advancement. Terminology such as modern–primitive and industrial–preindustrial accentuates these difficulties.

In multiethnic classrooms ethnic minority students can be reticent to contribute their experience for fear of the racist and ethnocentric evaluations which may lead to their identification as separate from their peers and the dominant culture of the school. As Mullard comments:

> . . . other cultures, other ways of life, whether introduced as part of the formal or informal curriculum are seen and often openly evaluated against not their own value and belief patterns but, instead, those of the school and the wider British society . . .[5]

Overcoming this depends, in part, on creating an ethos in the school and classroom where differing cultural values have been absorbed and all cultural experience is recognized as valuable and important. This necessitates a close investigation of the structures, processes and routines that comprise the hidden curriculum.[6] Breaking down ethnocentrism through the overt curriculum depends on students understanding that

> . . . there are alternative ways of thinking, perceiving, feeling and behaving and that these are broadly determined by culture, that they are therefore learned rather than innate and relative rather than absolute, that all human societies have cultures which are complex, sensible and in principle intelligible . . .[7]

Social science teaching has a clear opportunity and responsibility here. Some preparatory work is necessary to lay the foundation for the development of the anthropological approach. All present syllabuses contain some reference to socialization. Most teachers probably already illustrate that much of human experience is learned and not instinctive by using examples of children deprived of human socialization,[8] and they are likely to illustrate the role of family, school, community and media in maintaining conformity to the expectations of society. This teaching can be extended to show that what is regarded as normal is culture bound and culture specific. Students need to understand in a simple way the relative nature of cultural standards, and how shared conceptions of reality determine our ideas of normal. Students find these ideas hard to grasp, and teachers will need to utilize a variety of techniques to develop understanding. One such tool is to study accounts of typical events and situations in British culture which have been stripped of commonsense meanings and are described as they might be by a stranger from another culture, as in 'Ret-seh-cnam' (Shelton 1974), 'Samtirch' (Mears and Pearsons 1981) or 'Body Ritual among the Nacirema' (Miner 1956).[9] These extracts generate students' interest both in trying to identify the everyday events described and in finding clues from the passage about the nature of the writer's imaginary culture. These passages illustrate how events and situations are made 'normal' and meaningful by shared conceptions of reality, and provide a salutory lesson that, unless a social scientist takes account of the viewpoint of a member of that culture, anthropological and sociological studies will be ethnocentric. Such an approach can illustrate methodological issues of objectivity and the rationale behind participant observation and ethnography.

A more factual extract, 'Footprint in the Sand: Black Exploration of the White Community' (Chevannes and Reeves 1979), while designed for A level students, can be adapted for younger students.[10] It sensitively shows how British culture can be misinterpreted by other cultures. It can be used with great effect to encourage and give confidence to ethnic minority students to recount their experiences. The paper provides some fascinating insights into prejudice and discrimination which can lead to an understanding that while cultures may be equally sensible and intelligible to their members they may not be equally acceptable in society. It is important for students to recognize that there are groups which have power to define which cultural behaviour is socially and legally acceptable through the education system, media and so on.

In developing understanding through engaging pupils' feelings and experiences *Rafa Rafa* (Shirts 1976) is a valuable simulation.[11] It develops empathetic understanding by illustrating the frustrations, misunderstandings and sometimes offence which can be engendered in interaction between people holding different cultural norms and conceptions of reality.

Showing other cultures as coherent and intelligible may require a case study of a culture. This may prevent other cultures being viewed as a series of bizarre and meaningless customs. In a topic-structured syllabus a case study of a culture could serve as an initial section since it could be used to illustrate the distinctive terminology of social science. Thereafter, throughout the investigations of topics which make up the bulk of the course, the culture selected for the case study could be used for comparison. There are good reasons for suggesting that the case study should be of a world culture rather than a British minority culture. Singling out one British minority culture may result in ethnic minority experience being separated from that of British society, but it may also lead to embarrassment for the ethnic minority students, particularly if their culture is inaccurately portrayed. Ethnic minority experience in Britain is very varied and rapidly changing and it would be very easy for a teacher presenting a case study of a British minority culture to fall into the trap of overgeneralization and stereotyping. On the other hand, an impartial study of one world society is likely to lead to a greater empathetic understanding of all cultures.

In introducing examples from third world cultures it may be necessary to expose the stereotype of poverty, disease, starvation, jungles etc. and to foster greater understanding of the extent and reasons for global inequalities created by colonialism and imperialism; it is also important to illustrate the attempts of third world societies themselves in developing their own societies. Having exposed the stereotype it may be used as a fund of teaching data which can itself illuminate relative values, relative notions of poverty, the nature of stereotypes and the role of the media in their perpetuation.

The task of portraying a culture which is not the teacher's own, from the viewpoint of that culture, is a daunting task which really requires first-hand experience. It may face teachers with a resource problem. Despite the fact that social sciences are particularly fortunate in having rich sources of anthropological data, many of these are at a highly academic level. Sometimes Commonwealth Institute speakers can make excellent starting points, provided the speaker is well briefed and the class has completed initial work on the anthropological approach. The Commonwealth Institute makes an interesting visit, particularly to show the contribution and development of commonwealth nations. The exhibits at the Museum of Mankind, which reconstruct living cultures with objects and artefacts placed in their own settings, are particularly useful. Both the Commonwealth Institute and Museum of Mankind have helpful education sections and provide free work sheets, with the practical facilities which schools need on visits to London, such as provision for eating sandwiches. Some teachers may want to utilize the good anthropological films, particularly those in which members of cultures speak for themselves. These are available on loan from the Royal Anthropological Institute Film Library.

Photopacks produced by Oxfam, Ikon and Development Education Centres can provide very useful cheap resources and contain very full background notes and teaching suggestions. They are particularly useful to indicate the changing economic growth and development of societies and cultures, since teachers should guard against the tendency of the anthropological approach of showing cultures as static.

Anti-racist teaching

Recent developments in anti-racist teaching emphasize the importance of the academic curriculum, social and personal education and whole school policies in establishing more favourable racial attitudes crucial to the development of a multicultural curriculum. Some anti-racist teaching has focused on individual attitudes concentrating on morality and aiming to sensitize students to manifestations of racism. Social science can complement these developments by explanations of the structural influences of an economic, political and social origin which help to generate racist attitudes and ideologies.

Because race illustrates hidden structural features which influence behaviour, it is a vital field of investigation for the development of understanding of the approach and concepts of social sciences. Students find difficulty in isolating and identifying these features, but as Hall (1980) says:

> . . . the issue of race provides one of the most important ways of understanding how this society actually works and how it has arrived where it is. It is one of the most important keys not into the margins of society but to its dynamic centre. It is a very good way of getting hold of the political and social issues of contemporary Britain because it touches and connects with so many facets.[12]

Yet despite race permeating so many issues and illustrating so many of the concepts and approaches of social science, teachers and examiners appear cautious and reticent to discuss race in any way other than a superficial or commonsense discussion of the existence of prejudice and discrimination and attempts at government amelioration. To some extent this is understandable, as teaching race is complex and emotionally charged. Teachers have been discouraged by controversies over pedagogy (Stenhouse et al. 1982);[13] the doubts about annexing the territory of students' attitudes in the liberal ethos of the education system (Jeffcoate

1979);[14] the pessimistic tone of research on teaching race (Miller 1969;[15] Stenhouse 1982[16]); and finally the lack of teaching resources. Any approach to the question of race will generate strong emotional reactions from students, and sometimes unleashes attitudes and controversies which may tax the resources of the most experienced teacher. 'Teaching Race' (Hall 1980)[17] demonstrates many of the complexities and potential pitfalls attached to developing the issue. Hall advocates the creation of an atmosphere which allows a free flow of communication and allows children to articulate the commonsense racism 'which is part of the air that we all breathe', for 'without hearing it teachers can't engage it and defuse it'. Teachers may understand the necessity of creating this atmosphere and yet it is exactly this situation which is most difficult to manage. There is a very fine division between promoting the necessary communication, and degeneration into counterproductive trading in racial insults or into a confrontation between the views of the teacher and the student from which students may find difficulty in retracting or reassessing their viewpoints. Social science teachers are used to coping with sensitive issues and dissension but even in dealing with parallel issues such as sexism there does not seem to be the same potential for vicious and dehumanizing statements as there is in racism. With such dangers, and especially in multiethnic classrooms where teachers may be concerned to protect the identities of ethnic minority pupils, teachers may decide that they may do more harm than good.

Social science has a unique role to play here since the debate can be established on a more academic level, and from the morass of feelings and attitudes can develop a study which enhances understanding of social scientific concepts, evidence and data, using race, as Bob Ferguson (1981) suggests, to develop 'careful structured development of theoretical skills combined with the acquisition of necessary empirical data'.[18] Such a study would inevitably sensitize students to the existence of racism, inform and combat prejudice based on ignorance and explain the processes involved in the creation of racist ideologies and attitudes.

In permeating syllabuses it is necessary to reveal the social, economic and political inequalities associated with race – social inequalities which may result in low status and poor life chances; economic inequalities such as unfavourable distribution of income, lack of investment in inner-city areas despite low costs of reproduction of work force; and political inequalities of citizenship rights and access to decision-making mechanisms. Explaining the processes causing the inequalities is important, lest students are left blaming the victims and with the impression that the fault lies either with individual attitudes or ethnic minority groups themselves. In explaining racial inequalities at a micro level the concepts of labelling and stereotyping can be introduced. Examples from education, work, law and order and housing which illustrate the negative effects of prejudice and discrimination are plentiful. The film *Eye of the Storm* (see Resources, Section 3c) represents a very powerful and yet understandable introduction for 14–16-year-old students to these concepts.

At a macro level, social science can illustrate how economic-based class inequalities may engender social and political ideologies which help to perpetuate inequality. The simulation *Star Power* (Shirts 1969)[19] makes a useful starting point to this difficult notion. Basically a trading game, it divides the class into three unequally placed groups with little chance of mobility. The most successful group then creates the rules and almost without exception the rules they make perpetuate their power and privileged position. From the understanding which such a simulation gives, students can go on to reveal the existence of ideologies which perpetuate inequalities.

There are already three topic areas on many syllabuses which can illustrate the influence of ideologies – migration, media studies and global issues – and these are explored below.

Migration is an important issue for discussion since so much of the debate on race has centred on numbers. The study can be used to disentangle some of the myths regarding migration from the evidence. (Dickenson 1982).[20] It can be used to show how racist attitudes and ideologies may respond to economic factors. Some migration can be seen as a response to the need for cheap labour; the curtailing of immigration and the rights of immigrants in times of recession can be viewed as a political response; the politicization of race as an election and legislative issue can be analysed, together with the division of the working class by racist ideologies and the use of migrants as scapegoats.

Media studies research has shown the effects of media on children's attitudes (Hartman and Husband 1974).[21] Thus, encouraging a critical approach to the various forms of the media may discourage treatment of media reports at face value. Overt evidence of bias and distortion in newspaper reporting can be illustrated by comparing newspaper reports of the same incident or a comparative study of all the newspapers published on one day; analysing films such as *It ain't half racist, Mum* (see Resources,

Section 3c) or common examples from children's literature can be equally illuminating (Klein 1982).[22] Semiology or image analysis also makes a useful approach. This analysis takes familiar presentations from the media to illustrate how these images act as signs, which connote cultural meanings derived from economic, political and ideological forces of society. The study of media images clearly illustrates how the portrayal of racial groups reflects and perpetuates the power relations of society. It demonstrates how these representations may change as a response to changes in political, economic and ideological forces of society. 'Race and the Media' (Ferguson 1981)[23] makes a useful introduction for teachers and illustrates the potential of this approach. But the semiological approach has been thoroughly developed for teachers in the British Film Institute's teachers' resource pack *Images and Blacks* (1981).[24] This pack can be used to develop and illustrate social science concepts and also in developing skills of critical analysis. Such a study is particularly relevant and interesting to students, since it is mostly visual, based on materials from films and television, which are intrinsically interesting to students. It contains the potential for an investigative approach. But importantly it 'sets up a context in which students black and white can begin to understand how political, economic and ideological forces interact naturally, to endlessly produce racist . . . representation'.

A global approach to world issues integrates the disciplines of sociology, economics and politics to show how economic inequalities can engender a political and ideological response. The Institute of Race Relations' recent publications *Roots of Racism* and *Patterns of Racism*[25] can be used to examine whether colonial and imperial economic regimes created racist ideologies to justify and support their perpetuation. But also the portrayal of third world nations prevalent in media and in some social studies textbooks may be regarded as evidence of an ideology which supports notions of Western superiority and the apparent incompetence of non-Western nations in governing themselves. Emphasis is frequently placed on: the extent of third world problems, rather than global, economic and political inequalities which create these problems; the supposed positive role of foreign aid in development, rather than third world actions towards their *own* self-development; and the conception of development which equates with the Western view, rather than the third world nations' own values or views of their development.

Despite all the difficulties inherent in teaching race which necessitate the use of professional skills, imagination and sensitivity, social science teachers have a responsibility to use the potentiality of their subject to expose racism at all levels. As HMIs Slater and Hennessy maintain:

> Some views and attitudes are arguably unacceptable in our democracy, racism; suppression of opinion; exploitation of the defenceless. They are anathema to most people in our society. Education which identifies the evils we must resist and suggests how we may resist them is quite proper and likely to command wide support.[27]

Developing skills

Many of the resources and approaches recommended in this chapter have attempted to extend knowledge and understanding of social science and a multicultural society, but also to develop a variety of skills. Skills, such as finding and evaluating evidence, presenting a logical argument, identifying bias and distortion, showing empathy, and development of political literacy can all be developed through a study of social science. These skills are of vital importance to students' future participation in a multicultural society. While particular information may be forgotten or becomes outdated, skills may be more durable. However, acquisition of skills necessitates practice. The resources for classroom use listed below emphasize some of the participatory, experiential and investigative teaching strategies which are not generally found in traditional textbooks. These methods give students the opportunities to practice a variety of skills and also make difficult concepts and ideas relevant to 14–16-year-old students.

Resources

1   Multicultural education and social sciences

A real problem for teachers is keeping up to date with the theory and practice of both multicultural education and social sciences. The selected books and publications are particularly useful to teachers in keeping abreast of developments.

Crick, B. and Porter, A. (1978) *Political Education and Political Literacy*. London: Longman.

Gomm, R. and McNeill, P. (eds.) (1982) *Handbook for Sociology Teachers*. London: Heinemann Educational.

Hicks, D. and Townley, C. (eds.) (1982) *Teaching World Studies*. London: Longman.

James, A. and Jeffcoate, R. (eds.) (1982) *The School in the Multicultural Society*. London: Harper and Row.
Tierney, J. (ed.) (1982) *Race, Migration and Schooling*. Eastbourne: Holt, Rinehart and Winston.
Twitchen, J. (ed.) (1981) *Multicultural Education*. London: BBC Publications.
Whitehead, D. (1982) *Handbook for Economics Teachers*. London: Heinemann Educational Books.

A very easy and effective way of keeping in touch with developments is through membership of the following organizations; subscription entitles members to copies of the very useful association journals.

Association for Teaching of Social Science 3 Battlefield Road, St Albans, Herts.
Economics Association Temple Lodge, South Street, Ditchling, Sussex, BN6 8UQ.
National Association for Multicultural Education PO Box 9, Walsall, West Midlands, WS1 3SF.
Politics Association 16 Gower Street, London, WC1E 6DP.

2 Teaching culture

2a Resources for teachers

Bulmer, J. (1977) *Guide to Teaching of Anthropology in Schools and Colleges*. Available from Extramural Division, School of Oriental and African Studies, University of London, Malet Street, London WC1E 7HP.
Royal Anthropological Institute (1980) *Teachers' Resource Guide*. Available from Royal Anthropological Institute, 56 Queen Anne Street, London W1M 9LA.
Social Science Teacher Anthropology Editions: Vol 7 No 4 April 1978; Vol 11 No 3 April 1982.

2b Resources for classroom use

The ATSS Anthropology Advisory Panel produces Resources Broadsheets which are available from J. Corlett, Oxford College of Further Education, Cowley Road Precinct, Cowley Road, Oxford. Included here are details of the particular resources mentioned in the chapter.

Chevannes, M. and Reeves, F. (1979) 'Footprint in the Sand: Black Exploration of the White Community – an Autobiographical Approach'. *In* R. Meighan, I. Shelton and T. Marks (eds.) *Perspectives on Society*. London: Nelson.
Hurman, A. (1977) *As Others See Us*. London: Edward Arnold.
Mears, R. and Parsons, W. (1981) 'Samtirch', *Social Science Teacher* Vol 10, No 3.
Miner (1956) 'Body Ritual among the Nacirema', *American Anthropologist* Vol 58, June.
Shelton, I. (1974) 'Ret-seh-cnam' in 'The Sociology of Everyday Life'. In *Handbook for Sociology Teachers* R. Gomm and P. McNeill (eds.) 1982. London: Heinemann.

Shirts, R.G. (1976) *Rafa Rafa*. Available from Christian Aid Publications, Box 1, London SW9 8BH.

2c   Films and photopacks

Oxfam Educational Department, 274 Banbury Road, Oxford, produce photopacks on Jamaica, Bangla Desh, India, Botswana amongst others.

Royal Anthropological Institute Film Library. Distributors: Scottish Central Film Library, 74 Victoria Crescent Road, Dowanhill, Glasgow, G12 9JN.

Taylor, N. and Richardson, R. (1979) *Seeing and Perceiving*. Ikon. Comprehensive and useful suggestions on availability and use of film on all areas of multicultural education.

Voluntary Committee on Overseas Aid and Development. The International Development Centre, 25 Wilton Road, London SW1 1JS produce photopacks on Tanzania and Kenya; City and Village Life in Western India; Latin America.

2d   Exhibitions

Commonwealth Institute, Kensington High Street, London W8 6NQ.

Museum of Mankind, 6 Burlington Gardens, London W1.

3   Teaching race

3a   Resources for teachers

A very full and comprehensive guide to books, journals and organizations interested in race relations is available in Tierney's *Race, Migration and Schooling* (see Resources, Section 1). The resources identified below relate only to the theory and practice of teaching race.

All London Teachers Against Racism and Fascism (ALTARF) (1979) *Teaching and Racism*.

Carby, H. (1980) Multi Culture, *Screen Education* 34, Spring, pp. 62–71.

Dodgson, P. and Stewart, D. (1981) Multiculturalism and anti-racist teaching: a question of alternative, *Multiracial Education* Vol 9, No 2, pp. 41–52.

Green, A. (1982) 'In defence of anti-racist teaching: a reply to recent critiques of multicultural education, *Multiracial Education* Vol 10, No 2, pp. 19–34.

Hall, S. (1980) Teaching Race. *In* James and Jeffcoate (eds.) 1982, pp. 58–69. See Resources, Section 1.

Jeffcoate, R. (1979a) A multicultural curriculum beyond the orthodoxy, *Trends in Education*, No. 4, pp. 8–12.

Jeffcoate, R. (1979b) *Positive Image*. Chameleon, Richmond, Surrey.

Parkinson, J. and MacDonald, B. (1981) Teaching Race neutrally. *In* James and Jeffcoate (eds.) 1982, pp. 206–217. See Resources, Section 1.

Stenhouse, L., Verna, B.V., Wild, R.D. and Dixon, J. (1982) *Teaching about Race Relations: problems and effects*. London: Routledge and Kegan Paul.

Ben Tovim, G. and Gabriel, J. (1979) The sociology of race – time to change course, *The Social Science Teacher* Vol 8, No 4, pp. 141–148.

3b   Resources for classroom use

AFFOR (1982) *Race Relations Teaching Pack*. Available from All Faiths for One Race, 1 Finch Road, Lozells, Birmingham B19 14S (very useful for teachers who may not have taught race before).

Community Service Volunteers *Hassle* (a board game designed to explore prejudice and discrimination) CSV at 237 Pentonville Road, London N20.

The Economist Schools Briefs (1982) *Britain's Urban Breakdown*. The Economist Newspaper.

Institute of Race Relations (1982) *Roots of Racism* and *Patterns of Racism*.

Shirts, G.R. *Star Power*. Available from Christian Aid.

Wolsk, D. (1975) *An Experience Centred Curriculum* Educational studies and documents No 17, UNESCO (Activity 8, 'Faces', is particularly useful in illustrating processes by which we form stereotypes, but many of the experiential activities in the book can have application in social science).

3c   Films and photopacks

Doing Things in and about the Home. Booklet and photographs designed to explore sexism and sex roles but useful discussion exercises can lead into discussions of stereotyping, race, ethnicity. Available from Maidenhead Teachers Centre.

Eye of the Storm and *It ain't half racist, Mum*. Available from Concord Films Council, 201 Felixstowe Road, Ipswich, Suffolk, IP3 9BJ.

The World in Birmingham. A photopack showing various aspects of a multiethnic community. A useful starting point for discussion of race. Available from Development Education Centre, Gillett Centre, Selly Oak Colleges, Bristol Road, Birmingham.

Values, Cultures and Kids. Approaches and resources for teaching about family and child development. Designed by a working party of home economics teachers but touches on many areas covered by social scientists and uses some interesting teaching strategies which illustrate how multicultural perspectives can be integrated into present syllabuses. Available from Development Education Centre, Birmingham (full address above).

3d   Migration

Dickenson, P. (1982) Facts and figures: some myths. *In* Tierney (ed.) 1982. See Resources, Section 1.

Runnymede Trust, 62 Chandos Place, London WC2N 4HH. Information office can supply statistics on migration.

3e   Media

British Film Institute (1981)*Images and Blacks*, Teachers' Resource Pack. Slides and Notes available from BFI, 81 Dean Street, London W1.

Ferguson, B. (1981) Race and the Media: some problems in teaching, *Multiracial Education* Vol 9, No 2, pp. 27–41.

Hartman, P. and Husband, C. (1974) *Racism and Mass Media*. London: Davis-Poynter.

Klein, G. (1982) *Resources for Multicultural Education: an Introduction*. Schools Council Programme Pamphlet Series, York: Longman.

3f Global approach to world issues

These publications are not only useful for content and approach to world studies but also because of the teaching strategies which can be adapted and used in social science teaching. There is also a very comprehensive list of resources on world studies in Hicks and Townley's *Teaching World Studies* (see Resources, Section 1).

Birmingham Development Education Centre (1981) *Priorities for Development*.

Christian Aid (1980) *The Trading Game*. A very effective simulation for illustrating effects of global economic inequalities.

Nance Lui Tyson (1979) *The Development Puzzle*. Centre for World Development Education.

Richardson, R. (ed.) (1976) *Learning for Change in World Society: Reflections, Activities, Resources*. World Studies Project. London: One World Trust.

Richardson, R. (1978) *Caring for the Planet; World in Conflict; Fighting for Freedom; Progress and Poverty*. Walton-on-Thames: Nelson.

Richardson, R., Flood, M. and Fisher, S. (1979) *Debate and Decision: Schools in a World of Change*. London: One World Trust.

4 British ethnic minority cultures

Permeating syllabuses with the experience of British ethnic minority cultures may require teachers to develop a greater understanding and knowledge of minority cultures. The following academic research might help the teacher gain a greater appreciation of diversity.

Centre for Contemporary Cultural Studies (1982) *The Empire Strikes Back: Race and Racism in 70's Britain*. London: Hutchinson.

Dhondy, F. (1982) Teaching young blacks. *In* James and Jeffcoate (eds.) pp. 257–270. See Resources, Section 1.

Husband, C. (ed.) (1982) *'Race' in Britain: continuity and change*. London: Hutchinson University Library.

Institute of Race Relations (for CARF and Southall Rights) (1981) *Southall: The Birth of a Black Community*.

Khan, S. (1979) *Minority Families in Britain*. London: Macmillan.

Miles, R. and Phizacklea, A. (1980) *Labour and Racism*. London: Routledge and Kegan Paul.

Pryce, K. (1979) *Endless Pressure*. Harmondsworth: Penguin.

Rex, J. and Tomlinson, S. (1979) *Colonial Immigrants in a British City*. London: Routledge and Kegan Paul.

Wallman, S. (1979) *Ethnicity and Work*. London: Macmillan.

Watson, J. (1977) *Between Two Cultures*. Oxford: Basil Blackwell.

Wilson, A. (1978) *Finding a Voice*. London: Virago.

Teachers may also find the television magazine programmes *Eastern Eye* (Channel 4), *Black on Black* (Channel 4) and *Ebony* (BBC 2) useful in familiarizing themselves with the perspectives of ethnic minority groups, their problems, interests and aspirations.

Teachers may be able to use members of ethnic minority groups, either teachers or parents, to talk to students. In organizing such a visit it may be helpful to use the technique advocated in the Active Tutorial Work programme (Baldwin, J. and Wells, H. (eds.) *Active Tutorial Work* Book 5, (1981) Basil Blackwell, pp. xvi–xvii; Button, L. (1974) *Developmental Group Work*, Hodder and Stoughton, pp. 86, 110, 163). This overcomes the necessity of the visitor having to give a formal talk and places the responsibilities on the students to invite, meet and entertain their visitor. They are also required to ask the visitor the questions which will derive the information they need. The technique requires considerable preparation and rehearsal, but is most worthwhile.

Notes and references

1 For the purposes of this chapter social sciences refers to the integrated recommended statement of 16+ National Criteria for Social Sciences approach suggested in the GCE and CSE Boards' Joint Council for 16+ National Criteria (1983). The chapter therefore concentrates on syllabuses which are referred to as Social Science or Social Studies although it may be of help to teachers of the separate subject disciplines, particularly sociology and to a lesser extent economics and politics.

2 Hall, S. (1982) Teaching Race. *In* A. James and R. Jeffcoate (eds.) *The School in the Multicultural Society*. London: Harper and Row, pp. 58–69.

3 Mukhopadhyay, A. (1984) *Assessment in a Multicultural Society: Social Sciences at 16+*, Schools Council Programme 5 Pamphlet Series. York: Longman.

4 Joint Matriculation Board (1981) *Examiner's Report*, O level Social Science.

5 Mullard, C. (1982) Multicultural education in Britain from assimilation to cultural pluralism. *In* J. Tierney (ed.) *Race, Migration and Schooling*. Eastbourne: Holt, Rinehart and Winston.

6 Teachers interested in a 'holistic' approach to multicultural education will find the ILEA *Aide Memoire for the Inspectorate* very helpful.

7 Corlett, J. (1978) Social anthropology for general studies students, *Social Science Teacher* Vol 7, No 4, p. 13.

8 See, for example, Nagel and Brown (1978) The Wild Boy of Aveyron, *Social Science Teacher* Vol 8, No 2; and Hambling and Mathews (1974) *Human Society*, pp. 154–6 (Anna and Isabelle case studies). London: Macmillan Education.

9 For details see Resources, Section 2b, at the end of this chapter.

10 For details see Resources, Section 2b, at the end of this chapter.

11 For details see Resources, Section 2b, at the end of this chapter.

12 Hall, S. (1982) *op. cit.*

13 Stenhouse, L. et al. (1982) *Teaching about Race Relations: problems and effects*. London: Routledge and Kegan Paul.

14 Jeffcoate, R. (1979) *Positive image*. Richmond, Surrey: Chameleon.

15   Miller, H.J. (1969) The effectiveness of teaching techniques for reducing colour prejudice, *Liberal Education* 16.
16   Stenhouse, L. et al. (1982) *op. cit.*
17   Hall, S. (1980) *op. cit.*
18   Ferguson, B. (1981) Race and the media, some problems in teaching, *Multiracial Education* Vol 9, No 2, pp. 27–41.
19   Shirts, G.R. (1969) *Star Power*, a simulation game available from Christian Aid.
20   Dickenson, P. (1982) Facts and figures: some myths. *In* J. Tierney (ed.) *Race, Migration and Schooling*. Eastbourne: Holt, Rinehart and Winston.
21   Hartman, P. and Husband, C. (1974) *Racism and Mass Media*. London: Davis-Poynter.
22   Klein, G. (1982) *Resources for Multicultural Education: an Introduction*, Schools Council Programme 4 Pamphlet Series. York: Longman.
23   Ferguson, B. (1981) *op. cit.*
24   British Film Institute (1981) *Images and Blacks* Teachers' Resource Pack. Available from BFI, 81 Dean St, London W1.
25   Institute of Race Relations (1982) *Roots of Racism* and *Patterns of Racism*.
26   Slater, J. and Hennessy, A. (1977) Political competence. *Reprinted in* B. Crick and A. Porter (eds.) (1978) *Political Education and Political Literacy*. London: Longman, pp. 254–255.

CHAPTER 4*

RELIGIOUS EDUCATION

Angela Wood

I once dropped a pile of carefully sequenced papers which flew about and landed in random order, and I was heard, in front of the class, to utter a mild curse. 'Tut! Tut!' exclaimed Bola, somewhat tongue-in-cheek. 'You're an RE teacher!'

'So what?' retorted Ziggy. '*She*'s got as much right to swear as anyone else!'

It seemed to me then, and it does now, that Ziggy and Bola represented two ideologies and that they enacted a tension at the heart of the subject and the teacher's role: a tension between the cognitive and the affective, between academic study and moral application, between ideas of the mind and values of the heart. I was frankly grateful to Ziggy for a little social justification and because it *is* true that the Religious Education (RE) teacher draws on *humanity*. But Bola, too, was pointing to something very significant.

There was a time when RE in state schools in Britain was seen as a process of acculturation and Christian nurture: that is, it was based on the assumption that Britain was consistently and coherently Christian and that it was the aim of RE to affirm agreed values and foster the pupil's faith. Whether the basis for this is a fair or accurate picture of society is debatable; at any rate, that is not the view now. The (old) 'Bola', with the teacher as guardian angel and moral missionary, is fading out and a (new) 'Ziggy' has faded in –

---

* Some of the ideas in this chapter are an extension of those in *Assessment in a Multicultural Society: Religious Studies at 16+* by Angela Wood. Schools Council Programme 5 Pamphlet Series. Longman, York, 1984.

an academic study of world religions which requires of the teacher a fund of new knowledge and a bank of material resources, as well as a 'neutral' stance. Ziggy was correct: assuming anyone has the right to swear, the RE teacher is not a priestly figure or a person apart but has an equal right to be human. As the teacher acts as a representative of the subject and the process, it is clear that there has been a shift from 'Bola' RE to 'Ziggy' RE. A 'Bola'-free RE may *look* fairer and broader and more interesting to pupils, but it has its limitations. In particular, it has failed in some circles to recognize the extent of children's emotional needs and the value-questions inherent in and pertaining to humanity's religious experience.

A new RE is emerging, as yet formless but definitely not void. It combines elements of concern for moral living (though it probably cares more about world hunger than any linguistic impoverishment) and an implied demand for autonomy, authenticity and academic enquiry. New dimensions are also developing, and together they offer a greater chance than ever before of RE not only finding but also creating curriculum opportunities in a multicultural society. This chapter explores several aspects of RE as it is already being practised in some schools and which hint at these opportunities.

Teaching about, and learning from, religion

Three styles of RE are currently being practised, sometimes more than one by a single teacher, conceivably within a single lesson. Certainly, there are some who would vary their style according to the subject-matter and situation. The 'neo-confessional' style is an attempt to make confessionalism (the testimony of faith and the encouragement to believe) more modern in method and more acceptable in a multicultural society. In practice it is an open-ended form of Christian nurture, making token acknowledgement of 'other faiths'.

In a multicultural society, the 'implicit' approach, which draws on the religious dimension in human experience, must naturally reflect the diversity of such experience. This approach therefore abandons the 'confessional' standpoint altogether and adopts an unrestricted quest for ultimate meaning in life. This approach is more common at primary school level where immediacy and spontaneity are more feasible because there are fewer external constraints (such as examination pressure or rigid timetabling). In secondary schools, 'implicit' RE is evident in thematic work, in integrated programmes and in assemblies.

By contrast, the 'explicit' method begins not with the individual teacher and learner but with the overt phenomena of religious traditions and alternatives to religion. The relevance to pupils' lives is of less significance than the study of the phenomena as phenomena. This approach is no more confessional and no less enquiring or analytical than the 'implicit' style, but it deals with different subject matter and is travelling, so to speak, in a different direction. It represents a direct attempt to come to terms with the religious pluralism of our society and of the world. The emphasis is on intellectual qualities but there is no reason in theory why it should not fully engage learners emotionally: 'The "implicit" and the "explicit" belong together – the search for meaning and the study of religions' (Schools Council 1977, p. 13).

The single most decisive influence on contemporary RE has been the work of Ninian Smart, especially his book *Secular Education and the Logic of Religion* (1968). Based at the University of Lancaster, his writings throughout the 1970s were broadly phenomenological, that is, descriptive and external as in the 'explicit' approach, and this shaped the Schools Council project 'Journeys into Religion' which was centred there from 1969 to 1973. 'Journeys' was founded quite directly on the six dimensions of religion which had been delineated by Smart: *doctrinal* – believers' formal statements of belief, usually presented in a rational form; *mythological* – exploratory and allusive writings in poetic or narrative form; *ethical* – the 'way of life', based on an individual's or religious group's ideas of right and wrong, which might be strengthened by a system of law; *experiential* – each believer's personal, living faith as it flows from and into the life they actually lead; *ritual* – religious acts which might be highly stylized and which carry heavy symbolism; and *social* – the sense of togetherness shared by believers.

According to this view, RE would be concerned not to initiate young people into one religion but into the meaning of religion and religions. It is put most succinctly by Minton (1983): 'You cannot make children either Christian or religious – both are wrong. I regard school as a place where lots of views of life can cross one another. The job of the school is to make sure that this is done in a tolerant way.'

Related to this notion of tolerance – perhaps that which creates tolerance – is the notion of honesty. Two statements bear out the importance of being 'true' to truth:

> There should be no gossip, no stories about a religion which would not be told in the presence of its adherents. (Cole 1978, p. 23)
> ... present Jews, Muslims, Hindus ... in a positive and, if critical, constructively, appreciatively critical, way. At the very least, not say about them things that are *not* true. (Wood 1979, p. 28)

RE is clearly an exercise in standing in another's shoes – and in taking off your own to stand on their holy ground! A religious tradition should be seen from the point of view of those who belong to it and descriptions of religious phenomena should not be distorted by externally imposed value judgements: questions of truth and value should be recognized for what they are.

While the dominant religion of the society might warrant dominance in the RE curriculum, more than one tradition must be present in order to guarantee the awareness of diversity. Non-religion and irreligion might well have their place, too, because of the agnostic mood of adolescence and secular, atheistic interpretations of reality which are prevalent in the modern world. In recent years, there has been some attempt, especially through the British Humanist Association, to replace the term 'RE' with a phrase such as 'education in stances for living'. The Humanists involved feel this would engender a more 'objective, fair and balanced' approach (BHA 1975); it would be a more inclusive activity but would preserve all the depth, richness and subtlety of 'religion'. Stopes-Roe differentiates between the two terms:

> Life stance: whatever the individual finds to be involved in his response to ultimacy. Religion: a life stance which finds ultimacy in God – or, more generally, finds ultimacy to involve a reference beyond the natural world, to the Absolute, or to a transcendent order or process. (1976, p. 25)

The first curriculum manifestation of 'life-stance' was the controversial Birmingham Agreed Syllabus and Handbook 'Living Together' which advocated intellectual development through a 'problem-centred' curriculum, the individual's search for meaning and a concern for the social context of religion.

World religions and the world

It is apparent that RE is becoming increasingly directed towards developing a critical understanding of the religious and moral dimensions of human experience and away from attempting to foster claims of particular religious standpoints. However, that is not enough, because all religions point beyond themselves to moral and spiritual realities, and RE must be more than a watered down – or even dressed up – social studies. In fact, it is really quite a different subject altogether for it can only fully meet the needs of a multicultural society – in Britain and worldwide – if it considers also what religion has done, what it has failed to do and what it says about the behaviour of human beings regardless of their religious affiliation. RE is thus '. . . self-defeating if it is only concerned with the study of "the religious dimension of human experience" and not with the realities which religious experience tries to grasp and respond to' (Newbigin 1977, p. 87).

Multicultural education which focuses not only upon the peoples of Britain but takes the whole world as its arena suggests a global dimension to RE; there is, indeed, a growing link between RE today and 'world studies' or 'education for international understanding'. The Centre for World Development Education emphasizes 'those aspects [of RE] which bear on problems of social justice . . . both what a religion teaches in theory and also how its members behave in practice' (Davies et al. 1979, p. 12).

The most vigorous and articulate exponent of the link between RE and world studies has been Richardson, who rightly points to the imbalance in the teaching of world religions, to the emphasis on the external and the peripheral at the expense of the central issues of human concern:

> We teach about the 5 K's of Sikhism . . . more readily than about the massacre at Amritsar; about the gods and festivals of Hinduism more readily than . . . Kipling's infamous proposal that non-Europeans are 'half-devil and half-child'; about the prayers and mosques of Islam more readily than about . . . the second-class status of Muslim children in many European schools; about the synagogue, Sabbath and bar mitzvah more readily than about . . . the holocaust . . . to understand any particular religious community you have to understand the threats to its integrity and to its very existence which it has had to withstand from other human beings. (1982, p. 184)

To include such issues would not be difficult to arrange in an RE curriculum – for the religions of the world teem with issues of justice, equality and dignity. Less easy to provide is the willingness and the sensitivity and the courage required of teachers to handle such issues in an enlightening and creative way. The external constraints are many and the teacher will not embark on the venture in the face of negative answers to such questions as: 'Is it on the exam syllabus?', 'Would the parents object?', 'Can I open and close it in a 35-minute period?', 'Will it get them jobs?', 'Will colleagues say (again) that RE is a waste of everyone's time?', 'Am I sufficiently experienced to succeed in the venture? And these questions will come before the more searching ones such as: 'Where do I stand on colonialism and imperialism?', 'What is its relationship with religion?', 'Can I present religion as a force for peace in world affairs?', 'Am I manipulating minds?', 'Can I accept responsibility for the children's learning?', 'Will they be "creatively descontented" or merely frustrated and bitter?', 'Shall I let sleeping dogs lie?'

There are some religious communities – Jews and Rastafarians, for example – which have been much more responsive to, and much more reflective about, their collective experiences than other religious communities have been; perhaps because they have had more to respond to. In these two cases the phenomenon of anti-semitism and of being Black in Babylon offer penetrating insights into the Jewish and Rastafarian conditions; put negatively, it seems impossible to understand them without understanding these phenomena, so crucial have they been and so formative each of these communitys' character and creed. However devastating the sacking of the Tibetan monasteries, on the other hand, it is unlikely to offer any new angle or any deeper insight into Buddhism as such than was available before the catastrophe took place. The same might be said of the execution of Baha'is in Iran. We may mourn their loss and be angered at the injustice but the event tells us nothing more about their faith.

Where persecution is a key to knowledge we learn less about the persecuted than the persecutors – less about the done to and more about the doers: how the Muslims were treated during the Crusades tells us about the Christians – their values, beliefs, aspirations and their perception of their role in history. Similarly, the Muslim treatment of Christians tells us more about Muslims than about Christians.

The response to persecution is a vital area of study, too; in particular, how religious systems have dealt with, or why they have dodged, disadvantage and disaster. Richardson (1982) discusses the use of the parable of the Good Samaritan as an exhortation to 'love thy neighbour' in RE lessons. It is, indeed, well known and very popular with teachers – though less well liked by pupils – and can be used as a model of the relationship between the capitalist West and the Third World. Richardson is quick to point out that the thrust of the parable is about the badness of those who pass by and the goodness of the Samaritan who stopped out of universal love and who cared for the victim of violence. The greater badness, however, is of the thieves who beat up the man and took all he had in the first place.

> The political obligation on the thieves not to beat people up, or at least to make reparation once they have done so, is surely greater than the obligation on third parties to succour and comfort their victims. But anyway, supposing the Samaritan himself was a receiver of stolen goods? Perhaps the money he gave to the innkeeper had previously been slipped to him by the very thieves whose victim he was now helping? (1982, p. 185)

Clearly, Richardson is drawing a connection between the Church in the North as an agent of relief and its support for political systems, which may have created, directly or indirectly, by omission or by commission, the conditions which need so much relief.

In the RE context, we cannot right all the world's wrongs but we can alter – or at least stop perpetuating – the kind of thinking in teachers and pupils which provides an occasional Lady Bountiful but continues to permit the need for such bounty. To take Richardson's point a stage further, the parable fails as an image of a healthy relationshp between the North and the South because it advocates mercy when justice is more desperately needed. To serve as a role model for young people in a multicultural world characterized by inequality, injustice and indignity, the Samaritan might well have sought out the perpetrators of violence (perhaps the two passers-by could be enlisted to help; they might find it more practical); demanded that they fully compensate their victim for the financial, physical and emotional damage they caused him; worked tirelessly to create better protection for individuals travelling alone; joined a consciousness-raising group concerned to promote healthy interethnic relations; and voted for a government – or stood for office in it! – that was committed to the introduction and implementation of human rights . . .

Christian culture and the curriculum

Before, during and after the recent changes in the form and function of RE, voices of protest have been raised. Some committed Christian educators have argued that the expansion of content to include material from non-Christian sources has necessarily reduced the time and resources available in schools for teaching, or teaching about, Christianity.

There are two main elements of concern: the first, in its weak form, is that Christian teachers have less opportunity to introduce children to Christian belief and behaviour. The strong form of this is that teaching about world religions reduces the primacy of Christianity and suggests to children that there are viable alternatives to it. Clearly, those concerned with multicultural RE must refute these claims on both religious and educational grounds. It is dishonest to pretend that there are no viable alternatives to Christianity when millions in Britain and billions throughout the world are patently *not* Chrstian. RE is a process whereby – among other things – pupils can come to see patterns of belief, behaviour and belonging as they really are. It is not an arena for the wish-fulfilment of the teacher, a vehicle for soul-snatching. Such activites, if they are legitimate at all, are inappropriate in state schools.

The second element of concern is that the majority of the British people have been Christian (they still constitute the largest single religious group) and that the British way of life has been shaped by Christianity since its arrival. (Certainly there are some 'immigrant' Asian parents who see Christian education as a means of cultural assimilation for their children.) It is therefore an important part of the educational process of making pupils aware of their cultural environment that they should have some knowledge and understanding of Christianity and some appreciation of its contribution to their lives.

Within the framework of multicultural RE, there is a very important role for the teaching and learning of Christianity. But it must obey the pluralist rules and play the objective game. The Chichester Project is a group of teachers and teacher educators centred in and around Bishop Otter College, Chichester, who have been producing a series of textbooks for secondary schools which present Christianity in its phenomenological terms, alongside other faiths: the Project does not make Christianity a special case.

There is no special case for the intrinsic worth of Christianity but there is a special case for its volume: within an RE curriculum in British schools, it may reasonably occupy greater time and space in typological approaches to religion, it will probably be drawn upon more heavily in themes and it is likely to serve more frequently to illustrate and exemplify manifestations of religious phenomena whenever religion per se is discussed.

There are two distinctive contributions that the teaching of Christianity can make to multicultural RE. First, it can be presented not as a monolith but in all its richness and diversity, theological and otherwise. It should certainly not be limited to its 'white' or 'British' appearances, but should expose the full Christian experience and (especially in the spirit of positive discrimination) accord a place of honour to Black Christianity.

Secondly, there must be critical appraisal of the historic socio-political stance of Christianity and a serious consideration of what can be done through the mediation of Christian values to remove inequalities and redress injustices in British society and the world community. It means, in essence, an application of 'liberation theology' and the 'social gospel': there are parables besides the Good Samaritan which are capable of radical reinterpretation.

Commitment, neutrality and openness

'Must RE teachers have empty hearts?' (Hull 1982, p. 105)

It is theoretically possible for a Christian teacher to teach about Sikhs and a Buddhist about Islam without anyone being able to guess whether they are Christian, Buddhist or whatever. In practice, however, teachers' own affiliations, or lack of them, are evident to their pupils – rightly or wrongly. In RE it is more than an optional fragment of personal information, which it might well be in other school subjects: it is a value position which enters the teaching and learning itself.

The tension between personal commitment and professional neutrality which characterizes many subjects is especially poignant in RE because the content not only implies, it also contains value judgements. Every lifestyle requires some form and some degree of commitment, be it to a religious belief or to a non-religious outlook; even individuals convinced of their neutrality cannot avoid commitment to that persuasion, and there is no reason why an exploration of one's own commitments, and those of others in the classroom, including the teacher, should not form part of a study of religions. Indeed, it is vital that pupils see religion as a form, even a source, of life: it is not just in books and on film but flows from and into *real* people. It is not very tidy, either, but it is something that people take seriously. Indeed a component missing from much modern RE is the business of serious commitment: it is crucial that pupils see what happens when someone gives themselves to a set of values and allows their whole life to be affected by it.

To the problem of personal commitment and professional neutrality there can be a partial solution: it is possible to see that these two qualities or responses are not mutually exclusive but that there is a distinction between commitment to a particular life stance and commitment about it as a course for study. Even for the purpose of presenting an 'objective, fair and balanced' (BHA 1975) picture of stances for living there is a need and a challenge to produce a living model of personal commitment – precisely because, paradoxically, this is a vital component of all life stances. RE is incomplete if pupils are not allowed to see what it means to be committed: 'Teaching religion . . . is walking a tight-rope between commitment . . . and openness . . . Some positive tension between the two is . . . inseparable from anything that can properly be described as religious education' (Oliver 1974, p. 183).

Revealed religion and the hidden curriculum

In RE, as in all forms of education, the 'how' is as important as the 'what': classroom climate and teaching style as aspects of the hidden curriculum are as vital as the content which is made explicit. Ultimately, multicultural education is concerned to liberate, to educate for a fairer world and to free all children from the limitations of ethnocentrism. A classroom climate characterized by relationships of dominance and dependence would be inauthentic and contradictory. There must be in RE lessons an atmosphere of interpersonal liberation so crucial to free and open soul-searching, to mutual respect within the learning group, and to a full understanding of the dignity of being human which all life stances proclaim and which multi-cultural education seeks to make a reality through the curriculum. Education for liberation must itself be a liberating process.

The writings of Paulo Freire, while immediately applicable to education in overtly oppressed societies, have clear parallels with those minorities in Britain who see their struggle as part of the same fight for freedom. Throughout, Freire stresses the need for openness and dialogue between teachers and pupils; for depth of interpretation; for fostering responsibility through experience; for increasing the ability to perceive and respond to challenge; and for working to transform the world: 'education is cultural action for freedom' (1972a, p. 13) and the 'consciousness of consciousness' (1972b, p. 52).

The major emphases are thus on encouraging pupils to make informed choices; to adopt engaging roles in their learning; to enquire into, and reflect upon, ideas and social situations; to develop to the full their creative potential, in thought, feeling and action, and to share learning with others on a cooperative and collaborative basis.

Through the school assembly, that 'daily act of corporate worship' required by British law, the school's values can be articulated and the hidden curriculum actually revealed. As an institution, it provides a really positive opportunity, all too rarely taken, of forging knowledge, belief and action.

One of the reasons why pupils warm so much to the assembly 'incident' in *A Kestrel for a Knave* (*Kes*) by Barry Hines (1968) is that it represents – in a way exaggerated by poetic licence, perhaps – an hypocrisy which they find familiar, a form that is not consonant with its meaning. First, there is a disparity between form and content: Mr Gryce, the Headmaster, adopts an extremely authoritarian stance; he orders a reading from Matthew 18 ('Never despise one of these little ones . . .'); speaks aggressively about love; and contradicts the terms he has set for himself: 'Fast asleep during the Lord's prayer! I'll thrash you, you irreverent scoundrel!' Then there is a conflict between the content of the assembly and its application: Gryce

victimizes a boy for coughing who did not cough, verbally brutalizes him –
and, it is implied, will later brutalize him physically – to demonstrate his
authority and his loveless power. Everyone knows he picked the wrong boy
– he picked the wrong topic, too.

From the point of view of the emerging religious consciousness of the
children at that school, it has to be admitted that it would have been better
not to have had an assembly at all: it was daily, it was corporate in the sense
that all were physically present – though Casper was mentally absent and
day-dreamed about his kestrel – but in no sense at all was it an act of
worship. One wonders what substitute the pupils might have made if they
had been given the option of preparing and presenting *their* assembly –
though such an option would be improbable in such a restrictive and
oppressive school. And if it had been on a voluntary or loosely grouped
denominational (not quite multifaith in that region) basis, it might have
disappeared altogether.

It is clearly farcical to assume sufficient spiritual unanimity to hold acts of
worship in schools. Many do not worship and do not wish to; others differ in
the conception of the deity they worship – and, at any rate, worship in such
different ways that the logistics are impossible, and causing offence is
unavoidable. What can be hoped for and striven after is a sharing, but
non-worshipping, assembly where festivals and other special times are
celebrated together, where individual and collective experiences are
reflected upon and where caring action is motivated. This can be accomplished, or at least attempted, in a school that is multifaith, or one that is
(apparently) monofaith:

> . . . the best assemblies are often held weekly rather than daily, attended by
> two or three years of age-range at most and conducted by pupils and teachers
> instead of being imposed from the top. They should not be regarded as one of
> the tasks of the religious studies department, but of everyone.
>
> (Cole 1983, p. 193)

Creed and culture in the classroom

Multicultural education, and the RE that is part of it, is for everyone. We
are all living in a multicultural, multifaith world; it is only a matter of how
wide the boundaries are. In every family, in every classroom, in every
village one finds diversity of lifestyles, shades of belief and pluralism of
values. Beyond the local community, our children become aware of less
subtle differences in ways of life and views of life – as inhabitants of the global

village, through increased mobility and sophisticated media. Understanding Islam is an important part of the Norfolk child's education.

In a school which has a multifaith population; where children not only learn about but also learn with people of faiths different from their own, there are added dimensions to the teaching of religion: the sheer existence of a pluralist classroom makes the adoption of a pluralist stance in teaching and learning not only desirable but actually unavoidable.

It also follows that everything is more personal, more intense and more apposite: in a classroom without Hindus, say, an academic discussion can take place – a perfectly valid and respectful one – as to whether statues of Krishna are idols. There is an altogether different discussion where there are devotees in the class. It requires of the teacher additional skills – sensitivity to persons as well as to issues – but it is all the richer for the inside information, the individual insight. A specific case may highlight the point: how to shelve a copy of the Qur'an? In a school/class containing Muslims, it will be covered in cloth, on its own on the top shelf. In a class without Muslims, it will probably be filed with other books, according to size or class use. Teachers and pupils may well respect Muslims but that might not extend to the Qur'an; they might, indeed, consider it artificial – as well as pointless – to treat the book with such veneration when they themselves are not Muslim.

In a multifaith school members of religious minorities will have special needs that are seldom recognized by schools, and less frequently met when they are recognized. In some situations, the abandonment of religious identity – such as not wearing 'colours' or head-covering in the case of Rastafarians, or male Sikhs shaving and not wearing a turban – is a price that must be paid for social acceptance and educational success. And there are other situations where distinctive features of religious belonging – dietary laws, sexual mores, disciplined prayer – conflict with the school's learning experiences, working relationships and rigid timetable. A happy, harmonious school is one which sees itself as a community not merely composed of individuals but also created by them. It follows that structures of the system should not be imposed from above but forged by pressures from within.

Sometimes to respond to the needs of religious minorities requires very little effort: allowing girls to dress as modestly as their tradition requires, making available at lunch-time during Ramadan a room away from the dining-hall for Muslims who are fasting. The resistance to such provisions in so many schools points to ignorance, or institutionalized racism or a desire for uniformity.

At a secular level, schools have made considerable strides to meet the needs of their minority communities. Most notable is the area of language: there are translation/interpretation services for parents, English as a second language classes and mother tongue teaching. For many, religion and language are inseparable and other provisions are needed – what might be described as 'holy tongue teaching', that is, the facilitation, through whatever means it has at its disposal and with all the goodwill it can muster, of religious nurture for any and all. If a school wants to, or feels it must, arrange classes in Arabic and Gujerati, why not in Islam and Hinduism, too? All too often religious identity is treated by teachers as an unnecessary habit, like chewing gum which must be spat in the bin.

As well as needs and difficulties, there are rewards to be earned in teaching RE in a multifaith school – rewards of excitement and stimulation, or movement and growth, the cut and thrust of dialogue, the ebb and flow of human ideas and feelings acted out in evolving lives. But above all, for those involved, a mirror is held up to ultimate reality that is richer, more subtle and more complex.

RE and race

A burning question remains, that of the specific relationship between RE and race relations or indeed between religion and racism. It is most likely that RE teachers will consider racism a 'bad thing' and perhaps even condemn it publicly, so to speak, through the learning materials they procure or produce. So often they fail to demonstrate that non-Christian religions are also opposed to racism: that failure is itself a form of racism.

Theory into practice

This chapter has tried to communicate the excitement and hope of multi-cultural RE. For specialists who need practical guidelines and ready access to information, or non-specialists interested in RE, the single most useful publication is *Religious Education Directory* (Gates 1982). This contains details of providing agencies, priority areas, working examples, and some significant statements about RE, and is an excellent resource for those readers who are sufficiently encouraged and stimulated to wish to take further this exploration of RE curriculum opportunities.

References and further reading

British Humanist Association (1975) *Objective, Fair and Balanced: a New Law for Religion in Education*. London: BHA.

Cole, W.O. (1978) Approaching someone else's beliefs – some criteria. *In* Cole, W.O. (ed.) *World Faiths in Education*. London: Allen and Unwin.

Cole, W.O. (1983b) Meeting religious needs. *In* Cole, W.O. (ed.) *Religion in the Multifaith School*. Amersham: Hulton Educational.

Davies, B. et al. (1979) *The Changing World and RE*. London: Centre for World Development Education.

Freire, P. (1972a) *Cultural Action for Freedom*. Harmondsworth: Penguin.

Freire, P. (1972b) *Pedagogy of the Oppressed*. Harmondsworth: Penguin.

Freire, P. (1976) *Education: The Practice of Freedom*. London: Writers' and Readers' Publishing Cooperative.

Gates, B.E. (ed.) (1982) *Religious Education Directory*. Religious Education Council of England and Wales.

Hirst, P.H. (1976) Religious beliefs and educational principles, *Learning for Living* Summer 1976, pp. 155–157.

Hull, J. (1975) Editorial, *Learning for Living* March 1975, pp. 130–131.

Hull, J. (1982) Open Minds and Empty Hearts? *In* Jackson (ed.) (1982) pp. 101–110.

Jackson, R. (ed.) (1982) *Approaching World Religions*. London: John Murray.

Kelly, A.V. (1980b) Ideological constraints on curriculum planning. *In* Kelly, A.V. (ed.) (1980a) *Curriculum Context*. London: Harper and Row.

Minton, D. (1983) Interview reported in *The Teacher* June 24, p. 6.

Newbigin, L. (1977) Teaching religion in a secular plural society, *Learning for Living* Winter 1977, pp. 82–88.

Oliver, G. (1974) Religious commitment and the religious education teacher, *Learning for Living* May 1974, pp. 181–183.

Richardson, R. (1982) World Studies and World Religions. *In* Jackson, R. (1982) *op. cit.*, pp. 182–191.

Schools Council (1977) *Journeys into Religion*. London: Hart-Davis Educational.

Smart, N. (1968) *Secular Education and the Logic of Religion*. London: Faber.

Stopes-Roe, H.V. (1976) The concept of a 'life stance' in education, *Learning for Living* Autumn 1976, pp. 25–28.

Wood, A. (1979) Judaism in the home, synagogue and classroom, *Shap Mailing* (Commission for Racial Equality) pp. 28–30.

Woodward, P. (1973) Teaching world religions, *Learning for Living* March, pp. 21–24.

PART TWO

LANGUAGE AND LITERATURE

CHAPTER 5

ENGLISH

Jean Bleach

Introduction

English teachers who have worked in multicultural, inner-city areas have
needed to develop keener understandings of dialect and the nature of
language in order to understand and share the experience of all their pupils.
They have also seen the need to broaden the range of literature they use in
their classrooms. A multicultural English curriculum has begun to emerge
from reciprocal contributions of pupils and teachers. The pupils have
brought the experience and the expertise – linguistic and cultural: the
teachers have sought theoretical understandings, and have been forced to
read more widely in linguistics, in cultural and historical fields, in the
literature in English of writers with colonial pasts, and in Asian literature in
translation. All this has strengthened English teachers' growing awareness
that curriculum generally should be responsive both to the immediate
experience of pupils and to the questions about language and culture,
gender, class and race that are central in society now.

In trying to establish respect for the cultures of all pupils in their
classrooms teachers have had to realize how often their own views of
minority group cultures are idealized, oversimplistic and set in exotic
never-never lands, far from the actual struggle, including political struggle,
of the community cultures represented in Britain. The dynamic interaction
of the communities with indigenous British culture has produced surprises
for both sides. Schools and teachers have been open to criticism, deserved
but bewildering. Teachers have had to realize how limited their experience
necessarily is, to regret that so few of their colleagues are representative of

communities their pupils come from, and to recognize the right of community groups to act as consultants when the school is attempting to mediate aspects of their cultures, literatures and language to their own children, as well as to others. We have also had to recognize how deeply grounded are our own racist assumptions of superiority and inferiority, of competence and the lack of it, of rights to power and decision-making. We have had to rethink our most profound psychological and political assumptions. (There *is* a link, here, with women's experiences of gender-based discrimination, but it is my own view that feminists have to confront racism as a separate issue, also, in themselves and in society, as men who experience racism yet have to recognize sex oppression.)

This chapter draws together three strands of work that come under the curriculum heading of English: various aspects of language, literature, and the kinds of discussions and explorations that can be broadly labelled anti-racist. Many of the examples given, in the first two categories especially, relate to one central activity of the English curriculum: that of reading, telling and writing stories, especially personal narratives.

It is a tenet of multicultural education that schools and classrooms need to be hospitable to the cultures and experiences of all pupils. But until teachers accepted their pupils' language and understood their need to use it for at least part of the time, teachers excluded a large part of their pupils' lives and experiences from the classroom.

When white teachers – who largely staff our schools – began to understand the dialects that link black children with their communities, they had privileged access to writing and drama that made known hidden experience. Some of these texts are published by the ILEA English Centre; they are probably of major importance in charting the history of black culture in Britain, and for English teachers they are vital resource materials in the attempt to develop multicultural curricula for the society as a whole.

Written works produced by developing bilinguals also occupy a unique position in Britain today in bearing witness to many different aspects of our multicultural society. Because bilingual pupils operate in their less familiar language (i.e. English) at school and in all their contacts outside their home communities, English is the way in which a large part of their life experience is encoded. This is not to deny that pupils need access to their mother tongues in classrooms, but it does help to explain how powerful is the drive to make explicit in English certain parts of their experience and to try to create links between the public domain of their lives in the present, and the domestic domain that contains the memory of their past. Teachers have been awed by their pupils' motivation in writing such narratives in the face of the difficulties presented by writing not only in a new language, but often also in a new script.

This chapter aims to provide some ways for teachers and pupils in largely monoethnic white schools to begin to enter into an understanding of the multicultural society.

Language: a broader approach

This section starts by considering some of the work on dialect and bidialectism that English teachers have undertaken, challenged by the presence of West Indian dialect users in their classrooms. This may not seem an issue of direct relevance to many teachers outside the inner-city areas, but such studies have helped shape the movement towards language study as a significant part of the English curriculum. There are, of course, parallel cases of regional dialect, but moves towards convergence of dialects have been going on in Britain for a long time, and few native dialects have syntax that differs radically from standard. Secondly, by focusing on the ways teachers can make explicit to dialect-speakers how to move their written work closer to standard forms (when the writers choose to do so) this work has prepared the ground for English teachers in mainstream classrooms working with students for whom English is a second language. The section thus goes on to consider the issues associated with second language learners of English.

Understanding more about dialect

Teachers' initial work in this area was often concerned with discovering the syntactical rules of dialects – usually Jamaican dialects – using the expertise of pupils or teacher colleagues. John Richmond's (1977) paper *Dialect* first popularized linguists' awareness that West Indian dialects were rule-governed and were powerful instruments for communication. He showed that most children of West Indian origin in London had access to two or three dialects of English, and shifted between them at will. His work began to make English teachers aware of the emphasis on competitive verbal performance that is a strong feature in many West Indian speech styles: rapping, verbal duelling, dubbing and toasting and oral narrative performances, for example. (See also Mercer (ed.) 1981.)

McLeod (1980) and Richmond and McLeod (1980) trace the development of writers working from this kind of linguistic background. They document teachers at work who are able to make more explicit to themselves, and therefore also to their students, that they can make the choice to write in dialect, and/or in more standard forms. Through encouraging children to take up the task of originating ways of writing dialect, a truer language awareness is generated.

Language study

The various papers describing all this work are (except the last) collected in *Becoming Our Own Experts* (Richmond et al. 1982) which brings together the studies in language and learning referred to in this section. They were done by the Vauxhall Manor Talk Workshop, a group of teachers who collected data from their own classroom practice, and set about finding ways of analysing its significance for themselves. They were members of the Language in Inner City Schools movement which grew as a cooperative venture with the English Department of the University of London Institute of Education. Other outcomes of this movement included a survey of linguistic diversity in London schools (Rosen and Burgess 1980) and, indirectly, *The Languages Book* (Raleigh 1981). Not only is this book an attractive text for language study, its scope is broad enough for monoethnic children to enhance their awareness of their own language, of the roles and value of English-based dialects, including regional dialects, and to introduce them to some of the languages spoken as community languages in Britain.

Initially, the Talk Workshop teachers focused mainly on language form. Later, as they came to take dialect forms for granted, and as their encouragement allowed their pupils to use the full range of their language repertoires in the classroom, they became excited by what their pupils were *saying*. 'Brixton Blues' was an improvised drama displaying great verbal skill and code-switching ability by third-year girls. A full transcript appears in *Becoming Our Own Experts*. Much more recently, Elise Dodgson, now working at Vauxhall Manor School, directed a drama called *Motherland* drawing on the experiences of the girls' mothers. There are now a number of audio- and video-cassettes available to teachers who want to bring the voices and experiences of black people into their classrooms (see Resources at the end of this chapter).

Second language learners in mainstream classrooms

What teachers have learnt from dialect-studies A greater sensitivity to dialect has enabled English teachers to read the 'error' in children's writing as systematic, and has been of use in revealing to teachers the pupils' current understanding of the target language form they are heading towards. Teachers can then operate from a clearer understanding of *their* role, in dealing selectively with 'error' as it becomes part of the writer's consciousness. This theoretical understanding, and some experience of using it in practice, is of enormous importance when English teachers come to articulate ways in which they can intervene helpfully in the language development processes of *second language learners* of English.

The English classroom as a good learning environment for second language learners The presence of second language learners in mainstream classrooms is not new. Apart from some intensive short-term work in special classes, second language learners of English have always been the responsibility of ordinary classroom teachers for the major part of their learning. In areas where there are very few children from minority ethnic groups, classroom teachers have to take all the responsibility for supporting their learning of English. Many teachers place these children in working groups which already have high status in the classroom and where there is plenty of talking to learn. Through collaborative small group work the English as a Second Language (ESL) pupils develop working relationships with peers, which can give them the social and emotional confidence to take risks of trying out a new language. The native English speakers will be able – and probably more willing – to offer consistent help if the teacher makes explicit the roles they can play: encouraging participation in talk; interpreting tasks set and demonstrating how they can be performed; offering advice and help while the writing is under way or afterwards. (See Resources for some useful materials.)

In supporting the language development of second language learners, teachers can draw upon the powerful modes of learning developed in mixed ability English classrooms. These include interactive group work, a sense of cooperation and making explicit the goals of their activities so that children can plan, organize and evaluate their learning for themselves.

There is another aspect of the 'ordinary' English curriculum that is of great use to developing bilinguals. Short stories and novels read aloud, and stories told to the class allow inexperienced users of English to hear long, unbroken stretches of highly patterned language. The latter features expressive intonation, together with greater redundancy than is usual in expositional speech, and also predictability of the overall schema (they will be familiar with the forms of stories from their mother tongues) which make for easier understanding.

Our knowledge of the importance of stories in building English mother tongue competencies should help us see their importance also for helping bilinguals develop writing performance.

How hearing, telling and writing stories helps the language development of second language learners   Many older learners of a second language rely on the conscious application of syntactical rules in talking, and particularly in writing, their new language. This striving for correctness may block the learners from deploying a great deal of implicit knowledge that they are learning from the language environment. The greater facility with which young children learn a second language has almost certainly a great deal to do with their uninhibited taking on and practising of such aspects of their new language as intonation, speech rhythm, idiom, register and dialogue. It is my direct experience that inhibited older learners, 'frozen' at the level of producing non-native-like speech and writing, may find in retelling stories they have heard told and read to them a way of letting their unconscious knowledge direct their language production. Josie Levine calls this process 'following the tunes in their heads' (Levine 1981).

It is often easier for second language learners when they are writing stories successfully to make the overall shape of the story than it is for them to structure the details of the narrative (e.g. sentence structure) correctly. English teachers have been able to make use of this fact, and of the strong drive second language learners often have to make sense of the two parts of their life experience through writing personal narratives (see Introduction to this chapter). Here is one short example, written by Kam Lam Ngor, a Cantonese speaker. The title was the starting point for a class writing assignment. Note first how she exploits the assignment to build an imaginary bridge from an East London classroom to her home in rural Hong Kong, and, secondly, how confidently she handles the overall texture, and communicates her feeling and her meanings, despite great difficulty at the lexical and syntactic level.

Fantasy in an English lesson
The plane is travelling to Hong Kong, I am so happy and with a fright about when I see my friend in there. Feeling the time is so slowly as usual, at last the plane is reach. Hong Kong. lots things have to dos before I go out to see my friend and Grandma, relations, take back my case from the airport. The man checks the passport, not even only meself. When I go is strange people, I see

my Grandma, my uncle my aunt, my friend. and comson but they all strange to me. The house is no different of when I left four years ago. except is bit older and dirty then when I left. I see my labourer, only give a smile doesn't know what, would talk to them. The house is different of in London, the floor is so cold for my food, you have to boil the water, is not use gas. is use sticks, no bath room, you have to go wash at the kitchen, one thing is so ? is when I lie on the bed. not soft, so strong, like lie on a stone. I can't sleep well. and also is so many little insect want to get your blood. Next morning my Grandma wake up at six o'clock, early for me, I go out to the market with her. Then we turn up to my uncle's house, next few days, I only have one thing to do, is go to my relations house, a friend when I was four years old we go to school together, play together. because in that time she is live near me, she was moved to another place now.

Pupils who are taking on a new language are also necessarily divorced from a simple continuity with their own cultures, and, possibly, their own countries. Having to operate in a language not their own will cut children off from the past experience which is precisely the source of their most powerful feeling. The need to express the past, and use it as a base from which to make meaning of the new is shown again and again in the drive that carries inexperienced writers of English through the effort it takes to write long personal narratives.

To help pupils see that it is acceptable to try, teachers need to show that they care enough to understand the meaning, but they also need to indicate that students can feel confident that, over time, they will help them towards increased correctness. Reading *My Life* (Elbaja 1978) can remind students of their own experience, and often provides a way of getting started.

How to connect the need for pupils to hear stories at quite high levels of sophistication with their need for reading access to much simpler texts within a mixed ability classroom   One possibility is for pupils to adapt an exercise carried out by black sixth formers in the BBC *Scene* programme 'Why Prejudice' (See Resources, Section 1). The group examined a collection of children's picture books for racist and sexist stereotyping, and discussed the ways such images had affected them, and how books might help younger children form more positive self images. This is a way for students to perceive how their implicit racial and sexual attitudes have been formed. It is also a way of validating the reading of simple text for all. This is a good place to introduce some of the folk tales and religious stories from other cultures that are mentioned in the following section, including texts in the language of developing bilingual students in the class. All pupils can come in such ways to recognize the linguistic ability of students who are beginning to read English, but who can also read (and translate) texts in another language and possibly another script. This would be a good context, also, for playing some tapes, for example, of stories in West Indian dialects or of BBC radio's *Mother Tongue Story* (see Resources, Section 1). If swapping oral stories occurs in the class at this stage there will be gains for all – and possibly an atmosphere may be created in which second language learners can use their mother tongue. If students afterwards write their own children's books (with illustrations) unusual awareness of audience and form are likely to be shown by students with very different writing ability – including second language learners in the class.

Literature – cultural diversity explored

Literature is a most potent force in allowing us to enter a world of experience imagined by another person. These imaginary worlds will be shaped in part by the immediate social and cultural experiences of the writers, and will bear the imprint of the historical time and circumstances in which they are written. The work of writers with dual vision created by their experience of Western cultures *and* of another non-Western culture needs to be related to, not separated from, writers who inform and reflect the dominant culture. In every sense George Eliot, Dickens, Conrad, Faulkner, Achebe, Walcott and Evelyn Waugh need to be read and studied together.

English teachers who are readers of contemporary fiction and poetry have access to some of the most subtle and complex representations of what experience shaped by British cultural domination looks and feels like when viewed from outside British metropolitan culture. It would be hard to find any poet writing in English with greater claim to be called a major poet than Edward Brathwaite, Derek Walcott or Seamus Heaney. The poetic consciousness, facing the humiliation of past oppression in order to be free to make sense of experience in its own terms, is a central theme for each of these writers.

Amongst major novelists writing in English today, one would surely have to give central places to Doris Lessing, Nadine Gordimer, V.S. Naipaul, Chinua Achebe – and probably Toni Morrison (with *Song of Solomon* and *The Bluest Eye*), Maxine Hong Kingston, Ruth Prawer Jhabvala, Ngugi wa Thiongo and Salman Rushdie.

The use of Afro-Caribbean and South Asian literature in school

Teachers have been stimulated to read deeply into the literary traditions that nourished the Afro-Caribbean and Asian writers who *are* well known here. They have undertaken such reading to help them and their students to value the intellectual and cultural achievements of people whose recent immigrant status and past colonial position exposed them to racism and contempt, and to gain insight into cultures that have had long historical connections with Britain. In doing so they have found renewed literary enjoyment.

Novels of childhood for 14–18 year olds   Mphahlele, introducing Dadié's *Climbié* (1966), picks out two major themes in African fiction (in English and French): childhood between two cultures, and the struggle for independence. Goody (1983) introducing a list of books from the Caribbean, annotated for use in schools, suggests similar themes in Caribbean writing. Here, I am concentrating on novels that will also nourish the kind of autobiographical writing referred to in the previous section on language.

The stories of childhood are vivid. The poignancy of these recountings of childhoods is almost certainly the severing of the writers' own direct continuity of experience with their pasts: memory is especially acute and immediate. The vernacular, the behaviour, the environment is created in such detail it is almost possible to feel we share another culture. Selormey's *The Narrow Path* (1974), Laye's *The African Child* (1955) and Anthony's *A Year in San Fernando* (1965) are examples. In different, comic vein are *Swami and friends* (Narayan 1935) and *Poona Company* (Dhondy 1980).

Things Fall Apart (Achebe 1958), *Ambiguous Adventure* (Kane 1972), *A Brighter Sun* (Selvon 1979) and *Green Days by the River* (Anthony 1967) deal with similar disjunctions from the more analytical viewpoint of adolescence. All these novels are for older students looking back on childhood, and could be used alongside *There is a Happy Land* (Waterhouse 1968), *Joby* (Barstow 1977), or *A Northern Childhood* (Layton 1975, 1978).

In general ways English teachers know that there are strong literary cultures in South Asia. Many are aware of the poetry of Rabindranath Tagore and, perhaps, Najrul Islam in the Bengali tradition. Dr Ranjana Ash has done a great deal of work to make teachers more aware of the poems, novels and short stories available in English translation by writers such as Premchand (Urdu and Hindi) and Waris Shah (Punjabi). Dr Ash is a founder of the South Asian Literature Society, which meets at the Commonwealth Institute, and her edited collection of stories by Asian authors

(1980) is a very useful resource. (For radio support, and some bibliographies, see Resources.)

It is my view that to understand white racism children need to recognize Britain's role as the major nineteenth-century colonizing power, her consequent wealth, and the effects of colonization on black and Asian people. Autobiographical novels from Africa and the Caribbean, and modern Asian writing, as well as offering sympathetic access to different cultures, show the schisms of consciousness in individuals caused by the impact of cultural domination. Derek Walcott's caustic inversion of the Robinson Crusoe/Friday story for two actors, *Pantomime*, satarizes liberal white reaction when blacks begin to reassert their own cultural values in the post-dependence period. The script exploits a range of theatrical effects and discursive styles as well as verbal wit to make its points. Pairs of students could use the script effectively in English or Drama as a basis for reading or improvisation.

Older students might read at least one novel shaped by the struggle for independence; books by Ngugi, Beti, Bessie Head, Alex La Guma, de Vieiera have all been used successfully with fifth and sixth year examination classes. The London GCE Board's A level syllabus B has an Afro-Caribbean option paper that validates the study of some of these writers. Ballin et al. (1980) have suggestions about the use of texts like these, and also for modern Chinese writing that could be used in schools. (See also Resources.)

For younger secondary pupils There is a vast, and rapidly growing, library of books for children drawing on myth, folk tale and fable from societies which retain a rich oral culture. (See Resources.) Many of these collections are unsatisfactory as written text – poorly produced, with a great deal of social and cultural context left implicit, but teachers can often use them as the basis for storytelling. There are dangers, though, when one is not familiar with the culture-bound forms of storytelling, intonation, range of symbolic reference – even with innuendo or reference to taboos. There are now a few resources that bring into the classroom the voices, accents, dialects and the narrative styles of storytellers from the communities where the stories originate. There are also some beautiful individual-story or multiple-story picture books which are particularly useful with pupils who are learning English. It is important to remember, though, that ESL learners in mainstream classrooms will only be able to use these resources if they are in common use in the classroom.

Community writing in Britain

The single best source of texts written by young members of minority group communities is the ILEA English Centre, which published the collection *Our Lives* (1979). Perhaps less daunting to read are the individual short novels, especially Mohammed Elbaja's *My Life* (1978), Errol O'Connor's *Jamaican Child* (1978), Paul George's *Memories* (1977), and Chelsea Herbert's fiction *In the Melting Pot* (1977). The striking aspect about these, and others like them published by community bookshops, adult literacy groups and other cottage industry presses, is the way that fairly inexperienced writers find, in the extraordinary disjunction of their lives, an acute need and ability to reflect on both parts, and to find ways of relating their lives together again. They offer all pupils reminders of how to get in touch once more with similar, if less traumatic, forgotten early experiences.

Dhondy's story-collections *East End at Your Feet* (1976) and *Come to Mecca and other stories* (1978) are well known, generally available and indispensable. Set in and around Brick Lane, in London's East End, they do two things no one else yet does: they indicate the intercultural tensions of black and Bengali people in the area and the racism that presses on both, and they give us access to the consciousness of Bengali youth in ways that challenge teachers' stereotypes.

Multicultural children's books

Publishers' lists in the United States of America and here show an enormous growth in children's fiction about black children and their families, about intercultural tensions and resolutions, and many of the best of the American books are written by black writers.

One powerful reason for using children's books by black American writers with pupils here in Britain is that some of these writers touch on aspects of experience done nowhere else as well. *The Friends* (Guy 1977) is a classic example, describing the friendship between two girls in their early teens and its eventual dissolution. *Basketball Game* (Lester 1977) explores with realism the scars created by an adolescent boy/girl friendship across colour lines. It might be possible to compare pupils' responses to some texts on similar themes in books where they are presented from majority or from ethnic minority viewpoints. Such comparison could be formal, or informal: done by the teacher observing, or by children in discussion with one another after reading a pair of texts. So, for example, a basic list might include the following:

Themes	Multiethnic books	Monocultural books
Family friendships among women.	*The Friends* (Guy) *In the Melting Pot* (Herbert)	*Little Women* (Alcott)
Sexual dilemmas of young women	*Emma Jackson* (Guy) *Ruby* (Guy)	Any of the stories by Judy Blume *Goldengrove* (Paton-Walsh)
Humorous and inventive fictions dealing with the unexpected competences of girls, and with the ways that less able boys have other things to offer than academic success.	*Philip Hall likes me, I reckon, maybe* (Greene)	*Tyke Tyler* (Kemp) *Harriet, the spy* (Fitzhugh) *Thunder & Lightnings* (Mark)
Adventure stories in realistic settings	*My Mate Shofi* (Needle)	*The Machine Gunner* (Westell)
Infectiously funny books with very serious themes.	*3rd Class Genie* (Leeson)	*18th Emergency* (Byers)
Attempts to help young children come to terms with difficult family situations. For older children to evaluate.	*Daddy* (Caines)	*My Brother Stephen is retarded* (Sobol and Agre)
Closely paired texts on mismatch between school and life outside.	*The School Leaver* (Macmillan)	*A Comprehensive Education* (Mills)
Books that help children perceive the relevance of history to current social problems	*Long Journey Home* (Lester) *To Be a Slave* (Lester) *Taste of Freedom* (Lester)	*Stone Book Quartet* (Garner) *Eagle of the 9th* (Sutcliffe) *A Question of Courage* (Darke)

One important way of comparing such texts is by 'placing' them in relation to who wrote them, and the time in which they were produced. It is interesting, for example, to speculate about why so many of the books that place young and adolescent girls' experience centrally, as valid in its own right, are written by black American women writing now.

Anti-racist teaching

In debating and slowly testing out responses to the challenges our classrooms have offered us, English teachers, like others, have had to define the political assumptions on which our views of schooling, culture and society rest. A variety of perspectives have emerged, many represented in a reader compiled by James and Jeffcoate (1981). Jeffcoate represents the liberal humanist and, concerned with the way British culture proliferates nega- tive images of people from other cultures, he urges the formation of rational and moral intercultural relationships in the name of sanity for the whole emerging polis. Others adopt Jeffcoate's position, but deal much more in the individual psychology of, for example, formation of identity and self-image. James presents the Marxist viewpoint; he insists on the need for analysing what happens to children from community groups in British schools, to see where political power causes discrimination. He believes in 'multiculturalism' as a necessary *starting* point, but that the outcome of education should be 'cultural relativism' and that the debate and exchange of experience in an intellectually rigorous multiethnic classroom can encourage such an outcome. Others elaborate this viewpoint to argue that racism can be understood and tackled only in the context of teaching about British imperialism and the economic and political gains which colonialism gave to capitalist states. It is from, broadly, the second, Marxist, stance that 'anti-racist teaching' has emerged.

Across the broad range of ideas of what makes a valid English cur- riculum, English teachers, working from a multicultural perspective, have gained a great deal in coming to a truer sense of literary value in contem- porary literature; in meeting challenges to their own knowledge of language structure and function, and in the range and quality of debate in their classrooms over major intellectual, social and political issues, especially racism.

Two aspects of what goes on in English classrooms mentioned so far only by implication are of central significance to anti-racist teaching: class and small group discussion, and drama. In the past, and even to some extent now, it has been hard for teachers who have wanted to work towards racial harmony within their own schools to accept that racism is a part of the experience of all their pupils, black and white, in this society. Of course, even outside the inner-city areas, young people are exposed to the racism, explicit, and by omission, of media representations of reality – witness the behaviour of English fans to black players on the football field – and, from earliest childhood, build pictures of black poverty, and incapacity as opposed to white – and particularly British – enterprise and competence. Teachers have themselves had to recognize the racism in society and to understand that good intentions are not enough to dismantle discrimination deeply structured into society.

Nor is it enough simply to open the classroom to debates on how children view the presence of minority community groups in this country. The reason I see African literature as vitally important is that, more clearly than elsewhere, it puts on record how British colonial presence irrevocably altered African cultures. It also shows clearly the cost of liberation struggles to the people involved and, by implication or direct statement, the degree of self-interest Britain felt in maintaining imperial authority.

Debates on race in English lessons need to take place within such frameworks of understanding, for older pupils. For younger children a starting point can often be to ask how many have relatives now living abroad, for example, in South Africa, or whose family connections include soldiers and administrators, at all levels, who served in India, Africa, the Caribbean, Hong Kong or elsewhere in South Asia. Surveys of this kind can be helpful in countering simplistic notions of the 'unfairness' of immigration patterns to this country. Showing films like *Why Prejudice* is also a very good way to start discussions on race and racism.

Drama is recognized by its serious advocates as a powerful learning tool, particularly when the learning implies a need to move out of a taken-for-granted frame, in order to see social facts in a different way. Teachers of English and Drama have discovered that improvised drama allows black pupils to demonstrate their ability to move easily between West Indian dialect and standard. Dramatic improvisation has also allowed black children to demonstrate the verbal set pieces practised in black culture. Labov (1969) documents these in the United States; Mercer (1981) and Richmond et al. (1982) here. Improvised drama has also allowed children working together from one ethnic group to move into mother tongue at appropriate points in their improvisations. Out of improvised dramas, in and out of school, powerful depictions of community life have emerged, a very few of which have been published. Teachers have discovered the power of role-play and simulation as information-learning and attitude change techniques.

Saunders (1982) presents a model for a multicultural curriculum which is anti-racist, and suggests detailed curriculum strategies for countering the barriers to coming to terms with the reality of living in a multicultural society in the education of all children. The barriers the curriculum must address itself to are, in his analysis, that most pupils are unfamiliar with other cultures, that they have inadequate awareness of minority issues, that they have inadequate self-awareness, and that they have a need for positive first and second hand role models. Referring to these four areas for change, I will try to suggest some strategies that fit good English practice.

Helping pupils become familiar with other cultures

This can only be effectively done by a worked out cross-curricular multi-cultural policy for the school, with anti-racist intentions. In individual classrooms or departments, radio and television educational programmes can help. Some make deliberate and carefully researched efforts to show the struggle towards a multicultural society that includes community views and experience. Individual teachers, wherever they practise, can rarely match these resources.

Oral, aural and written English work can draw on documentary and dramatic media presentations for discussions of other cultures, prejudice and discrimination and intercultural tensions. Some relevant programmes are listed in Resources.

Inadequate awareness of minority group issues

It seems quite clear that the people to raise community issues in schools and classrooms are parents, older siblings and members of communities represented in the school. In the English curriculum, teachers, editors and writers should be invited in to talk about the literature the class is studying, if this is at all possible. Parents will often accept invitations to tell the class their memories of childhood, or at least be prepared to write or record them. As teachers become more confident, it becomes possible to ask parents and others to join with English classes, in debate and discussion on issues of racism and of community rights, and matters related to religious observances and cultural preference.

Inadequate self-awareness

Young people need to become less egocentric, and more able to take on the demanding nature of our multicultural society. The English class offers plenty of opportunity for discussion and informal comment which can help pupils explore their own attitudes towards those who have a different colour, religion or language from themselves. Greater awareness about others may hopefully give rise to clearer self-awareness. But Betty Rosen, ex-head of English of a virtually all-white school in Waltham Forest, an Outer London Borough with many Afro-Caribbean and Asian inhabitants, cautions that intellectual discussion will never touch the heart of white complacency. Pupils, she argues, only believe that racism is a potent force and that discrimination could affect them if they have more direct experience of racism and its effects. A way whereby pupils may experience (briefly) social ostracism, unjust treatment and a negative valuation of some aspect of themselves is simulation (see, for example, the film of an American primary classroom *The Eye of the Storm*) available from Concord Film Council. Such simulation should, of course, only be undertaken with extreme care, by experienced teachers.

Role models

English teachers, together with their colleagues, have to operate as role models of racial fairness, and be absolute in their challenging of racism. I have suggested for example, the importance of having black people visit the classroom to talk as experts on all issues that belong to the community. The expertise and knowledge, including language knowledge, of ethnic minority children, particularly non-white pupils, needs to be validated within the classroom in the same way. It is a good idea to look out for ethnic minority writers who can be invited to visit the school and for plays featuring ethnic minority actors.

Anti-racist materials and strategies should be central to the English curriculum, but that is not to say that everything English teachers already teach should be abandoned. That is not what I have been suggesting. Rather, I have been describing some starting points from which English teachers can develop their current practice so that they may begin to create classroom conditions which increasingly meet the learning and social needs of all groups in our multicultural society.

Resources

1   Audio- and video-tapes that share black experience

Language in the Multi-Ethnic Primary Classroom Vol. I. ILEA Learning Materials Service (available outside ILEA from the Central Film Library). This video comprises two programmes, intended for in-service work, but very usable with older pupils. 'Listen to Us' has examples of primary school users of community languages and discussion of the link between language and culture by John Singh, HMI. 'The Way We Speak' shows primary age children using dialect in different classroom situations. This is followed by Joan Goody's remarkable interview about language, dialect and achievement with black London sixth formers.

Motherland. ILEA Learning Materials Service. 70+ minutes. A drama by girls from Vauxhall Manor School, about the experience of immigration into Britain by West Indian women in the 1950s and 1960s. Directed by Elise Dodgson, this drama drew directly on tape-recorded memories of the girls' mothers.

BBC *Scene* programme, 'Why Prejudice'. About 20 minutes. Repeat transmission November 1983, means that videos of this programme may be used for a further three years. Duplicated notes are free from the BBC, and can be photocopied as a basis for group discussions. Sixth formers from Brent explore prejudice – especially in relation to race. Incidentally, the group activities shown as the pupils explore their topic in different ways offer very good models for ways of organizing group talk situations in the upper school.

The Caribbean Anthology. A pack from ILEA Learning Materials Service, containing a teacher's book, five pupil's books and two audio cassettes. The poems are read by their authors, or other appropriate readers.

2 A 'self-help' kit for English teachers to support the learning of second language learners in their classrooms

a. *Issues in Race and Education* No. 39, Summer 1983, price 50p. Available from 11 Carlton Gardens, Brecknock Road, London N19.

b. Materials from ILEA Unified Language Service Collaborative Learning Project (Director: Stuart Scott). Assorted materials will soon be available from Tressell Publications.

c. 'Developing pedagogies for multi-lingual classes' by Josie Levine in *English in Education*, the Journal of the National Association for the Teaching of English, Vol 15, No 3, Autumn 1981.

d. *Language in the Multi-Ethnic Primary Classroom* Vol II. ILEA Learning Materials Service (also available from the Central Film Library), with notes. This video contains two programmes: 'Learning English as a second language: working together in the classroom' and 'Supporting understanding'. Hilary Hester, the director of the ILEA SLIP (Second Language Learners in Primary Classrooms) Project presents work within primary classrooms, and helps teachers analyse what they need to know and to do to make good practice supportive of second language learners.

e. *Stories in the multi-lingual primary classroom*, Hilary Hester, 1983. ILEA Learning Resources Branch, Publishing Centre, Highbury Station Road, London N1. This booklet, the first of the SLIP Project materials to be published, is of particular interest to English teachers.

f. *Scope, Stage 2*, Schools Council, 1972. A language development course intended for use in mainstream classrooms. Written by Hilary Hester and Josie Levine, the teachers book, in particular, still has a great deal to teach people beginning work with second language learners.

3 Audio-cassettes of stories in dialects and languages other than English

BBC *Radio Mother Tongue Story*

i) *The Mice and the Elephant*, in English and seven Asian languages. Now available on cassette from Radio Shop, BBC Radio Cassette Service, Centre for Educational Technology, Civic Centre, Mold, Clwyd CH7 1YA. An illustrated book may be bought to accompany the programme.

ii) *Mother Tongue Story*, a new series going out in Summer 1984, with six different stories in languages including the Sylheti dialect of Bengali, and the Mirpuri dialect of Punjabi, each with an English translation.

ILEA Learning Resources *Share-a-Story* packs (for 5–11 years and beyond). Folk stories from the Caribbean, and from other countries that children in the ILEA originate from. There are six packs, each with two story books and a cassette, where the texts are read in appropriate dialects.

4 Afro-Caribbean and South Asian literature

BBC *Schools Radio Programmes*

i) *Multicultural Resources* This programme will give support for the reading of literature from the Caribbean and South Asia. BBC Nighttime Broadcast (the whole block transmitted at once), going out Summer 1984.

ii) *One World* Five TV geography programmes are accompanied by radio programmes of music, stories and poems from St Lucia, Barbados and Jamaica. Summer 1984.

Bibliographies

i) Ruth Ballin, Jean Bleach and Josie Levine (1980): *A wider heritage: a selection of books for children and young people in multicultural Britain*. National Book League.

ii) Judith Elkins (1971): *Books for the multi-racial classroom: a select list of children's books, showing the backgrounds of India, Pakistan and the West Indies*, Pamphlet No 10, the Library Association Youth Libraries Group.

Community Bookshops are important sources of information on books, local experts, groups meeting etc. ILEA Centre for Urban Educational Studies (CUES) has published a pamphlet 'A Selection of London Bookshops'. This is available from CUES, Robert Montefiore School Building (Top Floor), Underwood Road, London E1 5AD.

South Asian Literature Society c/o Ronald Warwick, Commonwealth Institute, Kensington High Street, London W8.

5   Multicultural children's books: book reviews

Rosemary Stones and Andrew Mann (eds.) *Children's Book Bulletin* uses stringently anti-racist and anti-sexist criteria in reviewing recently published children's books. Available from 4 Aldebert Terrace, London SW8. Useful sources for informed judgements on multicultural children's books are the review sections of: *The English Magazine*, The English Centre, Sutherland Street, London SW1, and the National Association for the Teaching of English (NATE) journal *English in Education*, The NATE Office, 49 Broomgrove Road, Sheffield S10 2NA.

6   Picture books

For example, Haley (1972) *A Story, A Story*, Methuen; Andree and Hana (1974) *The Enchanted Savannah*, Methuen; Myers (1981) *The Golden Serpent*, Julia MacRae Books; Ramachandran (1979) *Hanuman*, A & C Black; Thorne (1982) *The Voyage of Prince Fuji*, Macmillan (out of print). Important new collections include Radice (1980) *Striving*, Anvil Press Poetry Ltd, from the Bengali; and Davies et al. (1980) *Tales from Mozambique*, Liberation (out of print).

7   Radio and TV programmes

BBC
   i) *Multicultural Education*: ten programmes for teachers.
  ii) *Scene*: two programmes, 'Scene in Northern Ireland' and 'Why Prejudice'. This order of viewing recommended by teachers; racial prejudice in context of other kinds of prejudice.
 iii) *Wheels of Fire*: about development issues in India.
ITV
   i) *Tomorrow's People* (for 9–12 year olds): tackling racism through programmes about identity; home and family; friendship and community.

ii) *Our People* (for older students): six programmes on immigration in Britain.

iii) *Viewpoint 2* (suitable for older students): four programmes on how the media presents the world, including youth, black people, with a booklet by Andrew Bethell (1980).

These and many other videotapes of ITV programmes available on hire from Guild Learning, Guild House, Oundle Road, Peterborough.

References

Achebe, Chinua (1958) *Things Fall Apart*. London: Heinemann African Writers Series.

Anthony, Michael (1965) *A Year in San Fernando*. London: Heinemann Educational.

Anthony, Michael (1967) *Green Days by the River*. London: Deutsch.

Ash, Rajana (ed.) (1980) *Short stories from India, Pakistan and Bangledesh* (each extract has a list of further reading). London: Harrap.

Ballin, R. et al. (1980) *A wider heritage: a selection of books for children and young people in multicultural Britain*. National Book League.

Barstow, Stan (1977) *Joby*. Glasgow: Blackie.

Dhondy, Farrukh (1976) *East End at Your Feet*. London: Macmillan Topliners.

Dhondy, Farrukh (1978) *Come to Mecca and other stories*. London: Fontana Lions.

Dhondy, Farrukh (1980) *Poona Company*. London: Gollancz.

Elbaja, Mohammed (1978) *My Life*. ILEA English Centre.

George, Paul (1977) *Memories*. Commonplace Workshop.

Goody, Joan (1983) An annotated bibliography of books by Caribbean writers that have been used in the classroom, *The English Magazine*. ILEA English Centre.

Guy, Rosa (1977) *The Friends*. Harmondsworth: Puffin.

Herbert, Chelsea (1977) *In the Melting Pot*. ILEA English Centre.

ILEA English Centre (ed.) (1979) *Our Lives*.

James, A. and Jeffcoate, R. (eds.) (1981) *The School in the Multicultural Society: a reader*. London: Harper and Row, in association with the Open University Press.

Kane, Sheik Hamidou (1972) *Ambiguous Adventure*. London: Heinemann.

Labov, W. (1969) *The logic of non-standard English*. Washington DC: Centre for Applied Linguistics.

Laye, Camara (1955) *The African Child*. London: Fontana.

Layton, George (1975, 1978) *A Northern Childhood*: Vol 1 The Baladava Story and other stories, Vol 2 The Fib and other stories. London: Longman (Knockouts).

Lester, Julius (1977) *Basketball Game*. Suffolk: Peacock.

Levine, Josie (1981) 'Developing pedagogies for multi-lingual classes', *English in Education* Vol 15, No 3, Autumn.

McLeod, A. (1980) *Writing, Dialect and Linguistic Awareness*. English Department, University of London Institute of Education.

Mercer, Neil (ed.) (1981) *Language in School and Communication* (see especially

David Sutcliffe 'British Black English in British Schools'). London: Edward Arnold.

Narayan, R.K. (1935, new edn 1978) *Swami and Friends*. Oxford: Oxford University Press.

O'Connor, Errol (1978) *Jamaican Child*. ILEA English Centre.

Raleigh, Mike (1981) *The Languages Book*. ILEA English Centre.

Richmond, John (1977) *Dialect*. ILEA English Centre. Now available in Richmond et al. (1982).

Richmond, J. and McLeod, A. (1980) Art and craft of writing, *English Magazine* No 6. ILEA English Centre.

Richmond, J. et al. (1982) *Becoming our own Experts* Studies in language and learning made by the Talk Workshop Group at Vauxhall Manor School, 1974–79. Available from ILEA English Centre.

Rosen, J. and Burgess, A. (1980) *Languages and Dialects of London School Children: an investigation*. London: Ward Lock.

Saunders, Malcolm (1982) *Multicultural Teaching: a guide for the classroom*. London: McGraw Hill.

Selormey, F. (1974) *The Narrow Path*. London: Heinemann.

Selvon, S. (1979) *A Brighter Sun*. London: Longman.

Walcott, D. (1982) Pantomime. *In* Andrew Bethell (ed.) *Power*. Thames Television in association with Nelson.

Waterhouse, K. (1968) *There is a Happy Land*. London: Longman (Imprint).

CHAPTER 6*

MODERN LANGUAGES

John Broadbent

To grasp for the new experiences and new identity which can be reached by learning a new language is in itself both exhilarating and liberating. Too often, however, attempts to move beyond purely monolingual forms of education have resulted in frustration for both teachers and taught. Compact, well-organized courses with carefully graded, explicit objectives now make it easier for pupils to enjoy some sense of measurable achievement even after the shortest exposure to a new language. With sensitive management modern language classrooms can become islands of alternative culture in which prejudice and the tendency to stereotype those who are visibly different can be successfully combated, and where adolescents can be encouraged to develop confidence in the enormously varied linguistic abilities that they already possess. One logical consequence of such a learner-centred approach would be for the languages of minority group pupils to receive legitimation by inclusion in the timetable alongside those already more commonly taught. At secondary school level a wider range of open but properly informed choices, and within those options a measure of syllabus negotiation with room for individualization, can help all pupils confidently to extend their personal horizons.

Particularly in inner-city contexts, where patterns of migration have greatly enriched the linguistic environment, maximizing the potential of

* Some of the ideas in this chapter are an extension of those in *Assessment in a Multicultural Society: Community Languages at 16+* by John Broadbent, Mahmood Hashmi, Baikunth Sharma and Maroulla Wright. Schools Council Programme 5 Pamphlet Series. Longman, York, 1983.

diverse young people, often within a single classroom, is a singular challenge; it will require staff who are prepared to try out new ideas which are informed by a living interaction with the communities from which their classes are drawn. In some ways the English and Welsh system, in which decision-taking devolves upon local education authorities (LEAs) and the governing bodies of individual schools, makes it easier to devise solutions which are tailor-made for a particular locality and school. Although this chapter attempts to suggest principles and workable strategies for teachers to implement for themselves in their classrooms and beyond, it would be irresponsible not to stress the need for concerted policies at both local and national levels particularly with regard to the recruitment and training of future language teachers.

Modern languages in the United Kingdom

Too numerous to be catalogued here are the contributions already made by practising teachers on both sides of the Atlantic to forms of language education and assessment which are designed to make the learning of new languages a pleasurable and worthwhile experience for all regardless of class or cultural background. That their experiments have not yet met with total success is hardly grounds for pessimism when one considers how recent initiatives to democratize language teaching have been. Prior to the general expansion of comprehensive schooling, any languages other than English tended to be offered almost exclusively to able pupils selected for maintained grammar school places or within the private sector of education. This was as true for Welsh in Wales and Gaelic in Northern Ireland as it was for French and German in England. In the late 1960s, when grammar and secondary modern schools began to be merged into the comprehensive system of today, a tremendous expansion took place in language teaching. This expansion was in some ways parallel to the developments which occurred in the United States in the wake of the National Defense (Education) Act of 1958. Whereas the Newsom Report pointed out in 1963 that a modern language was taught to only about a third of the pupils in perhaps half the secondary modern schools of England and Wales, little more than a decade later a survey of 83 comprehensives conducted by Her Majesty's Inspectorate (HMI) revealed very high percentages of pupils studying languages into their third year of secondary schooling, as shown in Table 6.1.[1]

Table 6.1 Percentage of pupils studying at least one modern language across a sample of 83 comprehensive schools, 1975–76

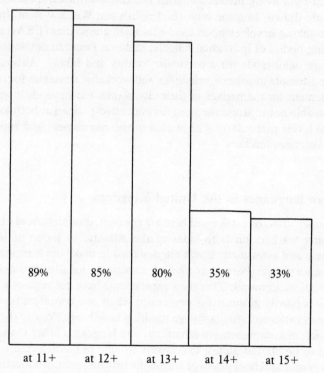

89%	85%	80%	35%	33%
at 11+	at 12+	at 13+	at 14+	at 15+

Source: Her Majesty's Inspectorate as quoted in the *Second Report from the Education Science and Arts Committee* (1983) House of Commons (Session 1982–3)

In 1977 the Department of Education and Science (DES) undertook a review of LEA arrangements for the school curriculum; it seemed from all of the responses that indicated a formal policy on the matter that at least one language was *offered* to all secondary school students.[2] Most LEAs reported that their schools generally required pupils to continue to the age of 16 with English, mathematics, physical and religious education, but there was great variation in the overall size of a school's curricular core, and only in some instances did the additional compulsory subjects include a modern language. Very few LEAs actually appeared to specify which language or languages should be taught, although in the United Kingdom as a whole French is overwhelmingly offered as the first modern language from the first year of secondary schooling onwards, with German frequently as the second, and usually made available one or two years later.

Figures provided by the GCE and CSE examination boards for Summer 1981 show the relative number of entries for English and the most commonly assessed modern languages (see Table 6.2).

It is significant that, at school-leaving age, for every ten entries in English there were only approximately three in French and barely one in all the other listed languages added together. These figures suggest that there is considerable room to move the mainstream curriculum beyond the monolingual insularity it has inherited from the past.

Table 6.2   Entries for the most commonly assessed languages in England and Wales, Summer 1981

	CSE	O LEVEL	A LEVEL
English	603,254	527,370	64,049
French	159,033	168,192	25,719
German	33,392	53,376	8,861
Spanish	6,205	13,381	2,883
Italian	679	2,962	652
Russian	279	1,471	384
Chinese	—	1,438	241
Greek	—	616	231

Source: GCE and CSE Examination Boards, England and Wales.

Even with regard to French, competence appears to be lacking where it is most demonstrably needed: the Foreign Affairs Committee of the House of Commons noted in 1981 that very nearly half of the Diplomatic Service Staff at the British Embassy in Paris were unable to speak French to an adequate standard!

That there are rich reserves of bilingual, even multilingual potential in major areas of conurbation has been revealed in surveys conducted by the Linguistic Minorities Project based at the University of London Institute of Education.[3] In Bradford, Coventry, Peterborough and the London Boroughs of Brent, Haringey and Waltham Forest, where the entire school population was surveyed, up to one-third of the students reported that they spoke a language other than English at home.

All of the surveys have indicated a clear predominance of one or two particular languages – see, for example, the figures for Brent shown in

Table 6.3.[4] Before discussing how the potential in those languages can best be developed, this chapter considers multicultural perspectives with regard to the languages more commonly offered in maintained schools.

Table 6.3 Home languages of pupils in Brent schools, July 1982

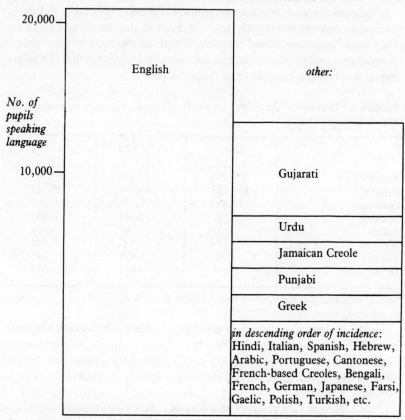

Source: Report 47/83 to the Education Committee of the London Borough of Brent from the Director of Education (1983).

Modern language classrooms as cultural islands

Much of the intrinsic delight and resulting motivation which supports the acquisition of a new language arises from contact with people who normally speak that language. Ideally, a massive system of international pupil exchanges sponsored at government level is called for. Lacking such a system, the school-based language teacher has to take on the task of encouraging the exchange of letters, shuttle tapes, reciprocal visits and the like, because human contact is demonstrably just as vital as the quality of classroom presentation itself. Ways of maximizing the illusion of being transported beyond Anglo-Saxon cultural norms in the modern language classroom have been well tried by committed teachers and well documented since the 1960s. Frequently changing wall displays, the use of a variety of resources, posters, maps, books, music, films and filmstrips, realia of all kinds, if need be carried from room to room in a 'teaching box', can contribute to an atmosphere in which the use of a language other than English is natural and pervasive.

A number of general suggestions have been made about the ways in which cultural phenomena can be satisfactorily contrasted to positive effect. First, it is wise to start by establishing a framework in which the sum total of the similarities can be shown to be infinitely more significant than the sum total of differences. Secondly, it is necessary to keep on revising the images presented, so that together they display as wide and accurate a picture as possible of the contexts in which the language being acquired is actually used. Thirdly, a properly sympathetic treatment of cultural difference has to be provided through the perceptions of people who see themselves as belonging to the society which is being studied.

It is frequently argued (and endorsed incidentally by teachers of Welsh in Wales) that language tuition succeeds best if it is used as a vehicle towards the acquisition of the skills and information which students desire. There are already schools in England which have established 'sections bilingues' to teach about the geography, history and civilization of France, in French. In order to ensure their continued existence, the DES should fund the arrangements whereby students of English in universities abroad come to work as foreign language assistants in British schools. The physical presence of a student who can relate his or her different experience more closely to pupils than can a teacher is much undervalued. Even a single visit of a black speaker of French from Martinique, Reunion, or wherever, has been known to increase motivation in multiracial schools, when the event is properly prepared beforehand. Teachers and occasional helpers in schools can of course be recruited from amongst those who have grown up in bilingual families here. The DES and Welsh Office (1983), however, do not appear to view this possibility favourably: 'It is widely held that foreign languages are best taught by teachers who are native speakers in English or

Welsh rather than by foreign teachers employed, as exchange teachers or otherwise, to teach their native language.'[5]

Part of the apparent lack of success of 'foreign' teachers may be explained by the fact that the forms of language use rewarded by the current range of examinations in England and Wales are often quite inauthentic. A particular example of this is the way in which candidates may be required to use past tenses to recount a story illustrated by a series of pictures, when in most languages present tenses would be more appropriate. The attitudes of boards examining French in England and Wales to accuracy and error tend to be even more stringent than their counterparts in France.

Despite the efforts of the Académie Française to codify standards of correctness, there is much regional variation in French, as there is also in German, Italian and indeed all languages. Moreover, there are in France, as elsewhere, well-established linguistic communities – in Alsace, Britanny, Flanders, Corsica, the North Basque country and so on. These, and more recently settled minorities also, provide evidence, if evidence is needed, of the narrowness of the nineteenth-century assumption that a communality of language necessarily implies a communality of culture. In the past, school textbooks have tended to limit themselves to middle or upper-class norms: language teaching and background studies materials must however reflect a wider view of individuals and social strata.

Languages and anti-racist teaching

French, German, Spanish, Italian and Russian tend to be identified as languages of white people and therefore – to extend the application of a phrase coined by James Baldwin – 'prisons for black people'. Success in these 'white' modern languages may often seem to black pupils to be no more than a further negation of their ethnicity; the refusal to succeed, or the decision to disrupt, can therefore become a form of affirmation for them which nevertheless results in general cultural impoverishment. Naturally much depends on the particular attitudes of the teacher and on whether it is made clear that no amount of racism can be tolerated, and that he or she takes pleasure in teaching pupils from different races and backgrounds.

French, Spanish and other European cultures, including British, encompass a variety of ethnic and social groups, a variety which needs to be made evident in the texts and visuals placed before all learners. As with different cultures, so with different races, educational materials must strive to show individuals with every type of human attribute; pictures of black athletes, footballers or musicians are not sufficient and may indeed reinforce existing stereotypes. (See Chapter 13 for a discussion of this point.) Course books such as *Éclair*, *Bibliobus* and *Action* which do avoid stereotyping deserve praise from and use by the discerning teacher; those which contain racist and colonialist overtones deserve to be criticized and not used. The same applies to set literary texts. An informed look at the currently available syllabuses suggests that those students who pursue language courses up to O and A level are proceeding through a minefield of explosive allusions, each of which runs the risk of permanently damaging their self-esteem. Verlaine, to offer one example, is undoubtedly a French poet of great simplicity and delicacy whose symbolic poetry represents such a milestone in European aesthetics that his work often appears as a set text. His great sensitivity was however no guarantee against racism (or sexism). A poem written by way of a manifesto for the style he was pioneering contains the following verse, which sharply illustrates his white ethnocentric perspective:

> Ô qui dira les torts de la Rime?
> Quel enfant sourd ou quel nègre fou
> Nous a forgé ce bijou d'un sou
> Qui sonne creux et faux sous la lime?*[6]

If Verlaine is to remain in the commonly accepted literary syllabuses, the narrowness of his world view must be complemented by the works of African and Caribbean writers like Aimé Césaire who belong to the same poetic tradition.

In the justifiable zeal to dispel the myth that this highly prestigious language is the sole property of white people, it is possible to overstress the impact of French beyond France, nevertheless, the forms of culture which are mediated through French transcend national and racial boundaries. Project work on major cities of the world in which French (or Spanish, or any language studied) is spoken, while providing greater chances for personal identification to pupils from ethnic minorities, can help all pupils to explore the effects of past colonial exploitation. Although former French territories are reasserting their identity and adopting their own languages as

---

* O who will tell of the wrongs of Rhyme?
What deaf child or mad negro
Made us this half-penny jewel
That sounds hollow and false under the file?

media of instruction, knowledge about black freedom fighters such as Toussaint Louverture and writers who have used French in their struggle for self-emancipation, provide an antidote to more conventional teaching in England about Wilberforce and the slave trade. To look at historical events through the focus of documents in another language is itself a valuable spur to critical insight.

Both Germany and Italy have experienced more deeply than most the extremes of inhumanity that racist government policies can reach. At advanced levels of study, language departments can supplement the work of history departments in teaching about the ultimate results of fascist ideology through the accounts of its victims.

A useful strategy from the very early stages of learning involves asking pupils to identify topics which interest them. This principle of consultation should extend to the range of vocabulary presented around a particular topic. Vocabulary lists will vary depending on the cultural background and acquired interests of pupils. For example, whereas most French course books will contain the names in French of only two places of worship (church and cathedral), pupils in multicultural classrooms who are using French to talk or write about themselves may well have more use for the equivalents of mosque, synagogue or temple. Word lists for fruits, jobs, leisure activities and many other topics need to be similarly open ended.

Languages and language varieties

Language awareness and the ability to apply that awareness is best inculcated through the practical activity of learning a new language. French is the language most commonly contrasted with English in our schools; in introducing students to its structures it is not necessary always to refer back to standard English. The language used in the playground can just as easily serve as a point of reference, and can be shown to have similarly consistent patterns. Word order, number systems, the marking of gender or of different levels of social distance ('vous' and 'tu') can be explained more easily to users of North Indian languages which have similar rules, whilst the inflection of verbs, the use of pronouns, and markers of plurality can be compared with dialect and Creole features, as much as with standard English. The acquisition of a range of adequate conceptual terms, useful in the discussion of how languages function, has clear validity in this connection; however, categories and forms of nomenclature evolved in the analysis of dead languages, most notably Latin, need to be scrutinized very carefully before being used for describing patterns in living ones. Classroom activities which investigate the derivation of words via languages in contact evoke a good response from students especially when they focus on the adoption by modern French of familiar English and American terms.

The socio-linguistic contexts of Germany, Italy, Spain, France or England can all be used to show that no language or variety can be thought inferior to any other. Some pupils in comprehensive schools in London have gained important insights from exchanging sets of tape-recordings made by users of English dialects, with sets of equivalent French and German ones. Although listeners brought up in England had no difficulty in deciding which variant of their own language sounded 'best', listeners unaware of the social conventions operating in a foreign language were not able to establish any kind of rank order. Students were quite astonished to discover that there appeared to be no objective basis for considering which kind of accent seemed to be superior. Here again the attitude of the teachers – for example the amount of interest shown in the different dialects which their pupils are able to adopt – can become just as important as the content and method of their courses. One underlying theme of raising language awareness – whether it is approached through French, English, or in its own right – must be a preference for 'appropriateness for communication in a particular context', rather than formal correctness. Children must learn to operate beyond current prejudices with regard to attitudes about 'good' and 'bad' language; they need to become cautiously aware of the ability of language to confirm social class, exerting power or exaggerating weakness.

Relating to the languages present in the classroom

Language teachers are concerned to promote communication in the particular language studied and also to provide a general insight into the processes of learning and describing any new language. Because French will probably continue to be for many years the most commonly taught language after English in British schools, the previous two sections have concentrated on pupil-centred and anti-racist strategies for the teaching of French, which was, by 1977, taught to well over three-quarters of all pupils in maintained secondary schools. A fair proportion of those excluded from modern language lessons in their first three years were pupils whose home language was not English. Sustained withdrawal from any particular lessons is now widely felt to have a negative effect on pupils' morale: it has racist implications when the pupils withdrawn share a similar cultural identity. Where the method of teaching French occurs mainly through the medium of French itself, the chances of success for such pupils are certainly no lower than they are for mother tongue English speakers and there may also be gains for their English language learning.

Quite often in schools with high numbers of pupils from ethnic minority families one used to hear the question: 'What is the point of teaching them French when they can't even speak English?' The negative assumptions behind such a question have begun, with the support of school language surveys, to be replaced with a more constructive formulation: 'These pupils are already potentially bilingual to an extent that monolingual English learners of French are unlikely ever to equal. Cannot their linguistic resources be developed in such a way as to benefit both them and their less fortunate peers?' Teachers (including the author) based in inner-city areas have perhaps been more fortunate than most because their students have forced them to adopt strategies for teaching fundamentally different from the ways in which they themselves learned French. It is particularly pleasant and rewarding when pupils who are starting to learn French, begin to take opportunities to demonstrate features of their own languages.

The professional organizations representing teachers of Italian recognized earlier than most the advantages of including in the range of available modern language options at least one language which is commonly used by ethnic minority communities. Italian is clearly within the scope of the EEC Directive on the Education of Children of Migrant Workers, circulated to interested bodies in the UK shortly before its formal adoption in July 1977. Article 3 of the Directive requires member states, in accordance with their national circumstances and legal systems, and in cooperation with states of origin, to promote mother tongue and culture teaching in coordination with normal education. The UK government has accepted that the benefits of the Directive should also be extended to the children of nationals of non-member states. A milestone in the formulation of education policies which cross national frontiers, the Directive offers distinct encouragement to LEAs and schools which have identified and are promoting the particular languages used by local populations. Even where LEAs are not following the intention of the Directive by taking initiatives in this respect, it is a reasonably straightforward undertaking for modern language departments in schools to survey the languages in use amongst their pupils. As long as teachers make it clear that the use of another language is to be considered a definite advantage, pupils will in most cases willingly declare their abilities. Such surveys can be conducted by private interviews, or individual questionnaires; alternatively, a group project can set out to discover one language or dialect that everyone can speak, and one that only one person, or a few in the group knows: follow-up work can involve further investigation of the languages known and methods of statistical presentation.

It is effort well spent for existing language teachers to familiarize themselves, however slightly, with the languages most commonly used by their school population. Some pupils may already be attending supplementary schools, and modern language departments should seek to discover their location and their needs, liaising with their teachers and identifying any of their own students who could usefully sit a public examination in the language of their community. The process of discovering this information is in itself instructive and highly encouraging for the pupils involved.

The DES circulated a questionnaire to all LEAs in England in 1982 enquiring about the measures taken to comply with the EEC Directive. The Memorandum on Compliance[7] reported that at least 25 community languages are now taught in mainstream and community supplementary schools to over 43,000 primary and secondary age pupils. This amounts to 12 per cent of the 375,000 children estimated to be from homes where English is not the first language.

Table 6.4 gives an indication of the languages most commonly taught. However, when one compares figures released by official cultural organizations it becomes apparent that the figures shown in the table are gross underestimates. For example, the Federation of Educational Associations of Greek Parents and the Greek Orthodox Church between them offer lessons in Greek to some 9,000 children in the London area alone, while the Agregadura Cultural of the Spanish Embassy provides for some 3,000 language students and over 10,000 are enrolled in language courses run by the Italian Embassy in Britain.

According to the same DES Memorandum 8,300 of these 43,000 pupils are receiving mother tongue lessons in maintained schools, but the proportion varies considerably between languages, depending partly on whether the community itself wishes to take responsibility for promoting its culture. It seems about 70 per cent of the children taught Urdu and Hindi, and 75 per cent of those taught Punjabi and Italian receive this tuition in state schools, whereas Chinese and Polish are taught almost entirely in the voluntary sector. Bringing the voluntary classes into the school building itself can represent a great step forward for the self-esteem of the children involved. Even then, language classes and clubs held out of school hours experience great difficulty in preserving continuity of teaching; and unless

Table 6.4 Numbers of children of school age taking lessons in the ten leading ethnic minority languages

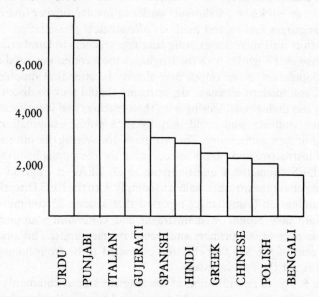

Source: *Memorandum of Compliance with Directive 77/486/EC on education of children of migrant workers*. Department of Education and Science (1983).

they are regarded as a move towards a future broadening of the mainstream timetable, they are only a limited school response to linguistic diversity.

Matters of choice

It is obviously important to seek the views of parents on including community languages in the mainstream curriculum, and schools need to improve interaction with their surrounding linguistic communities. Too often parents who speak languages other than English are discouraged from taking a full part in the education of their children. Even if they do not actually need translations of school literature, or interpreting facilities when meeting teachers face to face, parents from many cultural backgrounds, especially within the working class, lack knowledge about how to operate within parent teacher associations and governing bodies to influence the functioning of the schools their children attend. One starting point with regard to language education could be for a modern language department in a secondary school to find out from parents of children in feeder primaries, the balance of languages they would most like to see offered.

Similarly, pupils' perceptions need to be researched and taken into account. An article in *Time Out* (1980) quoted two pupils in their final year at a comprehensive school in Southall: 'We are not allowed to speak our own language at school. We can speak French, though, because French is in the school's curriculum . . . I remember thinking when I was younger that maybe, somehow, my language, the language of my parents wasn't a real language.'[8] A spot survey conducted by the author on a fifth-year German class in Kingsbury, on the other hand, showed how much pupils' attitudes may conform to institutional ones. Thirteen students, whose home languages included Gujerati, Italian, Polish, Punjabi and Yiddish were asked which they thought were the three most useful languages for them to study. All but the Italian speaker omitted the language used in the home from their lists. Although the perceptions about which languages are of most importance to them are likely to change somewhat with the introduction of community languages into the mainstream curriculum, the freedom to opt out of such instruction also needs to be guaranteed. At the Southall comprehensive mentioned above, an option scheme has been introduced which offers Punjabi instead of French from the first year onwards; although this is a significant advance, it still does not preserve the students' right to choose the balance of minority and majority group language and culture which best meets their desired identity as individuals. Students whose links with the language and culture of their relatives have become increasingly tenuous are unlikely to develop their full bilingual potential unless members of their peer group are also convinced of the value of their skills; this is one of the weightiest arguments for parity of community languages with French. Limited experience in a number of schools in England and Wales has already shown that propitious numbers of pupils are interested in learning the locally used languages. Indeed the range of ability encountered among students with roots in local linguistic communities is only marginally extended when absolute beginners join their classes. It is sensible therefore for each school to formulate an integrated model of language enrichment, not directed towards minorities in particular, but to all pupils.

In part this process of enrichment might well involve sessions in which pupils who have chosen different options come together to discuss the relative merits of their choices. Language awareness courses are now widely advocated as a useful first-term or first-year foundation for further language study. They should contain information which would help pupils to decide which language of the ones available in a particular school is best suited to their needs. A school in East London which has experimented with first-year introductory courses has concluded that 'tasters' are best limited to a maximum of three languages, with fuller cooperation with teachers of English remaining a desirable goal. The selection of optional languages in addition to English must not be allowed to become a mechanism by which children gravitate towards predictable subjects from the second year onwards – Azad Kashmiris towards Urdu classes, Jamaicans towards Creole, Mauritians towards French and so on. A requirement for each pupil to take more than one option would help to overcome the dangers of 'ghettoization'.

Opinions vary greatly about the size of school that can realistically consider offering more than one language. Table 6.5 shows a scheme for offering courses to various levels in a six-form entry school in a locality where Gujerati is widely used. Within this scheme, the opportunity of

Table 6.5   Language courses in a six-form entry school

Age	Level						
11+	Language awareness	First-year foundation course in Language and Communication with tasters in French, German, Gujerati					
12+ 13+	Two-year basic courses in one language	French		German		Gujerati	
14+ 15+	Intensive courses for continuers or beginners for two or three years to 16+ examination level	French	German	Gujerati	Computer Language	Extra English	Urdu/ Hindi
		'O' level or C.S.E.					
16+ 17+		Language and Community Classes (CEE or City and Guilds) Vocational Examinations (Institute of Linguist, RSA, etc.) 'A' levels in one or two languages					

Source: The Author.

finding out about two languages is offered to all pupils. Table 6.6, adapted from a study by the Schools Council Modern Langauges Committee (1982), shows a possible allocation of teaching time.[9] Such provision is clearly facilitated where a modern language is an element of the core curriculum up to 16+ and where the range of options extends right into the sixth form, in the form of intensive or Compact Courses. The characteristic features of such Compact Courses as have been developed so far include a clearly

Table 6.6 Possible school timetable

a) *Time division for a 35-period week*

	Number of periods	
	at 12+	at 13+
English	5	5
Mathematics	5	5
First modern language	5	3
Humanities	5	5
Science	5	5
Arts/crafts/music	5	5
PE	4	3
RE	1	1
Second modern language	–	3

b) *Time division for a 40-period week*

	Number of periods	
	at 12+	at 13+
English	6	5
Mathematics	6	5
First modern language	6	4
Humanities	6	6
Science	6	6
Arts/crafts/music	6	6
PE	3	3
RE	1	1
Second modern language	–	4

Source: Slightly adapted from *The Second Foreign Language in Secondary Schools: a question of survival*, Schools Council Modern Languages Committee (1982).

defined time span, and short-term clearly specified objectives, which the learner must regard as being attainable and as having a recognized validity. Since each Compact Course should be considered as self-contained, but forming part of a broader scheme of language education, the content should be substantial and meaningful in itself.

Such courses are naturally just as relevant in those secondary schools where students learn one language only and abandon it after their third year. Recognizing this fact, many LEAs have introduced local certificates based on graded tests; where students have spent time studying more than one language, their levels of attainment can be recorded in a school-leaving profile showing general language awareness, plus progress in all the language options taken.

Overcoming constraints

There have been frequent calls from within the modern language teaching profession for the kinds of reform advocated above. In England, the National Association of Language Advisers (1981) has supported the view that to facilitate a better balance between French, German, Italian, Spanish and Russian would 'fulfil only part of the cultural justification advanced for language learning since non-European languages are not included'. They argue that 'the present domination of the modern language provision in school cannot be justified, except in terms of the practical problems which could arise during a change-over from the existing position'.[10]

In working towards the kinds of reform advocated in this chapter, modern language teachers will find themselves confronting a whole series of external constraints. Falling rolls, and cuts in public expenditure, linked with the high cost of capitation, threaten the most enlightened approaches as often as do publishers' estimations of the most lucrative markets for their teaching materials. The world dominance of English is itself a disincentive to invest money or time in other languages, even those enjoying a relatively high status in our society. Socio-linguistic disincentives ally themselves with staffing policies in recreating a general inertia in many educational institutions including examination boards. A superficial comparison of the numbers said to be learning community languages (as shown in Table 6.4) and of the respective examination entries (as shown in Table 6.2) shows an enormous discrepancy between even the least taught European languages, and Indian ones, with a knowledge of Urdu, Punjabi, Gujerati, Hindi and Bengali being minimally validated by the existing range of examinations in England and Wales.

A number of conclusions flow from the realization that teaching particular languages, and the notions expressed in, or associated with, these languages, is not ideologically neutral. Nor is it possible to isolate purely multicultural aims from broader educational and political ones. In a society where racism has fed on unemployment, and on a general shift of funds from the public to the private sector, modern language teachers in state schools can have a vital influence in counteracting intolerance and in fostering empathy.

This chapter has outlined some of the ideas and strategies accessible to modern language teachers; it is hoped it will stimulate further discussion and innovation. In developing the power to use and make sense of new languages, dialects, even accents, there are, despite the constraints, plenty of opportunities for modern languages to make a positive contribution to the multicultural education of all pupils.

Notes and references

1   HMI survey of modern languages in 83 comprehensive schools, as quoted in the *Second Report from the Education, Science and Arts Committee* (1983), House of Commons.
2   Department of Education and Science and Welsh Office (1979) *Local Authority Arrangements for the Curriculum – Report on the Circular 14/77 Review*. London: HMSO.
3   Linguistic Minorities Project (1983) *Linguistic Minorities in England and Wales: a short report on the Linguistic Minorities Project*. London University Institute of Education.
4   Report 47/83 to the Education Committee of the London Borough of Brent from the Director of Education (1983).
5   Department of Education and Science and Welsh Office (1983) *Foreign Languages in the School Curriculum – a consultative paper*.
6   Verlaine (1884) 'Jadis et Naguère', reproduced in A. Hartley (ed.) (1959) *The Penguin Book of French Verse*, Vol 3, The Nineteenth Century. Harmondsworth: Penguin Books.
7   Department of Education and Science (1983) *Memorandum on Compliance with Directive 77/486/EC on the education of children of migrant workers*.
8   From an article by John Rose in *Time Out*, 11 July 1980; quoted more fully in Broadbent, J. et al. (1983) *Assessment in a Multicultural Society: Community Languages at 16+*, Schools Council Programme 5 Pamphlet Series, Longman, York.
9   Schools Council Modern Languages Committee (1982) *The Second Foreign Language in Secondary Schools*, Occasional Bulletin.
10 National Association of Language Advisers (1981) *Foreign Language in Schools*. London: Ashdown Press.

PART THREE

MATHEMATICS AND SCIENCE

CHAPTER 7*

MATHEMATICS

Ray Hemmings

Those nurtured in the Western tradition tend to think of mathematics as a unique flowering of European culture, and, insofar as the history of the subject is taught in schools here, this is the picture which is overwhelmingly conveyed. But in fact the evidence of cultures which have left written records suggests that mathematics has flourished all over the world; and it is this very universality which should make it one of the obvious contributors to a multicultural curriculum.

Of course other cultural activities such as music and literature are equally ubiquitous, but these have developed their own idioms, and are often difficult to appreciate by those outside the originating traditions. Mathematics is perhaps more accessible because its internal logic causes different developments to have much more in common; indeed it may be the feeling that two and two make four the world over which persuades teachers that there is little to be gained from looking at, say, Chinese or Indian mathematics. However, there is an interesting diversity within the unity which can considerably enrich the quality of mathematical activity in the classroom. This is understandably the first concern of a mathematics teacher; it is the intention of this chapter to suggest some ways in which the heritage of the component cultures of our multicultural society can contribute to the richness of a mathematics curriculum.

There are also important social implications of this fundamental unity underlying the diverse mathematical expressions of our common humanity.

---

* This chapter is adapted from two articles which first appeared in the NAME journal *Multiracial Education* Vol 8, No 3 and Vol 9, No 1, 1980.

Drawing on the mathematics of non-European cultures can communicate a recognition, and a valuing, of the cultural heritage of ethnic minority pupils actually present in the classroom (and not doing so communicates the opposite). This helps students from minority groups by increasing their knowledge of, and respect for, the cultures of their origins, whilst at the same time informing those from other groups about the mathematical riches of the various cultures whose people they now live alongside.

Apart from the social value of multicultural mathematics, there are also some general educational benefits which seem very significant. First, in recent years, teachers have felt it important to relate their teaching to children's experience of their 'everyday' social and physical environment. In the context of our multicultural society, this implies that school mathematics should draw on features of the cultural background of the various cultural minorities now living in this country. Secondly, it turns out that in doing this one becomes surprisingly involved in matters that traditionally belong to other subject areas – for example, to design, religious studies, history, and the social sciences. Perhaps this should not be so surprising since what we are concerned with is mathematics as a human activity, not simply with the mathematics which has been abstracted into textbooks. Thirdly, a multicultural perspective can make an important contribution to the education of awareness. Indeed one eminent educator, Caleb Gattegno, recently asserted that you can *only* educate awareness; or, in the words of a teacher I used to know, 'you can only teach anyone something they already know'. For example, most people know how to count but many people have problems manipulating the numbers they count with. Many of these problems can be resolved through a comparative study of counting systems in other cultures, which leads to awareness and understanding of 'our' counting system.

Counting and spatial relations in different cultures are discussed below. The use of games, the teaching of statistics and the history of mathematics are then considered for their contributions to the development of a multicultural curriculum.

Counting

The structure of our counting system is an ingenious and very powerful creation, and an awareness of it gives us a knowledge of an enormous range of arithmetical relations at the cost of very little effort of learning. As to the power of the system, consider that if you learn just ten words and one suffix

(-ty) you could, but for some irregularities in the English language, count to ninety-nine. You then have to learn only one more word to be able to count as far as nine hundred and ninety-nine (no irregularities here); one more word will take you to one short of a million. But to do this you obviously have to know the structure. Being aware of this structure then enables you, on the basis of knowing the equation 'three plus five equals eight', to say 'three hundred plus five hundred equals eight hundred', sixty-three plus five equals sixty-eight', or 'eight squillion minus five squillion equals three squillion'.[1] If anyone feels they have to work out any of these answers, when they already know the basic fact that $3 + 5 = 8$, then this indicates that they lack a proper awareness of the structure of the counting system.

Attention to the language of counting reveals that the structure is embedded in this language, and to hear this reflected in a variety of languages is an interesting way of directing attention to it. There is an added gain: most languages contain irregularities, generally in the words for the smaller numbers, presumably because they came into common use before the whole structure was established. Noticing these irregularities involves an awareness of the regularity – and then perhaps you can go on to create words so as to iron out the anomalies. For instance, the English words 'sixty', 'seventy', 'eighty', 'ninety' express precisely what is happening when we count in tens, but the words in the earlier part of this counting system – 'ten, 'twenty', 'thirty' – are somewhat distorted. To restore the regularity here we could say 'onety', 'twoty', 'threety', 'fourty', etc. The words 'eleven', 'twelve', 'thirteen' are even more irregular, and to bring them in line with the regularity of 'sixty-one', 'sixty-two', 'sixty-three' we would need to say 'onety-one', 'onety-two', 'onety-three'.

So in a classroom where there are members of ethnic minority groups it would be very useful for the teacher to encourage these children to tell others how they count in their several mother-tongues. Even if this is not taken so far as actually to learn the words, it is valuable to listen to them, to hear the sounds, to compare them with the more familiar sounds, to listen to the rhythm of the count and to note the irregularities and the occasional differences between one system and another. For instance, the count in Gujerati from 20 to 30 goes like this: wyss (20), ekwyss (21), bauwyss (22), dtherwyss (23), chharwyss (24), pachwyss (25), chherwyss (26), styawyss (27), utyawyss (28), ogntryss (29), tryss (30).

Two interesting things strike one immediately about this progression: first, in contrast to English, the 'units' sound precedes the 'tens' sound – though English is a little inconsistent in that it reverses the digit order through the 'teens', and sometimes the 'one-and-twenty' form is used; the second point of interest is the unexpectedly early appearance of 'tryss' (30) at 29 with the prefix 'ogn' which means 'one less than'. (What arithmetical advantages are there if your language tells you that 29 is 30 less 1? Would it help if we thought of 28 as 30 less 2?)

Counting: symbols

Although it may be less useful than listening to the counting words, there is value in paying attention to the symbols that are used in the various numeral systems – and again if possible it would be best to use the knowledge of the children in the class. The symbols now used in India (which are to be seen for instance on the Hindu calendars now easily obtainable in this country) bear a close resemblance in some cases to those used in Western Europe. The latter are in fact sometimes known as the Hindi-Arabic symbols, and they were adopted and transmuted by the Europeans in the Middle Ages when the clumsy Roman system was replaced by the more efficient place-value system that was developed in the East.[2] Apart from acknowledging our historical debt to those Eastern cultures for a system of representation, without which computation would be even more tiresome than it is, there is value in recognizing that the actual marks we make on paper are arbitrary, just as the base 10 we use in counting could be varied.

Finger counting

Another quite different form of number symbolism is that of using the fingers rather than pencil and paper. Teachers may have noticed some children of Indian origin counting on their finger-joints (not just their finger-tips), and it is worth encouraging them to bring their hands out from underneath their desks (they are likely to have understood the message that in this country using your fingers for this purpose is for some reason thought to be rather shameful), and to try to explain the system they are using. Throughout Asia, various methods of using this portable abacus that we have in our hands were developed from early days and are still in use, for example by merchants negotiating prices in silence through the medium of communicating clasped hands (Lemoine 1932).[3]

A striking system was developed in China which, by using three faces of each finger, given nine distinct positions corresponding to the numbers 1 to 9, and uses the successive fingers to denote the increasing powers of 10. Thus the five fingers of one hand are made to represent any number up to

100,000 – a remarkable demonstration of the economy of the place-value system (see Figure 7.1).

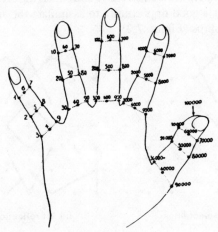

Figure 7.1

Space and geometrical ideas

The growth of an awareness of spatial relations is an important part of mathematical education. Not only is such awareness useful in practice (we probably draw upon this knowledge more frequently than we make use of our numerical skills), but it also gives access to sources of imagery which form the basis of so much mathematical understanding. There is more to this than learning to call a three-sided figure a 'triangle', and more than knowing that its three angles sum 180°. Notions of pattern, symmetry, transformation and equivalence are subtle and pervasive: they extend into all reaches of mathematics but they are most accessible in their geometrical forms. Situations which open up explorations of these ideas are therefore valuable, and doubly so if they also allow this exploration to be creative.

One such situation is to be found in the creation of rangoli patterns – those often intricate designs which are used by Hindu and Sikh families to decorate their homes on important occasions, most notably during the celebrations of Divali. Many of these designs are pictorial, but some are abstract and geometrical. One recipe which is often used is based on a square grid of dots. A few lines joining pairs of these dots are then reflected successively in each of the four axes of symmetry of the square. Very quickly a surprisingly complex pattern emerges; shapes form themselves which can be accentuated with colour; the lines threading amongst themselves can be interlaced. It is an effective and satisfying activity which at the same time affords a good opportunity to assimilate the subtleties of symmetrical relationships (Figure 7.2).

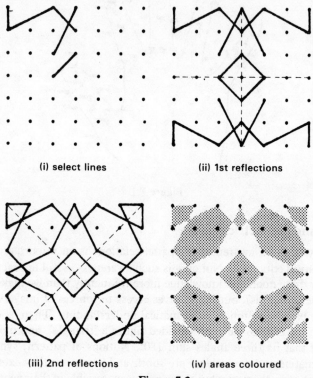

(i) select lines   (ii) 1st reflections

(iii) 2nd reflections   (iv) areas coloured

Figure 7.2

A rather different device, though still employing the dot grid, is often used in rangoli designs for space-filling (Figure 7.3). Similar devices are to be found in some kinds of African art (see, for instance, Zaslavsky 1975)[4]. They are examples of traditional folk-art which often involve breathtaking skill.

It requires a high degree of dexterity not to go off the rails in drawing these patterns; but also leads to at least one intriguing geometrical (or arithmetical?) problem, as the next illustration suggests (Figure 7.4). This

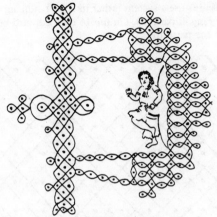

Figure 7.3

is taken from the Leapfrogs book *Lots* (1979) and the problem implied here is concerned with common factors.

A more sophisticated form of geometrical art is to be found in the intricate patterns that decorate many Islamic buildings. These are elaborations of the basic geometrical idea of the rangoli patterns, illustrated earlier in Figure 7.2. If one of these is repeated, new shapes are formed at the juxtapositions (Figure 7.5).

The artists of Islam did not restrict themselves to the square. They used a variety of shapes which tessellate – squares, triangles, hexagons or combinations of other polygons. The unit shape is then dissected by a number of obvious lines such as diagonals, joins of mid-points. Some of these lines, or segments of them, are then selected and the others removed. The pattern is built up by the repetition of these selected lines on the squares (or whatever) of the tessellation. Figure 7.6 shows a typical example of the basic construction, and the repetition of this results in the line drawing in Figure 7.7.

The quite striking effects can be enhanced by colouring, or by interlacing the lines; but the labour of drawing is considerable. Some reprographic technique is needed once the basic design is drawn. Photocopying, spirit-duplicators, tracing or carbon-paper may all be used. If simple printing facilities are available, as they usually are in a design department, this is probably the best medium. The basic square design can be made into a printing-block by sticking matches, strips of balsa wood, or string onto a stiff card base.[5]

Figure 7.4 The Hindus use a system rather like the bouncing of a billiard ball to make some of their rangoli patterns. On the 16 by 6 dot grid below, two lines are needed to complete the pattern,

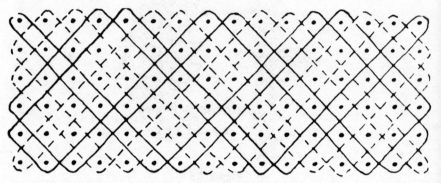

but on a 16 by 7 dot grid, one line goes all the way!

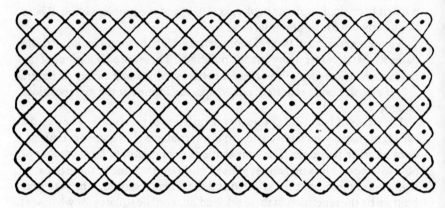

The activity and its products can be satisfying in themselves, and considerably more engrossing than most geometrical exercises. But, of course, teachers of mathematics will want to be sure that the activity does actually involve their students in a growing geometrical awareness. I think this comes about through the actual drawing in which they are inevitably involved, and it can be extended and made more explicit by a discussion of the finished products.

What is the implicit geometry involved? In the first place there is the existence, and implications, of the symmetries of various plane figures; and in the second place there are always a large variety of geometrical figures

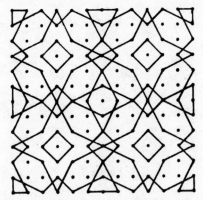

Figure 7.5   As the basic pattern developed in Figure 7.2 is repeated, new shapes emerge.

embedded within the constructions whose properties are implicit and often determine the nature of the final design. Look at the design of Figure 7.7. Are the large 8-pointed stars regular? What about the smaller 8-pointed stars? What are the angles at their points? How do you know? Are the small 4-pointed stars exactly the same shape as the large 4-pointed stars? Are you sure? How many times bigger are the large stars then?

If you look at the square Figure 7.6, with all the construction lines from

Figure 7.6

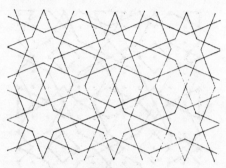

Figure 7.7

which this pattern was drawn, you will find a multiplicity of standard geometrical shapes: right-angled triangles, isosceles triangles (some of them right-angled) rhombuses, kites, trapezia, and of course squares. The basic properties of these figures are implicit in their symmetries. Many of the chord properties of the circle, as well as some of its angle properties, can also be extracted from this diagram. The reasons for the concurrency of many of the lines provide more complex problems. Certainly there is no lack of geometric potential; it is a matter of judgement how far this needs to be made explicit with particular students.

The introduction of the circle into the square (as in Figure 7.6) has an interesting effect on the kinds of shapes that then emerge in the designs.

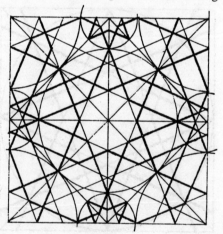

Figure 7.8

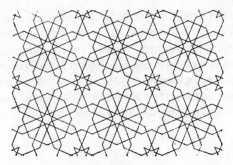

Figure 7.9

The Islamic artists exploited this with ever-increasing complexity. For instance the radius of the circle may be reduced to bisect the half-diagonals, and further circles introduced (Figure 7.8). The design in Figure 7.9 is one that has been generated from this figure. Over 200 examples are drawn in a book by Bourgoin (1973).[6]

Students at this level will also be involved in the study of rotational symmetry. The design in Figure 7.10 is an example of one way in which Islamic art employs this concept. The lines within the basic unit are selected so as to retain a four-fold rotational symmetry (in the case of the square). This figure is then rotated through fractions of this 90° symmetry, and the rotated figure(s) superimposed on the original one. In the photograph the

Figure 7.10[7]

effect is enhanced by a linking of these component figures and an interlacing of the lines – a device which was also employed in the designs to be found on Celtic monuments in this country. Finding the conditions under which this interlacing works is an interesting topological investigation; if you draw a continuous line, crossing over itself several times and coming finally back to the starting point, can you then always do an over-and-under interlacing? What if you also draw a similar kind of line on top of the first one?

Games

I was recently given a ten-minute lesson by three Vietnamese boys in their version of chess: I was then required to give one of them a game. This I lost fairly quickly in spite of some sympathetic help from the other two, but I am sure they were right that my best way of learning the game was to play it as soon as possible. In some ways it is easier to learn a variation of a game that you already know (note my ethnocentricity – I play chess: they play a variation of it! Where did chess originate?) but there is always a degree of interference. The names and moves of the pieces bore some resemblance to those in the game I knew, and this both helped and hindered my learning. My greatest difficulty, however, was in recognizing the pieces, which were all shaped like the pieces in draughts, and differentiated from each other only by the Vietnamese characters inscribed on their faces. My teachers had their difficulties, too: it is no easy task to explain the rules of a game, especially when you are doing this in a foreign language. When you play a familiar game you are barely conscious of many of the things that have to be explained when you introduce some new player to the system. This requires a careful ordering of information (should we make a flow-diagram of it?) if the learner is not to become hopelessly confused.

I am suggesting that this learning and teaching, and of course playing, of games is a very profitable classroom activity. But a mathematics classroom? Yes, particularly a mathematics classroom, because mathematics is a rule-governed activity, and the explaining and understanding of a set of rules for a game, and the subsequent devising of good strategies in playing, are very close to the kind of communication and to the thinking processes that are needed in mathematics. An added justification for games in a mathematics classroom is that they often involve some pieces of computation, or (as in the case of chess, for instance, or even noughts-and-crosses) some perception of geometrical relationships; but whilst this is true I think it should be regarded as a secondary argument.

If you are working in a classroom with different ethnic groups represented there is likely to be a good fund of varied games waiting to be uncovered. If you encourage the teaching and playing of these games, one thing that will probably emerge is the way in which different cultures have developed variations on the rules of games that are essentially 'the same'

Chess is a good example of this, as already mentioned: Chinese dominoes have no 'blanks' but eleven of the pieces are duplicated. In Hawaii people play dice games not with a cubical die but with four discs all blank on one side, the other sides being marked with one, two, three or four dots. Ashanti children have a game similar to noughts-and-crosses but played with four pieces of each of two colours. These are placed by the players alternately in eight of the nine places of a three by three square board. The pieces may then be moved alternately into a neighbouring vacant place until one player achieves three-in-a-row. This has obvious affinities to Nine Mens Morris, too; and there are variations on that game all over the world.

If the class does not have the benefit of its own cultural diversity the teacher may have to introduce these games (see Bell 1979).[8] Looking at a worldwide collection of such games may do a lot to raise an awareness of our shared humanity. On another level it can draw attention to the variety that is possible, as rules and equipment are slightly varied. The rules of the games are arbitrary, and yet they have to maintain an internal logic if the game is to be playable. If they are changed then play may be similar in many ways, but it can crucially affect the nature of the game. Mathematics, being also subject to human decision, has a similar arbitrariness in its ground-rules: by changing just one axiom you may move from Euclidean geometry to a geometry of a very different space; or if you change the usually agreed rules of the order in which you do operations in evaluating, say, $(8 - 3 \times 2) \times 7$, this may no longer have the value 14. Many people would prefer a rule which directs you to do the operations in the order they appear, reading left to right. Quite a number of people work on the assumption that the rules have in fact been changed in this way! Let us play the game that way then, for a bit, and see just what difference it does make. How would we write the above expression so that it still takes the value 14?

To be in control of one's mathematical dealing (and this is what I think 'numeracy' means) one needs an awareness of the way mathematics works. A part of this is the nature of the agreed (but sometimes changeable) rules of mathematics. Games provide a very accessible and enjoyable parallel.

Statistical work

The suggestions I have to make in this area really relate to the selection of data from which statistical ideas can develop. The main point emphasizes using 'live' data so that the students not only become more interested in the subject, but also become aware that it is a subject which has a strong relevance to their lives outside the maths room.

Now I am not at all convinced that students are greatly concerned about the distribution of pets amongst their classmates, or in the sizes of their friends' shoes, or the way the traffic flows along the road outside the school. Is it not possible to find some rather more significant statistics than these? Rather than this constant preoccupation with pets (which in any case are not a part of many of the minority cultures) would it not be more relevant to collect information, for instance, about the different languages that are used in the students' homes, or about the variety of religious backgrounds, or the time which students devote to religious observances and so on? The questions that are chosen for inquiry must be a matter for the judgement of individual teachers in consultation with their classes; but it strikes me that if questions are chosen which will increase the awareness (of both students, and teachers) of matters that really affect the life-experience of the students, this will be educationally helpful as well as fostering an interest in, and a respect for, the mathematical processes involved.

For older students one can look further afield, and I would like to suggest that there are interesting questions to be investigated in the statistics of world population, trade, the distribution of wealth and so on, particularly in the differentials between the so-called developed countries and the third world. Minority group students are citizens of this country; nevertheless, it is likely that they will find the study of questions relating to their country of origin particularly significant, since it will help them to understand more about the background of their parents and about the lives of their geographically distant relatives. But it is equally necessary that all of us should know more about the way that world economics affects the lives of people in different parts of the world.

If one uses data which relate to the world in which the students live, then they are far more likely to start asking questions such as: What does this mean? Why are things like that? Is it like this in my family, my village, my town? With a fairly adequate supply of pocket calculators in most classrooms now, there is no need for the textbook contrivance of manipulating the data so that the questions will 'work out'. We can use real data; the most ready source is in the many publications of the Centre for World Development Education (CWDE).[9] For example, their Development Puzzle contains a mass of interesting information on Trade, Aid, Population, Education, Industry and Agriculture etc. and includes quite a lot of statistical data.

Other useful material from the CWDE includes the World Population Data Sheet, the booklet World Population Report, and the larger World Development Report which gives a mass of data on most aspects of development, not simply population.

The problem of digging out this kind of data would no doubt be eased with the cooperation of the Social Studies Department in a school. Unfortunately (but understandably) teachers of social studies seem to prefer to underplay and oversimplify the mathematical problems. More cooperation between the Mathematics and Social Studies Departments would surely help both – as well as making this kind of study more intelligible to the students.

History

There is little profit in teaching the history of mathematics in any formal way, plodding through the centuries. Nevertheless, historical episodes can be used to illustrate the nature of mathematical enquiry, counteracting the misapprehension of inevitable finality. The development of algebraic notation was very similar to contemporary efforts to devise appropriate computer languages: it seems most likely that the now ubiquitous BASIC computer language will submerge, and come to be seen as clumsy as the early attempts at algebra. Yet those early versions express many of the same struggles as students now have to engage in; similarly, most of us meeting calculus for the first time have just the same conceptual difficulties as did the early pioneers.

So it seems likely that a historical perspective is a useful awareness for teachers, even if it is to be used explicitly only occasionally. There is difficulty, however, in finding suitable source material, and this is especially true if we wish to avoid what I consider to be the ridiculously ethnocentric version which is usually presented. In the process of conquest the cultures of occupied countries suffered the same fate as their political institutions, so that the surviving remnants are difficult to piece together.

We are almost completely ignorant of what was happening in Africa before the Europeans destroyed the culture there, and it is not easy to recreate a coherent picture of the achievement of Asian learning, though there is enough even in the standard works to suggest that it was considerable. (Boyer is probably the most readable and informative, though he views the Asians, and Indians in particular, with a grudging and critical eye.)[10] In both India and China there were efficient numeral systems – early on the Chinese used coloured rods (red for positive and black for negative) to represent the integers, and these are depicted in their written numerals:

These were used in a place system to represent numbers of any size, the symbols for 1–19 alternating with those for 10–90. Thus 1984 would be written: ▦ . In effect this was a centesimal system. The illustration (Figure 7.11) of Pascal's triangle (dated 1303 – over 300 years before Pascal's birth) shows some modification of these symbols. In India there was the decimal system, from which our present-day symbols are derived. In both civilizations these numeral systems facilitated considerable advances in both arithmetic and algebraic work.

The Chinese appear to have had an absorbing interest in pure number, and, for instance, produced some interesting approximations for $\pi = 3.1547$, $\sqrt{10}$, $92/29$ and $142/45$ – which all appeared in the first century AD. Later Liu Hui used the same method as did Archimedes – calculating with the help of Pythagoras' theorem the perimeter of a many-sided polygon – to find the circumference of a circle. Archimedes stopped at a 96-sided polygon: Liu Hui went to 3,072 sides to give a value of π as 3.14159. By the fifth century Tsu Ch'ung-chih had placed π between 3.1415927 and 3.1415926.

The algebraic work of the Chinese was likewise quite advanced, dealing for instance with the solution of simultaneous equations and with equations of higher degree using Horner's method some 500 years before Horner's time. They did a lot of work on the summation of series, and the appearance of Pascal's triangle indicates their knowledge of the binomial theorem for positive integral exponents (though they used it for the extraction of roots).

Although the Chinese civilization was advanced in its technological development – the early invention of paper-making and of printing, of

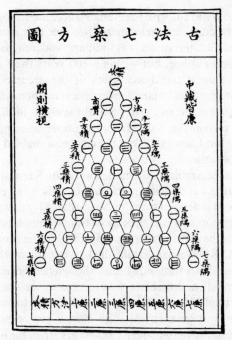

Figure 7.11   *Source*: Boyer (1969) *A History of Mathematics*, New York, John Wiley and Sons. Reprinted with permission.

gunpowder and the mariner's compass are well known – the study of mathematics appears to have proceeded as much for its own sake as for its applications to surveying and commerce, etc. The same may be said of Indian mathematics, but there an interest in astronomy was an additional motivation, and this led in particular to the invention and development of trigonometrical methods.

It is striking how similar in many respects was the mathematics of these two great Eastern cultures to that which was later developed in Europe. This is not entirely accounted for by the transmission from East to West via the bridging Islamic culture. The Arabs did not simply play the passive role of custodians and relayers which is often attributed to them in our ethnocentric story. In this the Greeks are the heroes of mathematical antiquity, developing the rudimentary ideas from Mesopotamia and Egypt into the first foundations of real mathematics. When their civilization succumbed to the invading tribes from the North, the Arabs, so the story goes, preserved this Grecian treasure until, with the Renaissance, the European genius was able to resume the creative development. It is true that initially the Islamic conquest of the Mediterranean was military and religious without any notable supporting culture, but within a 100 years their culture was fast growing, feeding upon the dying fruits of the occupied countries. By wedding the systematic and mainly geometrical mathematics of the Greeks with the more pragmatic and arithmetical expertise infiltrating from the East, was Islam responsible not only for the preservation of what otherwise might have been lost knowledge, but the amalgam enabled them to create a revitalized mathematics.

The most notable Arabic mathematician was Al-Khowarizmi, because it was he who created a systematic methodology which came to be known as Algebra. The word is derived from his book-title 'Al-jabr wa'l muqabalah' – 'al-jabr' means restoration (the process of transferring terms from one side of an equation to the other); 'muqabalah' refers to the process of cancellation of terms. Al-Khowarizmi established systematic methods for dealing with both linear and quadratic equations, though he worked in words not in the kind of symbolism which we now regard as an essential feature of algebra. Interestingly his justifications for the rules for manipulating his 'word-equations' was geometrical – he used a prototype of the Dienes algebraic materials ('invented' over 1,000 years later) for proving the complex procedures such as 'completing the square' to solve his quadratics. This is an example of the merging of the algebraic and geometric traditions of East and West. In the case of trigonometry – the other large area which the Arabs developed systematically – there was a choice between following Ptolemy's methods of chords (of a circle) and the Hindu use of the half-chord. They preferred the Hindu technique, and from this choice comes our present use of the sine function.[11] This was their starting-point, but they vastly extended the basic method, introducing the tangent function, computing tables of all six of the trigonometric functions and discovering many of the formulae which now form the bulk of A level syllabuses in trigonometry.

From the ninth to the twelfth century Islamic mathematics flourished with creative vigour. There is no space here to describe in detail this rapidly developing body of mathematical achievement. Perhaps it is worth mentioning the familiar name of Omar Khayyam (1050–1123); familiar as a poet, he was also a mathematician of very high originality, developing geometrical methods for solving cubic equations, inventing (or reinventing?) the binomial theorem, and investigating Euclid's parallel postulate by a method later attributed to the Italian, Saccheri – to mention just a few of his achievements. For a rather different reason (though it also indicates the sophistication of the mathematics we are considering) I would like to mention also one remarkable theorem due to Thabit-ibn-Qurra (826–90 AD) concerning so-called amicable numbers (i.e. pairs of numbers each of which is the sum of all the divisors – including 1, but excluding the number itself – of the other number). Such number-pairs are not easy to find: the smallest is 220,284 and was known to the Pythagoreans. It was not until 1867 that the next smallest pair (1184,1210) was found – by a 16-year-old Italian, Nicolo Paganini. However, back in the ninth century Thabit established the following method of generating a series of amicable number pairs: p, q and r are numbers of the form $p = 3.2^n - 1$, $q = 3.2^{n-1} - 1$, and $r = 9.2^{n-1} - 1$. Thabit showed that if all three of these numbers are prime for some value of n, then the two numbers $2^n pq$ and $2^n r$ form an amicable pair.

My purpose in mentioning this curious but remarkable piece of number theory (which incidentally was rediscovered 800 years later almost simultaneously by the two French mathematicians, Fermat and Descartes) is to suggest one way in which historical episodes might be used in school mathematics.

The computer now gives access to many such situations, enabling us quickly to rework the investigations of mathematicians of the past, and for instance it means that many 16-year-olds could now overtake the work of Nicolo Paganini!

The ideas presented in this chapter must be only a sample of the possibilities of opening up mathematics in such a way that students experience it as a part of a worldwide culture. It is to be hoped that teachers and teacher educators will develop further ideas and that they will find ways of sharing them.

Notes and references

1   The word was invented by Anna in Fynn (1974) *Mister God this is Anna*, a Collins Fount paperback. It is a form of invention which a lot of children delight in, perhaps feeling the power they possess when they have learned to count.

2   The course of this transmutation is illustrated in *Lots*, Leapfrogs, Devon, 1979, which is a compilation of ideas and pictures about numbers. It also includes some historical material about other early number systems. (Leapfrogs catalogue and publications can be obtained from Tarquin Publications, Stradbrooke, Diss, Norfolk.)

3   Lemoine, J.G. (1932) *Les anciens procédés de calcul sur les doigts*, Geuthner.

4   Zaslavsky, Claudia (1975) African network patterns, *Mathematics Teaching* No 73.

5   *Prints* published by Leapfrogs, 1967. Leapfrogs also publish two posters illustrating Islamic patterns, called 'Islamic patterns 1 and 2'. (For Leapfrogs address see Note 2 above).

6   Bourgoin, J.J. (1973) *Arabic geometrical pattern and design*, Dover Publications.

7   Bourgoin, J.J. (1973) *op. cit.*

8   Bell, R.G. (1979) *Board and table games from many civilizations*, Dover Publications, Revised edition.

9   Centre for World Development Education, 128 Buckingham Palace Road, London SW1.

10   Boyer, C.B. (1968) *A History of Mathematics*. Chichester: Wiley.

11   The word 'sine' has a curious etymology. In written Arabic vowels are often omitted: this resulted in the word 'jiba' (meaning 'half-chord') becoming confused with the word 'jaib' (meaning 'opening of a garment at neck and bosom'). European mathematicians in taking over Arabic trigonometry translated this into the Latin 'sinus' (meaning 'bosom').

CHAPTER 8

CHEMISTRY

Iolo Wyn Williams

On the face of it chemistry does not appear to be a very promising subject for discussion in a volume such as this. Hydrogen reacts with oxygen explosively wherever the mixture is ignited. Lead oxide heated with charcoal gives beads of lead in all parts of the world. Sugar ferments to alcohol whether extracted from beet or from cane. Chemical reactions are not culturally dependent. With very minor exceptions, such as the difficulty of maintaining hygroscopic compounds in a humid climate, or unstable compounds at high temperatures, chemistry laboratories at the school level are much of a muchness the world over. Chemical theory, the interpretation of chemical properties in terms of atomic composition, has for at least 100 years been generally accepted – speculative indeed, as theory should be, but not controversial in any national or ethnic sense. Chemistry, taught as the interplay of fact and theory might well be classified as culturally neutral, and over the last 20 years this is the way it has generally been taught.

Recent thinking about chemistry teaching and the place of chemistry in the curriculum, however, suggests that the pendulum may be about to swing away from the theoretical approach to chemistry towards one where the social aspects of the subject are given greater prominence (ASE 1979, 1981; Frazer 1982; Johnstone 1982; Fensham 1983). This should make it easier to introduce a multicultural dimension into the chemistry curriculum. However, to avoid making assumptions about the future of chemistry teaching this chapter will argue that a multicultural perspective is perfectly possible within the current secondary school chemistry curriculum.

What is chemistry?

In seeking to define the specific contribution which chemistry can make to multicultural education it is helpful to start with Fensham's (1983) discussion of what chemistry is all about, or in other words: 'What do chemists do?'

1. They convert raw materials into useful products by synthesis and extraction, for example, iron ore into steel; crude oil into plastics; soda and sand into glass; air and water into fertilizers; wood into alcohol; oil into dyestuffs, paints, glues, detergents, disinfectants and drugs. This is basically what chemistry is, and much of the teaching of elementary chemistry is the teaching of the elements of this complex web of inter-conversions. In order to carry out the process of synthesis chemists need some other basic skills:
   a. analysis, to be able to identify the raw material, usually in a mixture, sometimes present only in a very small proportion;
   b. separation and purification, to enable the process of synthesis to proceed, and to investigate the properties of the pure material;
   c. rate control, the speeding up or slowing down of the chemical process to bring about the desired result.
2. In addition to these practical purposes, chemists also investigate the properties and substances with a view to using them, or converting them into useable products.
3. Finally, and at a deeper level, chemists seek to explain and interpret the properties and behaviour of substances in terms of their chemical compositions and their atomic and sub-atomic structures.

Presented in this way chemistry is seen as a process of discovery and as a record of human achievement. It is also an account of current practice in a skilled profession. Pursuing this line of thought in a multicultural context the following points also seem as significant:

1. The origins of chemistry as a craft practice and as a science are diverse. They will be outlined later.
2. The raw materials of chemistry are found everywhere, although the uneven distribution of important resources (e.g. oil and mineral ores) has important economic and political consequences.
3. The products of chemistry are found everywhere and influence everyone's life.
4. There are chemists at work throughout the world in pharmacies and hospitals, in water purification plants and breweries, in agriculture and

the food industry, in oil refineries and in manufacturing industries of all kinds.

5. There is chemical industry in virtually every country in the world, ranging from the individual charcoal burner to the multinational petro-chemical complex.

6. People all over the world are involved in chemical processes whether they be making soap and candles, purifying salt, brewing beer or wine, spreading fertilizers and weedkillers, washing clothes, bleaching hair, applying suntan lotion, developing films, glueing joints, patching an old car with fibreglass, or a host of other activities carried out for pleasure, profit or self-preservation.

In seeking out the multicultural dimension of a chemistry curriculum we must always come back to the element of human achievement. In this context, valuing cultural diversity implies recognizing the achievement of human beings in different cultural, historical and environmental settings, with particular reference to the use and conversion of raw materials by chemical means into useable products.

The origins and growth of chemistry

Chemistry developed as a science in its own right in the eighteenth and nineteenth centuries, but only on the basis of experience and expertise built up over a period of hundreds, even thousands of years. Over 5,000 years ago in Egypt and Mesopotamia (around the rivers Tigris and Euphrates, the area now known as Iraq) copper was being extracted from its ores, glass was made and fabrics were dyed with natural colours. One of the most impressive discoveries of the period was that if the tin ores were mixed with copper ores, during the process of extraction, the metal bronze could be manufactured, which was harder and more useful than copper itself. Without any fundamental understanding of the nature of alloys such as we now possess, the ancient craftsmen were able to ensure that the mixture they produced had exactly the right composition to give the hardest possible alloy of the two metals (Bronowski 1973). Iron swords are known to have been produced over 3,000 years ago, and by 666 BC the technology of sword making had developed to the point where a flexible blade could be produced with a case-hardened edge to maintain sharpness. We know also that distillation was used in Mesopotamia as far back as 1200 BC for the production of perfumes.

The ancient Greeks in the last five centuries of the pre-Christian era contributed no technical skills to chemistry, for their culture rated the things of the mind more highly than those of the hand. They contributed, however, the first inklings of the atomic structure of matter (ideas which only came to fruition 2,000 years later), and the first theory of chemistry, advanced by Aristotle, who considered that all matter was either hot or cold, or fluid or dry; thus giving in combination earth (cold and dry), water (cold and fluid), air (hot and fluid) and fire (hot and dry). The four element theory dominated chemistry for many centuries without necessarily hindering its practical progress. Alexander the Great conquered the 'known world' for the Greeks, but his major achievement must have been the founding of the city of Alexandria with its library and university where the Egyptian practical arts and Greek thought came together in a great explosion of chemical creativity. The Alexandrian chemists invented stills for continuous distillation, furnaces, beakers, filters and other items of apparatus that have been in use virtually ever since. The chemical recipe books of the period, some of which are still in existence written on papyrus, show that the Alexandrians were expert at metal working, glass making and dyeing. Their instructions are clear and easy to follow. Later they became more and more concerned with the search for perfection in metals, that is for the conversion of other metals to gold, an idea which was perfectly acceptable within Aristotle's theory. This became known as Alchemy, the term 'Chemeia' being first used around AD 300.

Such developments did not occur only in one part of the world. Almost identical developments took place in China, where metal working and the making of gold was also well established at an early period. The alchemical tradition of China had a medical facet in that the perfection of metals was also felt to be good for the human body, so that the gold recipes were not only recipes for production of valuable metals but also recipes for medicines and human elixirs. Mercury and its compounds were well known to the Chinese, presumably with dreadful consequences for those who consumed them as medicines. (Li 1948; Ronan 1983).

The next major contribution to chemistry came with the spread of Islam and the expansion of the Arab world. The Islamic calendar dates from Muhammad's flight from Mecca to Medina in AD 622, and within 20 years the new force and religion had conquered Syria, Egypt and Persia. Within 100 years the Islamic influence had spread across the whole of North Africa and had conquered Spain. Arabic scholars in the ninth century translated the Greek Alexandrian manuscripts into Syrian and Arabic, and enthusiastically took up the study of chemistry. By this time there were well-established trade routes from China to the Middle East, and Arabic alchemy was undoubtedly influenced by the Chinese tradition. The Arabs knew of sal ammoniac (named after the temple of Ammon near where deposits were found) and knew the method of producing it by the distillation of animal products. Unlike the earlier alchemists, who had concentrated on metals and their compounds, they engaged in the distillation of all kinds of natural products and in the development of acids and alkalis as solvents. In the eleventh century ibn Sina (or Avicenna) became known as the greatest physician of Islam through his use of alchemical medicines. The tradition of medicine and alchemy known as iatrochemistry also flourished in India, reaching a peak in the period AD 1300 to 1550 just at a time when a similar movement was beginning in Europe.

In its turn Arabic alchemy faded away in the twelfth and thirteenth centuries, but by this time it had become sufficiently well established in south-western Europe, in Spain and in the south east in Byzantium (Constantinople, now Istanbul in Turkey), for a new thrust to develop in Europe. The old Alexandrian texts were retranslated into Greek and Latin together with the original works of the Arabs such as Jabir, al-Razi and ibn Sina. Many new works by European alchemists were attributed to these older authors to give them greater credibility. The importation of improved glassware from Italy allowed the Byzantine alchemists in AD 1100 to distil alcohol to a higher concentration than had been available previously. They also distilled vitriol (Iron(II) Sulphate) giving sulphuric acid in the twelfth century, discovered nitric acid in the thirteenth century and aqua regia in the fourteenth century. The availability of these powerful solvents extended the scope of chemistry considerably.

In the sixteenth century the German physician Georgius Agricola wrote his standard text on metals *De Re Metallica*, whilst the Swiss physician Paracelsus revolutionized medicine by discovering various chemical medicines, including the mercury cure for syphilis.

Thereafter, and until the twentieth century, the development of chemistry as a science and as a practical subject occurred principally in the West. One of the notable features of this period is how broadly European the development of chemistry was. The study of gases, pioneered by the Belgian, Van Helmont, led eventually to the simultaneous discovery of oxygen by Scheele in Sweden, Priestly in England and Lavoisier in France. The development of the first electrical battery by Volta in Italy led within a matter of weeks to Davy's isolation of sodium and potassium in England. The atomic theory of the nineteenth century was established by Dalton in

England, Gay Lussac in France, Avogadro and Cannizzaro in Italy and Berzelius in Sweden. Similarly the development of chemical industries in France, Germany and England can only be understood when studied together.

This sketch of the historical development of chemistry is relevant to the present discussion in that it illustrates the contributions of different cultural groups to the development of the subject, and thereby helps reduce ethnocentrism. The transmission from the ancient Eygptian and Greek to Islamic, Byzantine and European cultures recognizes parallel developments in China and India and possibly in other parts of the world. Many of the techniques and much of the terminology of modern chemistry derives from these ancient times: for example, alkali from Arabic *al qaliy* – the roasted ashes; soda from Arabic *suda* – a splitting headache; alcohol from ancient Hebrew – originally an eyeshadow, probably antimony sulphide (Flood 1963). Its incorporation into chemistry teaching, however, poses something of a problem, for in the past 20 years references even to recent history have been dropped from chemistry courses and textbooks. A number of older books which may be available in many schools provide useful background material (Lowry 1926; Holmyard 1931; Partington 1937; Leicester 1956; Taylor 1957). A recent volume by Ronan (1983) gives a balanced illustrated overview of the different cultural contributions to the history of the world's science.

If handled sensitively, reference to the multicultural history of chemistry can lead to an appreciation of the intellectual and practical achievement of each period and culture. It is important to avoid suggesting that more recent developments are in some way superior; older discoveries may now appear trivial, but in the context of their time they are equally important.

The European domination of the development of scientific chemistry should not be presented as the end of the road. In the twentieth century we have seen the growth of American science, and subsequently of an international scientific community. Scientists from many countries are making important contributions to the advance of chemical knowledge. What is arguably more important is that practical, technical and professional chemistry is practised in laboratory, factory and field all over the world by men and women with whom our pupils should be encouraged to identify themselves.

Chemistry in context

A study of current secondary chemistry syllabuses reveals a range of topics with multicultural possibilities. Some of these are reviewed below. Where the topics offer an opportunity to consider the multicultural history of chemistry, they have been denoted by (H). (C) indicates those topics with possibilities of referring to contemporary practice elsewhere in the world. (E) suggests that some ethnic minority groups may have different experiences to draw upon personally or through their parents.

1. *Raw materials and useful products*
   This provides a world perspective, and the search for a chemical process to bring about the transformation provides a constant reference point for the subject (C).

2. *Elements and compounds*
   Sources of elements; a geographical Periodic Table (C).
   The discovery and isolation of the elements (H).
   Naturally occurring salts and minerals (C).

3. *Separation and purification*
   Salt from rock salt, sea water, and from plant sources by ashing and leaching (C), (H).
   Sugar from beet or cane – involving pressing, precipitation of impurities with lime, concentration and centrifuging, decolourizing with activated charcoal and recrystallization (C).
   Distillation of fermented liquors for use as drinks, solvents and fuels (C), (E).
   Water purification (C).
   Chromatography of food colours (E).

4. *States of matter*
   Greek theories. Early techniques of distillation and sublimation (of sal ammoniac) (H).

5. *Acids, bases and salts*
   Use various plant extracts from ethnic food stores as indicators (E).
   Compare acidity of different fruits (E).
   Test alkalinity of different vegetable ashes (H).

6. *Metals*
   Iron smelting – traditional methods using charcoal (H).
   Working of iron for weapons and implements (H).
   Alloys – bronze and brass (H), (C).
   Aluminium smelting – case study of contemporary smelters (C).
   Corrosion and its prevention (C), (E).

7. *Fuels*

Compare wood, charcoal, dung, peat, coal, gas and oil (C), (H), (E).

Alternative sources of energy (C).

Methane digestors. Biomass production (C).

Fire fighting; bush fires in Australia resulting from high temperatures and eucalyptus oil vapour from trees (C).

Nuclear energy, now worldwide (C).

8. *Ethanol*

Fermentation of many starch- and sugar-containing plants, e.g. millet, grape juice, cassava, sugar cane (C), (E).

Alcoholic drinks (C), (E).

Industrial alcohol as a fuel (Brazil) and as a chemical feedstock (C).

Ethanoic acid and esters (C).

9. *Food science*

Apply food tests to rice, yam, plantain, banana, avocado etc. (E).

Food preservation, flavours and colouring – domestic and commercial (E), (C).

Drinks, soft and alcoholic (E), (C).

Fertilizers and soil improvers, herbicides and pesticides – natural and synthetic (C), (E).

Vegetable oils: castor, psalm, jojoba (C).

10. *Minerals*

Salt, sand, limestone and clay. Glass; pottery, ceramics and glazes; mortar, cement and concrete (H), (C).

11. *Household chemicals*

Soap. Detergents. Cleaning agents. Bleaches. Laundry work. Disinfectants (C), (E).

12. *Miscellaneous*

Cosmetics. Toothpastes. Denture cleaners (E).

Drugs and pharmaceuticals, traditional and synthetic (H), (C), (E).

Paints and dyes, traditional as well as modern petrochemicals (H), (C).

Glues and adhesives (C), (H).

Ink, writing materials, paper (H).

Explosives and fireworks (H).

Teaching and learning chemistry

Recent research in science education has suggested that many pupils find chemistry (and other sciences) more difficult than other subjects in the school curriculum. The three factors contributing to this difficulty have been identified as the level of abstraction involved in chemistry (Shayer and Adey 1980), the extent to which chemistry is 'overloaded' with information that the learner has to process simultaneously (Johnstone 1980), and the technical and semitechnical vocabulary and formal language involved in chemistry.

These three factors, especially the last, have particular relevance where pupils speak English as their second language or dialect. Chemistry teachers need to be particularly sensitive to these pupils' needs, and it is thus vital that they are fully aware of the linguistic difficulties associated with chemistry which are explored in more detail below.

Linguistic difficulties

Since Douglas Barnes et al. (1971) drew the attention of science teachers to the pitfalls of open and closed questions, studies of language and learning in science have proliferated. The Association for Science Education's study series booklet *Language in Science* (Prestt 1980) covers the field comprehensively and practically, and has an excellent bibliography. The Scottish Curriculum Development Service's in-service training pack *Language in Chemistry* (1980) is equally helpful. These studies may be summarized under the four main categories of language usage: listening, speaking, reading and writing.

The question and answer technique adopted by many teachers as an alternative to lecturing often seems to be employed as a means to maintain control over the class rather than to cause children to think. The teacher has a line of development to follow, with the result that unexpected or original answers are not well received or followed up. The line of questioning is not necessarily apparent to the pupils and so each question becomes something of a guessing game. The majority of questions are straightforward and factual, offering little scope for the expression of views or opinions. Cassels and Johnstone (1980) have speculated that the use of non-technical or semitechnical words in chemistry lessons may give rise to unexpected difficulties. In a research project involving many chemistry teachers, pupils were tested on their understanding of words such as disintergrate, negligible, spontaneous, simultaneous, displace, liberate, immerse, emit, converse and convention. All those quoted are taken from the list that more than 33 per cent of third formers seem to have difficulty with. The technical vocabulary of the subject itself may be less of a problem since the teacher will be conscious that he or she is introducing new terminology, but the similarity of sulphate, sulphite and sulphide, or of chlorate and chloride for example, must present difficulties to the unpractised ear. A consistent practice of writing the names as they are used would be helpful.

Studies of readability of scientific textbooks using one or other of the standard reading formulae (Prestt 1980) suggest that the reading ages of most chemistry books are far too high for the majority of pupils using them. Constant reference to this finding seems at last to be bearing fruit, and some more recent textbooks appear to be written in a more acceptable style, with shorter sentences and fewer complex words (Knutton 1983). *Chemistry for Today and Tomorrow* (Atherton and Lawrence 1978) is found to have a reading age of 15.5, which should just about make it suitable for fourth and fifth form 'O' level candidates for whom it is intended. The readability of notes provided by the teacher, printed or dictated, should be checked using one of the readability formulae. The simplest and safest guide to ensuring readability is to keep sentences short. The ease or difficulty of examination questions has also been shown to be related to their readability. A change of one word (e.g. fused to melted) can make a question significantly easier. Asking a direct question is preferable to an open-ended sentence to be completed. Positive questions are easier than negative questions. Blank-filling questions, unless the answer is obvious, can be very confusing.

The role of talk in learning has also been explored by, amongst others, Barnes (1975, 1977). He shows how pupils in dialogue with a teacher, or working on carefully structured small group tasks, talk themselves into understanding a problem. The importance of waiting for a pupil to formulate and express ideas has been well established though it is not easy to follow under the normal pressures of the classroom. Similar considerations apply to writing. The importance of encouraging pupils to use expressive writing, that is to write about their work in their own terms and in the language that comes most naturally to them, has been demonstrated by the Schools Council's *Writing and Learning across the Curriculum* project. It is not suggested that formal writing, as normally found in science, is unimportant. The teacher has an important role to play in producing formal summaries resulting from the pupils' own writing.

Clearly, the level of linguistic sophistication needed for chemistry learning presents particular difficulties for pupils for whom English is a second language or dialect.

New learning

One way for chemistry teachers to mitigate the difficulties associated with the level of linguistic sophistication needed is to explore classroom strategies which claim to make new learning easier for *all* pupils.

Fensham (1983) is a keen advocate of the theory advanced by the American psychologist Ausubel that new learning only takes place when it is linked to existing knowledge. Oversimplified in this way it is hardly more than a statement of the obvious. Pupils find it easier to learn about zinc and magnesium because they are already familiar with the metals iron, aluminium and copper. We introduce acids through the familiar acid drops, lemons and grapefruit. Even at this level, however, the suggestion that we should seek knowledge within the pupils' experience to which to link new learning is a helpful one. The advantage of project work, selected from the pupils' own experience, is that it does provide such ready-made foundations upon which new learning can be built. For ethnic minority pupils in particular such project work can offer opportunities to build on their own background; this can extend the knowledge and understanding of all pupils and also implies respect and recognition of cultural diversity.

Resources

It must be admitted at once that resources for a multicultural approach to chemistry teaching are difficult to come by. Few modern textbooks, for example, have more than a smattering of applied and social aspects. The revised Nuffield chemistry pupils' book *Chemistry in the World* (Hunt 1979) completely belies its title. *Chemistry for Today and Tomorrow* (Atherton and Lawrence 1978) is exceptional in that it has illustrations of chemistry in action from all over the world, and has frequent references in the text to chemistry in Africa. The historical aspects of chemistry are adequately provided for in the references already given, even though a considerable amount of work is required to turn these into useful teaching materials – a task currently in hand by the ASE and the Curriculum Subject Group of the Royal Society of Chemistry. Biographical details of important scientists of the world are provided by Asimov (1974), but are dominated by Europeans and Americans. Haber's *Black Pioneers of Science and Invention* (1978) may be useful in redressing the balance. On the contemporary side, information about the applied and social aspects of chemistry in the world at large is not easy to find at the right level. Raitt's *Modern Chemistry Applied and Social*

Aspects (1966), though dated, is still valuable. *Chemistry in the Market Place* (Selinger 1979) is one of the most useful sources, though its reference list is almost exclusively Australian. The literature of intermediate or appropriate technology (Dunn 1978; Moyes 1979) whilst providing a point of contact with the developing world is generally lacking in chemical content. Illustrative materials may be traced through the Centre for World Development's annual Catalogue of Resources (1983). Journals such as *School Science Review*, *Education in Chemistry*, *Chemistry in Britain* and *New Scientist* frequently contain useful snippets of information and, less often, longer articles. There is clearly a need for a collection of articles already published in this country and elsewhere.

The *Third World Science* project has attempted to gather together relevant material under different headings (Williams 1983). The following units have been prepared to date: Carrying Loads; Charcoal; Clay Pots; Dental Care; Distillation; Energy Converters; Fermentation; Housing; Iron Smelting; Methane Digesters; Natural Dyes; Plants and Medicine; Salt; Soap. Each unit contains Information Sheets for the teacher, extracts from relevant publications, illustrations and suggested activities. Sources of information include publications, teachers and pupils abroad, and science teachers in the UK with overseas experience. Further topics of chemical interest under consideration include Water, Sugar, Cement, Fuels and Vegetable Oils. These units were originally conceived as a contribution to development education, but they provide valuable resource material for the multicultural context, and could form the basis for practical activities and further curriculum development.

It is also important that multicultural curriculum content should be supported by visuals which reflect our multicultural society. Publishers are beginning to illustrate chemistry (and other) texts with photographs taken in racially and culturally diverse classrooms (Klein 1983).

Conclusion

To develop a multicultural approach within chemistry any further, we need more knowledge of chemists with international reputations from Africa, the Caribbean, Latin America and Asia, and even more about working scientists, technicians and operatives in chemical industries all over the world who could be used as models for our youngsters. We need detailed information about chemistry and chemical industry outside the industrialized countries and we need to know more about the potential chemical context in the domestic, personal lives of all our pupils, and how this context varies according to cultural background.

For chemistry, the challenge of multicultural education is to ensure that all our youngsters value cultural diversity, and devleop the self-confidence necessary for this demanding subject.

References

ASE (1979) *Alternatives for Science Education*. Hatfield: Association for Science Education.

ASE (1981)*Education Through Science*. Hatfield: Association for Science Education.

Asimov, I. (1974, 1978) *Asimov's Biographical Encyclopaedia of Science and Technology*. London: Pan Books, 1974. Newton Abbot: David and Charles, 1978.

Atherton, M.A. and Lawrence, J.K. (1978) *Chemistry for Today and Tomorrow*. London: John Murray.

Barnes, D., Britton, J. and Rosen, H. (1971)*Language, the Learner and the School*. London: Penguin.

Barnes, D. (1975) *From Communication to Curriculum*. London: Penguin.

Barnes, D. and Todd, F. (1977) *Communication and Learning in Small Groups*. London: Routledge and Kegan Paul.

Bronowski, J. (1973) *The Ascent of Man*. London: BBC.

Cassels, J.R.T. and Johnstone, A.H. (1980) *Understanding of Non-Technical Words in Science*. London: Royal Society of Chemistry.

Dunn, P.D. (1978)*Appropriate Technology, Technology with a Human Face*. London: Macmillan.

Fensham, P. (1983) *Conceptions, Misconceptions and Alternative Frameworks in Chemical Education*. Royal Society of Chemistry Nyholm Lecture, 1983 (to be published).

Flood, W.E. (1963) *The Origins of Chemical Names*. London: Oldbourne.

Frazer, M. (1982) *Chemistry All Around Us*, Report of a Seminar held at the University of East Anglia, School of Chemical Sciences, July.

Haber, L. (1978)*Black Pioneers of Science and Invention*. New York: Harcourt Brace Jovanovich. (By the same author: *Women Pioneers of Science*, 1979).

Holmyard, E.J. (1931) *Makers of Chemistry*. London: Oxford University Press.

Hunt, J.A. (editor) (1979) *Revised Nuffield Chemistry, Chemistry in the World*. London: Longman.

Johnstone, A.H. (1980) Chemical education research: facts, findings and consequences, *Chemical Society Reviews*, pp. 365–380.

Johnstone, A.H. (1982) Macro- and microchemistry, *School Science Review* Vol 64, No 227, pp. 377–379.

Klein, G. (1983) Multicultural teaching materials in maths and science,*Multicultural Teaching* Vol 1, No 3.

Knutton, S. (1983) Chemistry textbooks – are they readable?*Education in Chemistry* Vol 20, pp. 100–105.

Leicester, H.M. (1956) *The Historical Background of Chemistry*. New York: John Wiley.

Li Ch'iao-p'ing (1948) The chemical arts of old China, Easton, Pa., *Journal of Chemical Education*.

Lowry, T.M. (1926) *Historical Introduction to Chemistry*. London: Macmillan.

Martin, N., D'Arcy, P., Newton, B., Packer, R. (1976) *Writing and Learning Across the Curriculum*. London: Ward Lock Educational for Schools Council.

Moyes, A. (1979) *The Poor Man's Wisdom. Technology and the Very Poor*. Oxford: Oxfam.

Partington, J.R. (1937) *A Short History of Chemistry*. London: Macmillan.

Presst, B. (ed.) (1980) *Language in Science* (Study Series No 16). Hatfield: Association for Science Education.

Raitt, J.G. (1966) *Modern Chemistry Applied and Social Aspects*. London: Edward Arnold.

Ronan, C. (1983) *The Cambridge Illustrated History of the World's Science*. London: Cambridge/Newnes.

Scottish Curriculum Development Service (1980) *Language in Chemistry*. Dundee: SCDS.

Selinger, B. (1979) *Chemistry in the Market Place*. London: John Murray.

Shayer, M. and Adey, P.S. (1981) *Towards a Science of Science Teaching*. London: Heinemann.

Taylor, F.S. (1957) *A History of Industrial Chemistry*. London: Heinemann.

Williams, I.W. (ed.) (1983) *Third World Science*. Bangor: University College of North Wales, School of Education.

CHAPTER 9*

BIOLOGY

Michael Vance

Biology, together with other science subjects, has so far remained relatively untouched by changes in other curriculum areas regarding education for a multicultural society. However, the needs and circumstances of many inner-city schools with ethnic minority pupils are stimulating some biology teachers to question approach and content within the subject. At present there are more questions than answers, but discussion will lead to ideas and initiatives which should permeate the curriculum, leading to a biology more appropriate to the needs of a multicultural society.

Biology and the needs of the wider school community

All children in Britain are growing up in a multicultural society; their school experiences should lead them to appreciate the multicultural origins and manifestations of knowledge; it must lead them to see beyond their own ethnicity, and it must prepare them to respect and value other cultures and traditions. Biology has a major role to play in establishing a framework where discussion and enquiry can dispel racist images and stereotypes which are often based on ideas which appear to have scientific justification. The questions that pupils have about different attributes and physical form should be dealt with in biology, not only when they arise but as part of a coherent anti-racist theme throughout the school curriculum. Without this,

---

* Some of the ideas in this chapter are an extension of those in *Assessment in a Multicultural Society: Biology at 16+* by Michael Vance. Schools Council Programme 5 Pamphlet Series. Longman, York, 1984.

stereotypes will continue to be reproduced by an unchallenged racism. Such an approach should not be confined to urban communities, but should include schools which are predominantly monoethnic. Failure to do this will result in the development of a 'bipartite' curriculum and further widen the gap that exists.

Biology and the needs of minority ethnic pupils

Educational underachievement among some ethnic minority pupils is well documented and widely accepted (Rampton 1981). Biology teachers who do not accept this are unlikely to see the need for change, nor to recognize the needs of minority ethnic pupils. The Rampton Committee suggested that factors contributing to underachievement might include 'the inappropriateness of the curriculum, examinations, a lack of responsiveness to the needs of minority ethnic pupils and an inability to develop new curriculum materials'. The biology curriculum is no exception.

My experience as someone of West Indian origin, educated in England during the late 1960s and early 1970s, is one of receiving images of a backward and deprived third world rife with disease and needing the science of the West to combat its problems. Today, in the early 1980s, the biology curriculum has yet to redress the imbalance, for it still prepares minority ethnic pupils for entry into a monoethnic body of knowledge, and does not provide a framework whereby they can examine, dissect and make decisions about their culture. These students should find some explanations of their origins, practices and physiology within the biology curriculum. Care should be taken to ensure that these explanations include a range of views from differing cultures, including the pupils' own. There will be difficult areas, where morals or scientific practice conflict because of the particular experiences of cultures; in these cases there are no answers that can be given other than a sensitivity of approach and an awareness of the dangers of cultural chauvinism.

Biology and the multicultural curriculum

Science, and in particular biology, can play a key role in defining the ideological context of society. In South Africa 'apartheid' (living apart) is underpinned by a racist ideology. Within the school curriculum of South Africa there are subdivisions of material and content serving the varying social groups in their largely separate schools. In addition theories of eugenics, racial variations and the evolution of Homo sapiens occupy an important part of the biology curriculum (Van Rensberg 1973). The key purpose of the biology curriculum in South Africa is to provide a scientific basis for racism. The British biology curriculum has an opportunity to promote anti-racism.

The Association for Science Education (ASE) has commented that science subjects as presently taught tend to emphasize theory and restrict personal involvement, and fail to help pupils see science as one of the most important cultural activities devised by man. Where science is demystified and seen as part of everyday life, it can become accessible to pupils of all the diverse cultures which exist in contemporary Britain. Making science accessible to the minority ethnic communities involves all areas of the science curriculum, promoting multicultural and anti-racist content, aims and objectives. Townsend and Brittan (1973) tested the ground for such change when they surveyed schools and their science departments. Twenty heads of science departments listed six topics within the scope of biology as areas which prepared pupils for life in a multicultural society. These six areas were genetics, evolution, blood groups, skin colour, adaptations to environment, food and nutrition. A few departments suggested greater emphasis on human biology, physiology, heredity and health education.

Eleven years on, there has been no change which has become generally accepted in the secondary school biology curriculum. However there is some innovation at the level of policy, as well as the initiatives and practice of some biology teachers. Willey (1982) refers to some of the approaches that can be taken up by a biology department reviewing the courses it is offering:

> The curriculum should aim to promote an awareness of racial differences and their origins, and to explain these differences in terms of the biological principles of variation, evolution, natural selection and adaptation to environment.
>
> By avoiding racial stereotyping and offence regarding religious or other observances/beliefs. Taking care in choice of illustrations of physiological and biochemical phenomena.
>
> By using examples from minority as well as the majority groups in explanations and descriptions of society and man's development. Where we deal with matters which affect race we take a broad multicultural view and attempt to avoid a negative approach when dealing with biological and environmental problems associated with Third World countries, and particularly the countries of origin of our own pupils.

Further good practice is mentioned by Her Majesty's Inspectorate in their report on 'Aspects of Organisation and Curriculum in Seven Multi-ethnic Comprehensive Schools' (1979):

> In four of the schools, work in science was seen which could be described as cross cultural. An Asian teacher of science described the food he ate at home and compared its content and food value with comparable Western dishes. Another teacher outlined the science of pigmentation using different pupils in his class as a living resource. In yet another school genetics was being taught with sensitive reference to current theories about racial types and their supposed characteristics.

Both these publications point to biology as the science area which most readily lends itself to a multicultural perspective. The good practice outlined implies a perspective of emphasizing cultural diversity, rather than focusing on the sort of anti-racist perspective which is a feature of some contemporary and complementary humanities courses (ACER 1982). If the positive initiatives are to be built upon, then there are two main tasks to be undertaken. First, to develop a range of resources drawing upon the differing biological experiences of the minority ethnic communities, and secondly, to stimulate discussion about the role biology can play in setting up whole school anti-racist policies.

A starting point might be to consider biology's role within a whole school language policy which embraces the recommendations of Bullock (1975), on community languages and dialect issues. Writing in biology is usually teacher directed and involves answering questions and recording experimental work with an emphasis on the use of transactional prose. Rosen and Brittan (1971) have described this as writing for an audience, with the teacher as assessor. This approach can hardly be avoided, if the department offers biology at GCE O level, and indeed many teachers argue that this type of writing helps pupils to think through both logically and sequentially an experimental record or discussion.

Biology has its own jargon, which, together with the formal language of science, may pose particular difficulties for pupils whose first language or dialect is not English. Where cultural language boundaries do not match subject boundaries, and where the meanings are not easily translatable between languages some ethnic minority pupils are at an additional disadvantage. A challenge to biology teachers would be to establish features of biology which are especially complex for pupils for whom English is a second language or dialect; the next step would be to work with a specialist teacher of English as a second language to identify strategies for dealing with this problem. It might be possible to produce worksheets with key words translated; better still, it would be useful to make a number of recordings to explain meanings, since pupils often cannot read their own mother tongue. A language policy for identifying the language needs of individual pupils within the biology department would also need to take into account, and make allowances for, the powers of expression used by the pupil communicating in non-standard English.

Teachers working with pupils from minority ethnic backgrounds will usually be aware that many feel that they should cast off the language of the home in return for acceptance by peers and members of staff, and entry into the 'life' of the school. Biology teachers seeking to develop a language policy and appropriate resources should also seek out the support of colleagues from minority ethnic communities so that strategies can avoid paternalism.

The importance of genetics and race within the biology curriculum

Pupils have ideas about each other which they derive from their parents and their own culture. These often include racist views, based on all sorts of scientific and pseudoscientific ideas. It is not uncommon to find pupils who believe that whites are more intelligent than blacks or that blacks are better at running than whites. Pupils with such ideas should find them challenged by the content and approach of contemporary biology courses; if pupils see that ideas which they believe to be scientific are *not* tackled, then the school has failed. The National Front has now made two nationwide interventions outside school gates: during 1977/78 school year, and in the early summer of 1983 before the General Election. These interventions have included leafleting and the distribution of their newspaper for young people, *Bulldog*. The first two issues of this 'race-hate' paper contained articles on 'race-mixing', 'the Jews' and 'the race problem'. Their ideology is perhaps summarized by the following passage.

> The claim that integration is harmless and that 'all races are equal' is totally false. Races differ, not only in the colour of their skins, but in other physical ways and especially in temperament and innate intelligence.
>   Scientists tell us that these differences are not the result of environment only, but mainly of heredity. 'Men are not born equal' says Professor Francis Crick, a Nobel Prize winner . . . It is not bigotry to oppose multi-racialism. It is a natural healthy instinct to preserve one's own kind. A leading scientist, Sir Arthur Keith, has said that what is called prejudice is simply Nature's way of improving Mankind through racial differentiation. (*Bulldog* 1977)

What the passage does is to pose racism as a scientifically proven theory and therefore as 'truth'. Race cannot be treated as unproblematic, and Clayden et al. (1978) writing about the position of aborigines in Australia argue that: 'The genetic inferiority thesis is not new to Australian science literature and the effects of the debate permeate through all levels of society . . . The quality of education can only be improved if debates around such ideas are organised in a structured manner within the classroom . . .'

Biology teachers have to guard against the stereotyped images being received by pupils from those human biology texts which portray negroes as synonymous with Africa. Within these books there is often little reference to the manner in which division and subdivision can be made – for example, in Europe there are a number of races and not just *one* European race. First, biology teachers have to address themselves to the question of whether it is desirable to define an individual race. Linked to this is the 'concept' of race purity which is an essential part of racist ideology. Physical anthropologists have sought to rationalize this by using the terms primary and secondary races. A primary race is defined as a fundamental extreme, and a secondary race as the intermediate of two populations. Notions of racial purity often lead pupils to ask: 'Have races been pure in the past?' Most physical anthropologists answer this question by arguing that there were fewer people, and therefore social groups were more isolated in the past, resulting in greater differentiation. Biology teachers should add to this by showing pupils that the history of people is one of migration and encounter, a fact often neglected in most biology and human biology texts.

As well as tackling the origin of human variation, the biology curriculum needs to provide a base whereby pupils can come to terms with arguments about social/genetic inferiority such as those put forward by Jensen (1969) and later supported by Eysenck. Here biology has an important role to play in the anti-racist education of pupils, by taking them through some of the evidence that shows the effect of environment in regulating the expression of genes. This is usually crudely posed as the 'nature versus nurture' argument in explaining ethnic differences in raw IQ scores. The assumption that intelligence is essentially inheritable and due to genetic expression can be challenged by the use of valuable and interesting examples such as those cited in Whitten and Kagan (1978).

Ashley Montagu (1957) was one of the first anthropologists to argue that the term 'race' be abandoned. He sees culture as being a major factor in the development of the human species – 'a unique zone of adaptation' – available only to people, and believes that race is far too emotive and subjective a term to be useful to anthropologists. Instead he suggests that we consider humanity as a series of differing breeding populations within a species varying in the frequency of one or more genes, and has coined the term genogroup.

Teaching about cultural diversity through the medium of biology

If race and eugenics represent one side of the coin, the other side is educating pupils to respect, know about, and understand, the range of cultural diversity. This is most relevant within the themes of health, human population, world resources, diet and nutrition, which are established areas of the biology curriculum. Regrettably, these are often treated as marginal topics, partly because of the scarcity of resource material for multicultural biology.

These themes are areas where pupils could be encouraged to recognize that each society has its own traditions and styles of everyday living which are different and not necessarily superstitious or primitive, as often portrayed by the mass media. One strategy for combating both ideology and resource deficiency is to use the pupils' own experience, and even to involve parents. Such an input may help to make the pupils from a minority ethnic background, experiencing the alienation that is almost synonymous with inner-city schools, feel that they have something unique to contribute, thereby increasing motivation and participation. On this matter the ASE comments that a good course should 'allow youngsters to gain a sense of social meaning and identity as well as personal autonomy' (1980).

In the laboratory or classroom the biology teacher should ensure that the texts which are used show scientists from all races involved in investigation and experiment. This should be supplemented with the use of displays which show flora and fauna typical of countries where pupils' families originated, and which take up issues of unequal and diminishing resources and conservation. Some of the overseas (Tropical/Caribbean) biology texts share these perspectives in that they promote an image of a changing and developing third world. It seems, however, that the majority of biology texts widely used by British schools tend to relegate social biology to a chapter at the end of the text, or not to consider it at all. One exception is the revised Nuffield Biology Text IV *The Perpetuation of Life* (1976) which is part of a well-established course for 13–16 year olds. It gives a large amount of attention to questions of race, heredity and intelligence. It commences by raising questions about the myth of social superiority, then quotes the famous 1951 UNESCO statement on equality, and goes on to reinforce the statement by declaiming that:

> Some biological differences between human beings within a single race may be as great as or greater than the biological differences between two races . . . Available scientific knowledge provides no basis for believing that the groups of mankind differ in their innate capacity for intellectual and emotional development . . . Social changes have occurred that have not been connected in any way with changes in racial type. Historical and sociological studies thus support the view that genetic (that is inherited) differences are of little significance in determining the social and cultural differences between groups of men. (p. 19)

The Nuffield text, however, tries to 'balance' this view:

> Not all biologists were completely happy about this statement. One eminent geneticist had this to say 'I feel at times that it was bending over backwards to deny the existence of race in the sense that this term has been used for political purposes in the recent past. I of course entirely agree in condemning the Nazi race theory, but I do not think that the case against it is strengthened by playing down the possibility of statistical differences in, for example, the mental capacities of different groups: (p. 19)

and then quotes another geneticist:

> By trying to prove that races do not differ . . . we do no service to mankind. We conceal the greatest problem which confronts mankind . . . namely, how to use diverse gifts, talents, capacities of each race for the benefit of all races. For, if we were all innately the same how should it profit us to work together?. . .

The above 'balanced' argument is unnecessary, pupils get enough exposure to the ideas of inherited race difference. Teaching about the way in which culture may affect the development of individuals through diet, attitudes to health etc. provides the alternative to the myth of racial superiority. As the Nuffield authors themselves conclude: 'The great paradox of the problem of racial conflict is that the people who take part in it inevitably call on biology to justify their actions' (p. 20).

Biology teachers have to be clear about their own position in this area if they are going to teach it in such a way that questions are answered and stereotypes challenged. Whitten and Kagan (1978) argue that it is the inability of intelligence tests to respond to the diversity of cultures of peoples that has allowed 'scientific' racism to become a very powerful force in contemporary society.

The revised Nuffield Biology Text provides an example of how the question of race in biology can be discussed:

What were the features or characteristics that the Nazi regime used to identify the Aryan race?

How accurate or satisfactory, as guides to identification were these features in practice?

Give examples to support your view.

The data in table 6 show some of the features of the different races of mankind:

	Number	Complexion	Hair	Stature
Features	1	dark	dark/wavy	short
different	2	fair	dark/straight	short
human	3	medium/dark	dark/straight	medium tall
races	4	medium/dark	dark/straight	tall
	5	very fair	fair/straight	tall
	6	yellow	dark/straight	short
	7	brown	dark/wavy	tall
	8	yellow/brown	dark/wavy	short

Can you classify the races into groups or sub groups?

Show your scheme of classification by joining the numbers 1–8 by lines or brackets. (p. 20)

In a similar manner other different or common features of cultures with a biological relevance can also be examined. For example, differences and similarities in diet or food source can be investigated and compared within the laboratory. Sources of carbohydrates might be compared for a number of ethnic groups present in the class, using the pupils themselves as the source for compiling the table. This naturally leads into extending the contribution of the pupils, familiarizing classes with other words and expressions for materials and living organisms encountered in biology. Certainly, if the biology curriculum is to increase its account of cultural diversity, then it must expand the forms of communication used in the laboratory, and in particular make more use of the rich linguistic background present in many schools through the use, for example, of recordings and interviews, not only of pupils but also of parents and of those working for ethnic minority organizations and community agencies. Some local history projects are structured in this way, and they can provide a useful exemplar, even extending to involving embassies and high commissions, who often see this sort of work as complementary to public relations.

Embassies and high commissions may also provide a source for guiding teachers to, or providing them with, resource material which paints the world in a positive light. One of the problems of most standard school biology texts is in the photographs and images of the third world conveyed to the reader. These images are often misleading to all pupils.

One text used in my school is the generally very good Roberts *Biology for Life* (1981). In the section 'Food and Diet' there are two photographs of a child, in one seen suffering from severe lack of protein (kwashiorkor) and in the other shown after being given a full diet for several weeks. The first picture of this African baby is one of a scowling infant and in the second, after a 'full diet', the baby is happy and smiling. A fourth-year pupil of West Indian origin teased Kwame, a Ghanaian pupil, remarking that the picture was of him. Kwame was distressed, so I asked him if he had suffered from 'kwashiorkor' as a child. He replied 'NO', and went on to explain that not all Ghanaians suffered from malnutrition. He said that his mother had told him that it was not so common when she was a child in Accra, but that today many people do not want to eat traditional foods, such as pounded ground nuts (peanuts, cola nuts), which, he added, 'were good for them', and thereby have an unbalanced diet leading to malnutrition. I decided to show the class a video about farming in Ghana from the 'Disappearing World' series. This shows how development projects emphasize the growing of cash crops in place of food crops. From this we were able to discuss how, through aid programmes, food production is reduced in order to grow crops that bring in foreign exchange. This was a valuable lesson for the class and had an encouraging effect on Kwame.

Another illustration from a commonly used text, *Introduction to Human and Social Biology* by Mackean and Jones (1975), caused a similar situation from which different lessons were learnt. The diagram shows a negro male passing eggs of the blood fluke schistosima mansoni into a river by urinating, while other men were swimming in and drinking the river water. Donna – a girl of West Indian parentage – said: 'Those Africans are nasty pissing in the water.' We then had a short discussion about the origins of our own drinking water. The implications of the diagram to Donna confirmed her own view of Africa; although it could have been from almost any area of the world she automatically assumed that it referred to Africa. This illustrated to me the extent to which images permeate and develop a 'false consciousness' in children from minority ethnic groups; and how ignorant they can be about their own cultural background, especially if they have little support at home, are in a small minority, or are isolated. In this case the incident stimulated the pupils to examine the situation comparatively and to be critical. People in the third world countries where water is untreated normally boil it before drinking. To supplement this, we 'plated' samples of tap water and grew bacterial colonies on the agar so that the class would realize that water does contain micro-organisms even in 'advanced' Britain, and hopefully would begin to think about their assumptions. Practical work like this can be used to exploit the mixed experiences of any class, introducing pupils to a range of lifestyles, and awakening an informed interest in each others' differences through linking the home with the biology curriculum.

Multicultural education and biology: teachers' initiatives

My research for *Assessment in a Multicultural Society: Biology at 16+* (Vance 1984) allowed me an opportunity to communicate with other biology teachers and to appraise the current practice concerning multicultural issues within the curriculum. None of the 39 school biology departments that responded to a mini-survey of Mode 3 syllabuses referred to the multicultural nature of their school as a major reason for developing such biology examinations, although 'the needs of their pupils', and 'improving exam results' were cited as typical reasons. Some respondents expressed a willingness to adopt a multicultural perspective, but added that resource material was scarce. One respondent wrote about a discussion that had taken place at her school within the department: as a black British teacher, she felt that the most important task was to get her colleagues to be aware enough to draw out the particular cultural experiences of pupils during question and answer sessions as well as to use examples from other cultures. Her department had made a start by widening the scope of their practical work in the third year to embrace looking at a wide range of foods, examining different styles of hair and skin care, and leading to a consideration of the types of pupils in the class, using the *Science at Work* – Cosmetics (1979) as a guide.

Respondents listed the following topics already included in their biology 16+ syllabuses, as being of relevance to a multicultural approach to the subject:

Energy requirements and actual energy intake in different countries.

Testing a wide variety of foods (including yam, sweet potato, pasta and green peppers) for starch, fat, sugar, protein and vitamin C content.

Oral hygiene and the incidence of dental caries in relation to diet.

Hay fever and its incidence amongst ethnic minorities.

Origin of blood groups.

The role of melanin in the skin, carotene.

Diseases of world wide significance.

How we taste spicy food.

The genetics of sickle cell anaemia.

The distribution of races.

Racial morphology.

The respondents also considered which topics of a multicultural nature might be included in future Mode 3 courses; some of those included overlap to a certain extent with the list above:

Sickle cell anaemia, frequency and heredity.

Blood groups and race.

Heart disease and diet.

World diets, energy values of, significance of, comparison with UK diet.

Food tests to incorporate foods of cultural minorities.

Diet deficiency diseases treated alongside obesity.

Famine and starvation, world food resources and inequalities.

Diseases of the 'developed' and 'underdeveloped' world.

Racial variation and adaptation, evolution of races.

Pigmentation, its significance.

Comparative medicine and hygiene.

Two respondents suggested project work as a vehicle for bringing multi-culturalism into the mainstream biology examination curriculum, and that, coupled with an integrated curriculum where biology, mathematics, craft and humanities complement each other, this could provide a major opportunity for innovation. This approach is already working in some junior schools, and secondary schools have much to gain by following their lead.

Towards a multicultural content in biology

The argument so far is that good biology is multicultural biology, with a content arising from anti-racist aims and objectives and emphasizing cultural diversity. These should be reflected in the assessment structure of any biology curriculum.

The following section outlines biology topics which are particularly relevant to multicultural education. However it is important to stress that biology teachers should use these only as starting points. Where departments follow hard and fast rules laid out by 'experts' then they will miss out on the value of the discussions leading to the formulation of a multicultural biology course. A 'magic formula' handed out to biology teachers will not effect a great deal of change; it is the consciousness-raising aspect of researching, arguing about and preparing resources that eventually becomes part of classroom practice which is the most important consideration.

Plants and animals

Plants and animals used as examples should include those of significance from countries represented by pupils from minority ethnic backgrounds. Particular emphasis should be placed on those with particular economic significance. Where possible these examples should be illustrated by slides or living specimens (e.g. maize, cocoa, carite). The botanical and zoological gardens, embassies and the Natural History Museum are all rich in resources and provide valuable opportunities for school visits.

Food and nutrition

Consideration of food chains should include those from all over the globe and include their interrelationship with people where appropriate. Complexity of food webs can be shown by looking at examples from around the world in differing environments where the number and type of food sources available to people can be compared and contrasted.

Dietary practice should include examining examples available within each of the food classes, and food used by different groups of people. Special consideration needs to be given to the proportion of and importance that is attached to particular foods and food classes. For example, rice provides the major carbohydrate source for the Chinese, who form one-quarter of the world's population. Foods which are tested, for example for protein content, should be those consumed by people in Britain today (including pupils) and not be limited to the gastronomic experiences of teachers. Diet can be explored in a comparative manner and linked to any work being carried out within areas of Home Economics, such as examining vegetarianism among Gujeratis and comparing this to the 'Ital' diet of Rastafarians. The teacher may wish here to broaden the experience of pupils by having examples of these foods brought to the classroom to eat and analyse.

Closely related to this area are questions of food and health. World food resources and health (including diet deficiency diseases such as beri beri, kwashiorkor, rickets, scurvy and pellagra) can be considered comparatively alongside problems of diet in the West, such as obesity.

Oral hygiene varies from country to country and different methods of care can be compared for effectiveness in dental health; for example fluoridation, use of salt and diet can be related to the incidence of caries.

Examining zoonoses and other parasitic diseases would also bring pupils to consider the manner in which diseases are transmitted and controlled, some of which are important to hundreds of millions of people.

The relative productivity of crops such as sugar cane can be examined in comparison to the productivity of, say, the British wheat crop.

Respiration

This might include respiratory adaptations to altitude and temperature, including the role of humidity.

Transport

This topic can cover the adaptation of the circulatory system to temperature, origin and significance of blood groups, sickle cell anaemia and thalassaemia. It should include examining the blood of pupils from negro and Cypriot backgrounds for sickling of blood cells.

Growth

A comparative view of growth rates, and the effects of diet on growth, should both include consideration of genetic differences at the onset of puberty, interacting with dietary factors.

Homeostasis

The incidence of diabetes in various ethnic groups and its relation to diet could lead to a study of how water and salt contents change in differing climates, and the regulation involved.

Reproduction

Starting from a discussion of family size in different societies, the teacher could lead on to perspectives of childbirth and pre-natal care throughout the world, including methods of delivering babies. Child care should be treated as a number of different methods of rearing children, and birth control presented as different practices which have a long history but which are dependent on morality, religion, and level of technology. Birth control programmes which include trials of 'new' contraceptive drugs in the third world, such as Depo Provera, can be discussed as:

a) one society imposing its values on another
b) necessary regulation following lowered child mortality
c) using people in the third world as guinea pigs, as in the use of Depo Provera in Mexico
d) needed globally so that the problems of increased population and unequal sharing of resources and aid can be offset.

Genetics and variation

It is important to treat sensitively work on genetic-related disorders, such as sickle cell anaemia, and their incidence within racial groups. Other topics include how skin colour and other racial characteristics are transmitted. Careful and discursive treatment is necessary when debating the relative importance of environment on the expression of genes, using 'intelligence' as an example.

The variety of peoples represented within the school and throughout the species can be studied. Skin colour can be used as an example of continuous variation, thereby counteracting such terms as 'half-caste' (half-made). Biological definitions and their validity, human morphology and its relationship to environment, and variation within racial groups are all related topics. An example of practical work in this area might be to look at nose shapes, skin pigmentation and so on.

Environmental issues

These might include some of the following:

a) conservation and pollution – resources and their differing use
b) the relation of culture to resource use
c) global conservation issues
d) disease and health – diseases of global significance (e.g. influenza, yellow fever, herpes)
e) a comparison of health care in relation to needs and health 'technology'
f) public health, i.e. health care for large numbers of people, differences in structure and provision
g) the World Health Organisation
h) the notion that what a healthy body is varies enormously between societies

i)   the use of pharmaceuticals in 'developed' and 'underdeveloped' societies
j)   folk medicine and its role (homoeopathy, 'bush teas', acupuncture etc.)

The process of implementing a multicultural biology curriculum is by no means easy. Science has traditionally steered away from considering its relationship to society, and consequently biology teachers have had little preparation for teaching in a multicultural society. Ideally implementation needs the support of the local authority in developing biological materials more appropriate to a multicultural society. This will usually involve forming groups of biology teachers who will be able to pool experience and do the necessary research to develop materials. A guide to resource materials follows, which outlines agencies and books including some not already mentioned, and which may assist colleagues interested in starting discussion who agree with the spirit of the arguments outlined within this chapter.

Resources

Texts

John Baker, *Race*, Oxford University Press, 1974. Definitive book on racial evolution, origins, meaning of, trends, colour, odour, physical differences.

D. Baldwin, *Then and Now*, Longman child development series, Arnold, 1982.

Fraser Brockington, *World Health*, Pelican, 1958 (out of print). A very informative but dated book.

C. Clarke, *Human Genetics and Medicine*, Studies in Biology Series No 20, Arnold, 1977.

A.G. Clegg, and P.C. Clegg, *Man against Disease*, Heinemann, 1973. Good background information and detail.

L.B. Cook, *Caribbean Agricultural Science*, Books 1 & 2, Collins, 1978. Good section on economic crops of the Caribbean, their cultivation, diseases and use.

T. Geoffrey-Taylor, *Principles of Human Nutrition*, Studies in Biology Series No 94, Arnold, 1978.

A. Godman and C. Webb, *Certificate Human and Social Biology*, Longman, 1973. Gives a simple treatment of the relation of Vitamin D synthesis to sunlight.

D. Harrison, *Patterns in Biology*, Arnold, 1974. A very good section on blood group polymorphism.

J.J. Head, *Society Through Biology*, Arnold, 1976. Reasonable section on sickle cell anaemia.

Health Education Council, *Health Education for Ethnic Minorities*. Recommended.

D.G. Mackean, *Introduction to Biology* (Tropical edition), 1969. Excellent section on food storage plants, e.g. yams, cassava, their growth and cultivation.

Van Overbeck, *Lore of Living Plants*, Natural Science Teachers Association, Washington, 1964. Has a complete section on nutrition science and the individual.

Simon and Schuster, *Book of the Body*, USA, 1979. Comments on hair and skin pigmentation and their origin. Some good pictures.

R. Taylor, *World Health*, Macdonald Educational Colour Units, 1977.

T. Williams, *Drugs from Plants*, Sigma Books, 1947. Excellent specialized book. Includes chapter on the contribution of Egypt to modern medicine.

Agencies and individuals

Community Health Group for Ethnic Minorities, 28 Churchfield Road, London W3 6EB. Wide range of information on diet, morbidity, mortality, race, hypertension, mental health and race, rickets, women's health. Available from group serviced by GPs, pharmacists and nurses.

Ealing and Hammersmith Area Health Authority's health education service have compiled a list of resources including films and speakers on many aspects of minority ethnic health, facilities in Asian, Greek and Turkish languages.

Organisation for Sickle Cell Anaemia Research, Wood Green High Road, London N22.

G. Khontiorghes, researcher on thalassaemia, University College Hospital, Gower Street, London W1.

Third World Science Project, Professor Iolo Wyn Williams, School of Education, University College of North Wales, Bangor, Gwynedd. The project has produced a series of readers including practical work, for UK teachers to enrich school science and their view of science in the developing world. There are units on Salt, Soap, Housing, Carrying Loads, Fermentation, Clay Pots, Dental Care, Distillation, Vegetable Oils, Methane Digesters, Iron Smelting and Useful Plants.

References

Afro-Caribbean Education Resource Project (1982) *Ourselves*, a series of units for 9–13 year olds. ACER.

ASE (1979) *Alternatives for Science Education*, Consultative document. Hatfield: ASE, p. 38.

ASE (1980) *Language in Science Education*. Hatfield: ASE.

Bulldog (1977) Issues 1 and 2, September and October.

Claydon, L., Knight, A., and Rado, M. (1978) *Curriculum and Culture Schooling in a Pluralist Society*. London: Allen and Unwin, pp. 59–61.

DES (1975) *A Language for Life* Report of the Committee of Inquiry appointed by the Secretary of State for Education and Science (Bullock Report). London: HMSO, para. 20.

DES (1981) *West Indian Children in Our Schools* Interim Report of the Committee of Inquiry into the Education of Children from Ethnic Minority Groups (Rampton Report) London: HMSO, p. 7.

HMI (1979) *Aspects of Organisation and Curriculum in Seven Multi Ethnic Comprehensive Schools*. DES, p. 12.

Jensen, J.J. (1969) How much can we boost I.Q. and scholastic achievement? *Harvard Educational Review*, 39(1), pp. 1–123.

Mackean, D. and Jones, B. (1975) *Introduction to Human and Social Biology*. London: John Murray, p. 199.

Montagu, A. (1957) *Statement on Race*, New York: Schuman, pp. 1–110.

Nuffield Foundation Science Teaching Project (1976) *Text IV, The Perpetuation of Life and Teachers Guide IV*. London: Longman.

Roberts, M. (1981) *Biology for Life*. Walton-on-Thames: Nelson.

Rosen, H. and Brittan, J. (1971) *Language, the Learner and the School*. Harmondsworth: Penguin, pp. 84–106.

Science at Work series (Project Director, John Taylor) (1979) *Cosmetics*. London: Addison Wesley.

Townsend, H. and Brittan, E. (1973) *Multi Racial Education – Need and Innovation*, Schools Council Working Paper 50.

Vance, M. (1984) *Assessment in a Multicultural Society: Biology at 16+*, Schools Council Programme 5 Pamphlet Series. York: Longman.

Van Rensberg (1973) *Education for South Africa's Black, Coloured and Indian Peoples*. Johannesburg: Erudition Books.

Whitten, P. and Kagan, J. (1978) Race and I.Q. *In* D.E. Hunter and P. Whitten (eds.) *Readings in Physical Anthropology and Archeology*. New York: Harper and Row.

Willey, R. (1982) *Teaching in Multicultural Britain*, Longman Resources Unit for the Schools Council.

CHAPTER 10*

HOME ECONOMICS

Sue Oliver

Opportunities

Both the content and context of Home Economics teaching are directly concerned with cultural expression, and (it may be argued) provide exceptional opportunities for the development of multicultural education. The *content* of Home Economics includes human relationships and family patterns, child-rearing practices, division of labour within the home, the sex-role relationship in meal preparation and household chores, consumer choice and the use of fabrics in interior design and for clothing. All these examples constitute relatively intimate, 'immediate' aspects of pupils' lives and are also highly culture-specific. The *context* or teaching environment of Home Economics usually involves comparatively small groups, working in a practical situation which demands a high degree of pupil/teacher interaction; the teaching environment also strengthens the close association with the home through the presence of 'domestic' equipment. Within a sensitive, perceptive and reasonably informed approach this combination of content and context can provide a sound basis for an understanding of cultural diversity.

In recent years Home Economics has seen a change of emphasis from a content-based curriculum, focusing on limited craft skills and an end-product, to a process-based curriculum in which a range of cross-curricular

---

* Some of the ideas in this chapter are an extension of those in *Assessment in a Multicultural Society: Home Economics at 16+* by Sue Oliver. Schools Council Programme 5 Pamphlet Series. Longman, York, 1984.

skills, such as observing, analysing, communicating and planning are developed and applied in the context of home and family.[1] Such a change of emphasis should also facilitate cross-cultural reference, and thereby lessen the reliance solely on the culture of the majority. This is an important area for development within Home Economics.

Home economics – a sociological perspective

'Originally Home Economics involved cookery, sewing, housewifery and laundry work, which were seen as essential elements of the curriculum for girls.' (DES 1978)[2] Although the subject has changed substantially since its inception, the image of Home Economics in many schools is still one of a subject which prepares girls for the role of wife and mother and for running a home, an image which unfortunately is perpetuated by the majority of books on home management.

The diversity and multidisciplinary nature of Home Economics is now widely acknowledged, and is illustrated by the following definition:

> It involves studies of the needs of the individual in the community, and of the best uses of human and physical resources in the context of home and family life. The title points to the present day emphasis within the subject on an increasing awareness of the importance, both of the family and of the home, in an ordered society. The subject now assists in the general development of girls and boys as individuals who will contribute positively to society . . . Its particular contribution is that it combines knowledge drawn from sciences and arts and applies it to experiences which pupils can relate directly to their own lives. Such experiences, which may be practical, give meaning and reality to theoretical work and help many girls and boys to understand and accept otherwise difficult concepts. (DES 1978)[3]

The writer believes that studies of people form a central theme within Home Economics, closely aligning the subject with the social sciences. Others would not concede so central a position to this aspect of the subject but an exploration of this sociological context of Home Economics could provide a major contribution to the developing multicultural curriculum. It is ironic that these very elements of the subject which have direct access to cultural expression are, because of their interpretation, often the source of sex, class and culture bias.

Ethnocentric interpretation

Traditionally the aspect of Home Economics which is concerned with the study of the individual, family and community or society has been inter-preted as representing only the immediate or majority culture. It is excep-tional for such study to be extended to ethnic minority cultures within Britain or to the cultural patterns of other geographical areas. The extent to which interest in British regional variations has been encouraged within the Home Economics curriculum is also very limited.

The issue of interpreting the sociological context of Home Economics is explored in a recent Schools Council discussion document on Home Eco-nomics examinations at 16+ (Oliver 1984).[4] Although the majority of CSE examinations make reference to the 'individual within the home, family and community and/or society', there is virtually no acknowledgement of the multiethnic nature of British society or of the cultural variation which is an integral part of such a society.

It may be argued that such reference is unnecessary as 'society' at least implies the total society, inclusive of ethnic minorities; yet one's concept of 'society', and even more certainly of 'community' and 'family', is likely to be based on one's immediate experience. Thus the experience of many teachers and examiners will be based on their own white, middle-class, traditional British backgrounds. Meanwhile, the experience of many children is increasingly of a multicultural society, and for some of being an ethnic minority within a multicultural society. The two experiences do not match and unless explicit reference is made in syllabuses and course out-lines to the multicultural nature of society, it is likely that 'the family', 'community' and 'society' will be interpreted as those of 'English' pupils by both teachers and pupils of ethnic minorities.

Anti-sexist and anti-racist conflict

Sex-role stereotyping is both a complex and sensitive issue. In theory, but particularly in practical Home Economics lessons, there will be situations where an anti-sexist approach will not necessarily be an anti-racist one. In the interests of greater cultural fairness it is important to understand the sex-role relationship within different cultures. For a subject whose origins and development are so closely related to women, surprisingly little atten-tion is paid to the changing role of women in British society. Such attention could provide an introduction to a better understanding of the traditional and changing sex roles, especially with regard to the division of labour within the home as illustrated by various cultures, and of the dilemmas experienced by many ethnic minority boys as well as girls in this society.[5]

Class bias

In many areas the work produced in Home Economics (and presented for assessment) is representative of 'middle class' rather than 'working class' culture. How frequently, for example, do London school children prepare pie and mash with liquor, or children in South Wales prepare faggots and peas? A revival of the traditions of British regional cookery might be helpful here. Class bias is also evident in the presentation of food, table laying and in interior design; in budgeting and in the emphasis on house *purchase* and in the structuring of social situations in both theory and practical assignments.

Developing a multicultural perspective

Content

The study of food and related customs offers a range of opportunities for an understanding of social and cultural diversity. Food has always played a major role in the Home Economics curriculum; it has, however, been almost exclusively associated with cooking. While this is an important aspect in a cross-cultural context, the relatively neglected sociological context of food provides an introduction to the concept of cultural variation, and may integrate both linguistic and religious factors. The traditional use of food is an aspect of culture which 'survives' immigration, and foods from minority cultures are increasingly available in this country. Both the theoretical and practical study of food can be used to stimulate research, for example, into meal patterns and their close association with religious belief and traditional festivals or into cross-generational changes in meal patterns and food choice (Douglas 1975).[6]

Food also plays an important part in encouraging children to relate experience; the effect on a child from an ethnic minority of recognizing a hitherto unfamiliar food can be dramatic, and the use of less familiar foods in displays and for drawing or photographing can stimulate discussion and provide valuable 'incidental' experience. Unfortunately it is particularly easy to isolate and exploit the *overt* cultural expression, within the study of food (and textiles), through lessons on 'international cookery' or 'international evenings' at school. Such gestures must be seen only as supportive and illustrative of a deeper understanding of social and cultural diversity.

The following example illustrates the social and cultural diversity of one teaching group – using a thematic approach to the topic 'soup'. The pupils were asked to prepare a soup from their town or country of origin. The soups chosen included Turkish 'Taharna' in which yoghurt, mint and tomato are specially prepared as a flavouring; Nigerian soup with dumplings and spinach (in place of bitter leaf) made bright yellow with curry powder; Portuguese potato and watercress soup; Scotch broth made thick with pearl barley, and West Indian soup with meat and 'ground provisions' (sweet potato, yam) as well as plantain and pumpkin and a pea soup which evoked discussion of the 'pea-souper' fogs of London in the 1950s. All were interpretations of a food familiar to the child, from home, with adaptations demanded only by availability of ingredients and the pupil's particular expertise.

This example also serves as a vivid illustration of the different concepts of the word 'soup' and of the imagery provoked for children from different cultural backgrounds. It is a striking contrast to the stereotyped classification of soups, taught and assessed within examinations. It is also significant in that traditional British regional variations were represented.

Another example illustrates highly contrasting cultures. When a teaching group was asked to write about 'their favourite meals of the holiday', one boy of 11 from Zimbabwe wrote: 'My favourite meal was when my Mum made porridge – not like the porridge you have here, it has meat in it. At home it's called "Sadza". My next favourite meal was when my friend and I went to the Wimpy and I had a King-sized cheeseburger and chips.'

This is an interesting example of 'bicultural accommodation' and a perspective to be valued. It differs from the first example (in which children were asked to refer to their own cultural backgrounds) in that the choice to refer to his cultural traditions was entirely his own. It is important that information from ethnic minority pupils is not exploited, and that all pupils should be given the opportunity to choose the cultural base for their work.

It is also important that there should be genuine *exchange* of cultural experience – especially when a group is multiethnic – as in another lesson on cereals, where African maize porridge was made and tasted by pupils of English background, and where processed breakfast cereals were tasted by some pupils of Asian origin. Such exchange can highlight cultural similarities as well as contrasts; for example, a lesson on breads might compare Indian roti with roti eaten in the West Indies.

The cooking of food necessitates close pupil/teacher interaction, and the sharing of meals involves further communication between pupils, and often teachers. Such situations provide an exceptional opportunity for contact between different ethnic groups or for the initiation of discussions based on social and cultural variations – even when the group does not include pupils from highly different cultural backgrounds.

The above examples are, sadly, far removed from the typical demands of 'external assessment', where food – which forms a major area of the examined curriculum – is mainly treated as an ethnocentric way (Oliver 1984).[7] This treatment is most obvious in the classification of methods of preparation and cooking, meal patterns (names of meals, times, occasions and courses, including the concept of sweet and savoury), methods of presentation (concept of formal and informal and methods of table laying, and of serving and use of serving dishes). Within these areas it is all too easy for a particular social or cultural perspective to prevail, allowing no provision, for example, for the candidate of West Indian origin who arranges plates 'upside down') on the table (for reasons of hygiene), or for the candidate of Asian background who chooses not to use knives and forks but chapatis for eating with. 'The *correct* method' and 'use of *correct* equipment' are commonly used criteria in assessment – but both 'method' and 'equipment' are culture specific and therefore not universally applicable. So often the assessed curriculum becomes the taught curriculum.[8] The current formulation of national criteria for 16+ Home Economics examinations is an important opportunity to resolve issues in relation to majority and minority cultures.

Clearly Home Economics has numerous links with many other subjects. The study of food, for example, provides an obvious and important overlap in a multicultural context with geography and history. Geography includes study of food production, distribution and use, and there is scope for an overlap with development education, not only in the exploration of the interdependence illustrated by world trading patterns, but also in the political, social and economic structures which dominate that relationship. In the context of 'world food problems' an appreciation of these forces is important in understanding the causes of malnutrition of developing countries. Historical elements of Home Economics could be developed in an attempt to understand the concept of change. Contemporary changes might be given historical parallels, for example the potential influence of West Indian and Asian foods can be compared with that of the foods introduced by the Romans, which still contribute significantly to our diet, or with foods 'discovered' by colonizers (like the potato from Peru).

The importance of anthropological skills in the international context of nutrition education is increasingly recognized.[9] This has an immediate application within the secondary school curriculum. The diets of different ethnic groups vary significantly and 'recommended daily intakes' and 'dietary goals' must be related to religious requirements and culturally based food preferences and taboos as well as economic considerations. Instrumental to this approach is the need for accurate and up-to-date research information, specific to ethnic minorities, which should also help to avoid inaccurate or harmful stereotyping. Two areas come to mind – those of rickets and osteo-malacia among pupils of Asian background (Robertson et al. 1982)[10] and the vegetarian diets of Rastafarians (of West Indian origin),[11] where recent research indicates possible cause for concern (Springer and Thomas 1983).[12] Allied to the above is the desperate need for an inexpensive table of nutritive values which include the most common foods of ethnic minorities.[13]

Malnutrition is a particularly sensitive area of nutrition education; it is often equated with the protein-energy deficiency of developing countries (an image firmly established by the literature of international agencies). The overnutrition of the 'developed' world must be also viewed as malnutrition, and in this context, especially as many of the major diseases are now thought to be closely related to diet, there is an urgent need for recent findings to be collated so that they may be incorporated within the development of nutrition teaching programmes in schools.[14]

Child development studies also offer scope for multicultural education: 'It is now widely recognised that there are many possible forms of family structures, all equally valid, and that there is no one right way to bring up children[15]' (Birmingham Development Education Centre 1982). Such recognition is a crucially important basis for the study of child development and 'family-related' studies. Whether these subjects are to be taught solely within Home Economics or not, there are many traditional areas of overlap, both within the curriculum and assessment; in the area of nutrition teaching, for example, it is important to appreciate that the diets of young children will reflect the (culture-specific) diets of their parents. As this is a sensitive subject, and one of which many children have direct experience, it is important that the cultural backgrounds of pupils are taken into account in the planning of the courses.

There is also scope for the development of an international perspective in the study of housing, in which climate, building materials as well as cultural tradition and economic pressures are explored. In a multiethnic teaching group there may be opportunities for discussion based on direct experience of different housing styles. In the context of interior design there is opportunity for curriculum development which involves the concept of taste within cultural tradition and the implications of transference from one culture to another – areas largely neglected within the present curriculum and examinations.

Similarly, textiles can be reviewed in an international context. There is scope for an exploration of cultural traditions based on availability of materials and on religious beliefs and requirements, particularly in clothing. It is important here that teachers are aware that their pupils from ethnic minorities may face some practical dilemmas, for example, the 'irrelevance' of commercial dressmaking patterns to Asian pupils.

Context – the teaching environment

The opportunities which the practical lesson provides for close pupil/teacher and pupil/pupil interaction have already been mentioned. The use of language is an integral part of such interaction. In a practical situation the accurate interpretation of an oral instruction is often instrumental to the performance of a task. Unfamiliar expressions or sentence structure can hinder comprehension for both pupil and teacher, but vocabulary used in connection with names of materials and processes can also stimulate discussion and encourage an interest in regional variations and dialects.

The teacher's attitude and approach is of central importance. Recent discussions[16] held by the author with Home Economics teachers in inner-city schools with a high proportion of ethnic minority pupils focused on a reappraisal of the role of the teacher: 'It is important not only to impart knowledge, but to be able to *receive* it from pupils.'

This point was forcibly made several years earlier:

> While most [teachers] would fairly claim to know something of what it feels like to be a child growing up as a member of the white majority in Britain, having shared that experience . . . there is no way in which it is possible to tell what it feels like to be a Bengali in the East End of London, a Liverpool-born black, or a Sikh child in Bristol – unless of course the children themselves are asked and listened to' (New Society 1978).[17]

Such an exchange of knowledge requires sensitivity, as the following example of pupil/teacher interaction (in a biology lesson) illustrates:

> *Teacher*:   It will be what you call a pea shoot so you've got . . .
> *Boy 1*:   What kind of pea is it?
> *Boy 2*:   It's just an ordinary . . .
> *Teacher*:   It's a dried pea, probably a dried pea that you buy in a shop.

In this example a pupil of West Indian background raises a question about varieties of pea, which is certainly relevant to biology (Delamont 1976).[18]

Delamont argues that the teacher's definition of relevant lesson content is 'paramount, unexamined and undefended . . . if control of content is the teacher's strongest resource, it is also [his or] her Achilles' heel'.

To relinquish 'control over content' in the above example would probably have allowed the pupil of West Indian background to describe the peas which are most familiar to him – blackeyed, pigeon (gunga), etc.; this volunteered information could have served as an additional resource for the class and an opportunity to succeed for the boy concerned. It is this type of expression of cultural variation which should be encouraged and developed; further discussions, for example, might have led to cross-cultural comparisons, with the pupil offering to bring in some of the peas and (in Home Economics) his preparing 'rice and peas' with details of the way in which they are cooked and eaten at home – a good introduction to cultural 'awareness'.

The above quotation also pinpoints the way in which teaching may be interpreted as racist. Initially the teacher uses an ethnocentric approach, and then refuses to allow further comment from an ethnic minority pupil. Syllabus content may be important but the attitudes within the hidden curriculum are equally potent. The informality of Home Economics teaching (and assessing) contexts, provides every opportunity for conveying personal attitudes and value judgements. These situations also provide an opportunity for perceptive and sensitive interaction in which there is opportunity for the expression of cultural variation.

Summary

Developing a multicultural approach to Home Economics teaching (and assessing) therefore involves:

— recognizing and developing those aspects of the subject which, through cross-cultural study, could help create positive attitudes towards the expression of cultural variation.
— analysing curriculum content, with the aim of isolating factors which may be the cause of cultural disadvantage and consequently of unfair and inaccurate assessment of ability.
— using opportunities provided within the subject – especially within the informal context of practical work – to counter expressions of racism when they occur. This demands an overtly anti-racist attitude on the part of teachers, since only '. . . by adopting . . . a positive stance and by using opportunities to replace ignorance with factual information about other cultures and reasons for immigration to this country will teachers show that they are anti-racist . . .' (NUT 1981).[19]

Such opportunities exist within Home Economics – not least through the traditional teaching technique of demonstrating. The teacher's careful initial choice of topic, the use of an international perspective with cross-cultural references, the involvement of pupils, particularly those of ethnic minorities, in the demonstration and the refusal to allow racist comments to go unchallenged are all positive steps.

There is currently a move by some working within education away from a culturalist approach to one which gives priority to the elimination of racist attitudes at individual and institutional levels. It is no compromise to suggest that Home Economics provides opportunites for both approaches.

A child . . . becomes a person through interaction with others, with other thoughts, with explanations, systems of values and different behaviours . . . we are both made by and yet make our culture (Gamma 1983).[20]

The cultural patterns of ethnic minorities and the majority are constantly evolving. Home Economics is a subject which has 'access' through both content and context, and it is vital that its teaching should contribute to such change.

Resources

All about Food by Helen McGrath makes an obvious attempt to include men and ethnic minorities in text and illustration.

The Foods of the World series published by Time/Life Books contain excellent colour photographs of foods, including ways in which they are grown and used – a valuable and accurate reference for commodity studies. (Now out of print.)

Let's Eat published by the Multicultural Support Group, London Borough of Haringey, contains an outline of the foods and meal patterns of the ethnic minorities of Haringey. (Now out of print.)

Food in History by Reay Tannahill is basic reading for the origins of the use of foods. Eyre Methuen 1973. Palladin 1975 (paperback).

Health Education Council publications include leaflets on diets for children, adolescents and adults of Asian origin.

A Guide to Asian Diets available from the Commission for Racial Equality includes background information on religious and cultural customs.

Asians in Britain by Van den Berghs and Jurgens is a similar and useful guide. 1979.

Heinemann World Studies themes are teaching packs with units on 'food' and other aspects of life in different countries, which include Africa, China and India.

Priorities for Development produced by the Birmingham Development Education Centre (1981) is a valuable text and a comprehensive review of publications in the field of development education.

Issues and Resources published by AFFOR (All Faiths For One Race), 173 Lozells

Road, Birmingham, is a handbook for teachers in a multicultural society and includes a section on teaching about food.

Education in a Multi-Ethnic Society, Multi-Ethnic Education Review (Vol 1, No. 2, Summer 1982) is published by ILEA Multi-Ethnic Inspectorate, and contains valuable articles on anti-racist policies in schools; curriculum development in subjects related to Home Economics and a discussion on the meaning of 'Race', 'Ethnicity' and 'Culture'.

Values, Cultures and Kids – Approaches and resources for teaching child development and about the family, published by the Birmingham Development Education Centre (1982), is a valuable publication and possibly one of the first to tackle an area of Home Economics from a development/multicultural point of view. It collates work by Home Economics teachers in local schools and on in-service courses and emphasizes attitudes and approaches which are important in teaching this sensitive area of Home Economics. Much of what it says is applicable in a wider context.

Doing Things – in and about the home (1983) is a booklet and set of photographs drawing on a wide range of social and ethnic backgrounds and an important resource for discussion of sex roles within Home Economics. It is compiled by a group of teachers working from the Maidenhead Teachers' Centre, and is available from Sevawood House Ltd, 21 High Town Road, Maidenhead, Berkshire.

Nutrition Guidelines, providing nutritive values on a wide range of foods, and a computer nutrition programme called *Nu-Pack* have both been developed in ILEA specifically for ethnically mixed teaching groups. The guidelines will be published by ILEA in July 1984; the computer programme will be available in July 1984 from Inner London Educational Computer Centre, Bethwin Road, London SE5 0PQ. The recommendations for intake are in line with those of the report of the National Advisory Committee on Nutrition Education, 1983 (see below).

'One Step Nearer – a national campaign for nutrition education', is an article in the February 1984 issue of *Nutrition and Food Science* which reviews the 1983 report of the National Advisory Committee on Nutrition Education.

Notes and references

1 These are among the skills listed by the *Teacher's Guide* of the Nuffield Home Economics Basic course, Hutchinson Education, 1982.

2 Department of Education and Science (1978) *Curriculum 11–16*, A working paper by the Home Economics Committee of H.M. Inspectorate.

3 DES (1978) *op. cit.*

4 Oliver, S. (1984) *Assessment in a Multicultural Society – Home Economics at 16+*, Schools Council Programme 5 Pamphlet Series. York: Longman.

5 *Doing Things – in and about the home*, Maidenhead Teachers' Centre, 1983 are new materials which begin to explore the sex roles within Home Economics (further details in Resources List).

6 The anthropological background to the way in which meal patterns encode social

relations is explored in 'Deciphering a Meal' in *Implicit Meanings: Essays in Anthropology* by M. Douglas, RKP, 1975.

7 Outlined in Oliver, S. (1984), *op. cit.*

8 A point made in a report from the Schools Council Home Economics Committee, 1981 – *National Criteria for a Single System of Examining at 16+*.

9 The social, cultural and economic aspects of nutrition education were the focus of an international conference, 'New Developments in Nutrition Education', held at the Institute of Education, London, in July 1983. A book based on the conference papers is to be published by UNESCO in Spring 1984.

10 I. Robertson, B.M. Glenkin, Janet B. Henderson, W.B. McIntosh, A. Lakhani and M.G. Dunnigan (1982) Nutritional deficiencies among ethnic minorities in the United Kingdom, *Proceedings of the Nutrition Society* Vol 41, p. 243.

11 Vegetarianism still tends to be viewed as a 'fringe' issue in Home Economics. The increasing interest in vegetarianism, based on health as well as economic and ideological grounds, plus the predominance of vegetarian dishes among some ethnic minority groups, calls for a reappraisal of attitude within this area of Home Economics.

12 Springer, L. and Thomas, J. (1983) Rastafarians in Britain: a prelimary study of their food habits and beliefs, *Human Nutrition: Applied Nutrition* Vol 37A, pp. 120–127.

13 The Ministry of Agriculture and Fisheries *Manual of Nutrition* is quite inadequate; the comprehensive table of nutritive values in McCance and Widdowson's *The Composition of Foods* is prohibitively expensive for many schools.

14 See report prepared for the National Advisory Committee on Nutrition Education by a working party under the chairmanship of Professor W.P. James (Sept 1983). This is a discussion paper on proposals for nutritional guidelines for health education in Britain; the report is produced by the Health Education Council and is at present only available to those involved in nutrition education. However, the report is reviewed in 'One step nearer – a national campaign for nutrition education' in *Nutrition and Food Science*, February 1984.

15 Development Education Centre, Birmingham (1982) *Values, Cultures and Kids*.

16 Reported in detail in Oliver, S. (1984) *op. cit.*

17 Race and Teachers, *New Society* 16 February, 1978.

18 Delamont, S. (1976) *Interaction in the Classroom*. London: Methuen.

19 National Union of Teachers (1981) *Combating Racialism in Schools*.

20 Gammage, P. (1983) *Children and Schooling*. London: Allen and Unwin.

PART FOUR

THE ARTS AND
PHYSICAL EDUCATION

Chapter 11

MUSIC

Jack Dobbs and Frances Shepherd

Music in our multicultural society

Music is all-pervasive in our society. Radio, television, transistor, disc, musak and now the personal stereo make it easily accessible to us wherever we are. It takes many forms – pop, folk, rock, classical, light, electronic, avant garde – with the recent addition of a considerable amount from other cultures. This non-indigenous music enlivens the pop scene, acts as background to drama productions, is inherent in many television documentaries and sells commercial products.

At the same time the world has become more accessible to us. Greater mobility and ease of travel enable young people to visit countries which were formerly considered remote. Here they encounter unfamiliar sounds and different types of performances, and return home with a new conception of music. Rigid divisions between categories of music are disappearing, so that the ritual music of Tibet now takes its place with the latest pop group's offering and the work of contemporary composers as an equally acceptable component of a young person's auditory experience.

But we don't have to depend on radio, television and the cassette or overseas travel for our experience of unfamiliar music. In our midst are fellow citizens who have brought with them the music of their own traditions, and who are able to share it with us in our schools, community centres and concert halls, during our celebrations and on our television sets – a wealth of resources for us to enjoy.

In many ways, then, young people encounter a great diversity of music 'outside' themselves. But all of them also have within themselves such elements of music as rhythm, pitch, dynamics, tension and resolution. Music is basic to their lives, and this is true of their peers all over the world.

Music is not a universal language, but it is nevertheless a universal medium for the expression of deep feelings and aspirations, speaking in ways that belong to its historical period, geographical area and culture. It is a universal form of communication, able to elicit a response even when its structure and vocabulary are not fully understood.

Music in schools

Much music education, then, happens incidentally outside school without our assistance, and can lead to a more comprehensive approach to music than is customary in schools where the approach often remains Eurocentric, with a concentration on music of a particular type during a limited historical period. This sometimes causes a conflict in the pupils between what they think of as 'school' music and the music with which they choose to be involved outside school – 'their' music. Together teachers and learners need to recognize that music has many manifestations, each with a specific context and each worthy of respect. This means that the music of all schools, not just those with pupils from ethnic minority cultures, must be looked at critically to see if it truly reflects our multicultural society in the late twentieth century. This is perhaps even more necessary in rural areas, where pupils rarely have direct contact with people from unfamiliar backgrounds. Attitudes bred in blinkered isolation can easily succumb to persuasive racist propaganda. Since music so intimately represents the people to whom it belongs, an understanding of it can help towards an understanding of those people even before they are met.

This is not to suggest that the European tradition has lost its relevance. It remains basic to our culture, and for most pupils, although not the majority in some schools, it is the natural medium of communication. But it is also only one of many different and equally valid musical systems of the world.

What do we hope secondary pupils will gain as they move outwards from their 'home base', towards the music of other cultures?

1. A keener aural perception, for music teaching in the West has concentrated on aspects of the sound experience that can be notated, diverting emphasis from the ear to the eye, and limiting performance possibilities.
2. The introduction of new scales and rhythmic patterns, timbres and textures which extend the pupils' musical vocabulary and enrich their means of expression.
3. Group music-making which is aurally based, with the group members relating to each other rather than to a conductor, with spontaneity and

improvisation playing important roles, and with the composer and performer often being the same person.

4. The encouragement of audience participation and of social involvement, bringing together members of the community in celebrations and seasonal festivities.
5. A knowledge of the influence of non-Western music on twentieth-century composers, and of Western music on the music of other cultures, also of the elements which non-Western music shares with folk, jazz, rock and various types of popular music (e.g. the aural approach, improvisation, group interaction).
6. The relatedness of the arts, and the relationship of music to other activities and areas of knowledge.
7. An intellectual stimulus for pupils who choose to study in depth another culture for its own sake.
8. Tolerance and respect for other systems of music, developing attitudes in pupils which will, we hope, find expression in their relationship with people from other cultures.
9. An understanding of the function of music in the societies whose music is being studied, posing questions about the purpose of music-making in Western society.

What about the overcrowded curriculum?

There may be general agreement that a multicultural society requires a multicultural approach to music education, but how far can this be realized in practice? With an already overcrowded music curriculum can we possibly add anything extra? If what is being suggested is the addition of detailed teaching *about* the musical systems of India or Japan or wherever, then clearly this raises enormous problems. But so, already, does the current practice of introducing pupils to a large body of Western musical literature before they are able to speak its language expressively. There are plenty of opportunities if we begin to think conceptually and devise a methodology that can be applied to all types of music. If we take 'rhythm', for example, we can extend the pupils' ideas about this element and their practice of it beyond their present limited experience. To the rhythms of pop and rock and familiar classical and romantic music let us add those of Messiaen and Xenakis, not forgetting Stravinsky and Bartok, which some of them will still not have met, even at sixth-form level. It is not a far step to the additive rhythms of the tal (the metric system of Indian classical music) and the quite different use of rhythm in the Nōh music of Japan.

But before we take even that step let us encourage our pupils to experience the rhythms of their own bodies – often neglected because of our obsession with the printed page. They will discover the rhythm within themselves through movement as individuals, and in interaction with their fellows, and through the extension of their bodies into various types of percussion instruments including, perhaps, African drums. After experiencing rhythm at this personal level they are better equipped to use it in their own compositions, to listen with more sensitive ears to its use by other composers and in improvisation, and to recreate with greater sensitivity the music of other eras and traditions.

An extra musical activity is not being added to the curriculum; rather, an extra dimension is being discovered within the musical activity that already exists. What has been suggested for rhythm can be adapted for pitch, dynamics, timbre, combinations of sounds and the production of those sounds by voices or instruments. In so doing, three of the essential components of any music course are brought together – creation, performance and listening.

The activities of creating, performing and listening are referred to separately for clarity's sake: in practice they will not be isolated in water-tight compartments. Fundamental to all of them is the training of the aural faculty, with any notation that is necessary growing out of musical experience. The aural/oral approach will be familiar to some pupils from their primary school, as also the way music does not belong to the music lesson only. In secondary schools, where the structure favours specialization, it is more difficult for music to move into other areas of activity. But if music is to play an essential part in the life of the school, rather than be just a subject for study, this is what must happen.

Creating music

Until recently music education was more concerned with a re-creation of music than with its creation. Many more teachers are now producing their own music with the abilities and resources of their classes in mind, and are encouraging their pupils to do similarly. This is more evident in primary schools, although the Schools Council's Music in the Secondary Curriculum Project has done a valuable service in stimulating thinking at the secondary level. Inherent in this compositional approach is a savouring of musical sound for its own sake – beginning with the experience of a single sound. Such concentration on the essence of one sound, although common in the East, is the antithesis of the busyness inbuilt into Western concepts. The Indian alap (a melodic improvisation in free time, structured to reveal a rāg, the modal system of Indian classical music on which musicians improvise) begins, in this way, with the contemplation of one sound – the tonic – before it moves off to explore the relationships of other sounds to this and to each other within the rāg.

At this secondary stage it is important that any instruments used to explore sounds should be suitable for the age group, and not exclusively Western. It is possible to obtain many traditional instruments from other parts of the world (e.g. xylophones and sanzas from Africa, gongs and bells from Tibet and Burma) more cheaply than Western instruments. It is important, too, that the pupils should be taught to use the instruments with respect, even when they are not skilled in the technique of playing them. There are likely to be many more instruments available amongst the pupils than at first appears, since they may not think that the instrument they play at home has any relevance to what goes on in school. Many pupils have their own electric guitars, keyboards and drum kits, and there will be pupils from the ethnic minority groups who have been taught instruments by their parents and who will be able to use them in the creative group music making. Nor should the use of the voice be forgotten.

It must be stressed that creative work is not an 'anything goes' activity. Although the ideas to be used and the decisions to be taken are the responsibility of the pupils, encouragement and stimulation as well as help in finding a structure may be needed. The use of different types of scales and modes, rhythmic groups and ostinati (repeated patterns of notes) involves elements of music which can be found throughout the world. An Indian tal, for instance, makes an excellent rhythmic ostinato for improvisation, and for this purpose Indian instruments are not essential.

Group work is not only of value musically, it is also excellent social training, with each member adding his or her own contribution, to be considered carefully and accepted, rejected or modified; with the dynamic coming from within the group, and with mutual respect being essential to the process. The approach is aural: the cohesion of the group and the worth of the product depend on the way each individual listens to and cooperates with the others. As in Africa, this may well involve verbal exchange. The development of such sensitive interaction greatly improves the general quality of communication among the pupils.

Listening to music

Pupils who make music this way will have a deeper understanding of the music of other composers, and as they listen will discover new scales, rhythms, harmonies, timbres, and structures to stimulate their own musical thinking. To what will they listen? The possibilities are endless, and are limited only by time, the knowledge of the teacher and the resources available. If the school is equipped with good listening facilities – and booths or individual headphones are clearly desirable – the pupils can do a great deal of individual listening themselves.

With critical listening will come, we hope, equally critical questions. By listening to blue grass, Chinese opera, the choir of King's College, and Bhutanese chanting, pupils will experience many different styles of singing. Instead of a model voice they will discover as many 'natural' voices as cultural situations and styles of music. And what about the way the violin is used by a folk fiddler, the leader of a string quartet, the member of an Indian ensemble or a cosmopolitan experimental group? An investigation into the way percussion is used around the world opens up new horizons, provides further resources for our creative work and listening, and encourages us to examine our own performances more critically.

As they listen, pupils will discover that at a superficial level the differences may be considerable: at a deeper level there are fundamental elements which make for unity.

Another thing pupils will learn from their listening is how the music of one culture influences that of another. This may appear in fairly superficial ways – as in the imitation by Mozart of Turkish Janissary music; or more profoundly, as in the case of Debussy and the Javanese gamelan (a South-East Asian ensemble, which varies slightly from area to area, composed chiefly of metallophones, gongs and drums); or at a philosophical level as with Cage and Stockhausen. The number of recent Western composers who have been influenced by music of the Orient is very considerable: Britten, Messiaen, Boulez, Stockhausen, Partch, Reich and Chavez come immediately to mind, and the influence of such Afro-Caribbean idioms as reggae on popular styles is perhaps even better known. There have also been attempts at fusions, some partially successful, others just an artificial locking together of dissimilar closed systems, doing disservice to both.

The more pupils listen to instruments, the more they will recognize derivations from a common source – the oboe of Europe, the serunai of Malaysia, the shahnā'i of India, the sona of China – and they will discover that the bagpipes were not a Scottish invention, any more than the scale they use. Some instruments will not fit easily into the classification of strings, woodwind, brass and percussion, but they can all find an appropriate place in the classification of idiophones, membranophones, aerophones and cordophones, devised by Curt Sachs on the basis of an ancient Indian treatise.

The knowledge of this influence of one culture on another is necessary for a serious study of twentieth-century music by any pupil preparing for higher education. It becomes more meaningful through performance. Pupils hear about the new world of sonorities opened up to Debussy by the Javanese gamelan at the Paris Exposition Universelle of 1889, but what this actually meant to him as a musical experience becomes much more real to anyone who has the opportunity to be involved in a gamelan ensemble. Some inkling of it may be discovered by performances of gamelan music on Orff-type instruments, but if simulated instruments are used, the appropriate tuning should also be. As a way into the music of another culture the use of class or home-made instruments may be acceptable; as an attempt to reproduce the original sound it has its limitations. What we badly need is more workshops up and down the country where the authentic instruments are available to be played by our pupils.

Performance

Wherever possible we should include in all schools the performance of music from other cultures. For half a century the repertoire of suitable songs from beyond the British Isles has greatly increased and now includes folk songs from Europe, the Americas, Australia and the West Indies. These have introduced new idioms, and given pupils a glimpse into different kinds of living. They have also shown that there can be many versions of the same song, each of which is equally valid. In the call and response songs and calypsos of the West Indies this variety can be increased still further by pupils fitting their own words spontaneously to the melodic structure, and responding with physical movements to the rhythmic patterns of the song.

Songs from the Near and Far East and Africa have been slower in gaining popularity. There are reasons for this. There is the difficulty of language and of finding translations which fit the melody and still convey the sense of the original. In addition, there is the question of giving the folk song real relevance. This already applies to European folk song: how much harder with folk songs transplanted from other cultures.

Moreover, songs which come from an oral tradition cannot be notated precisely, and their melodic line and rhythmic groupings become distorted when forced into an inadequate notation. Then there are problems peculiar to specific cultures. For many children of Indian origin in our schools the only music they know comes from film songs, a hybrid music made up of traditional elements, but with Western style accompaniment and instruments. But there are other Indian songs which are possible and, as with some songs from Africa, these can give pupils the experience of new vocal techniques and of using a wider vocal range, particularly in the upper register. Singing them against a drone can develop a more secure sense of pitch and a greater accuracy of intonation.

Songs from non-Western cultures should, if possible, be taught live by a singer in the classroom, or from an authentic recording. Only then can the pupils learn how to ornament a melody with conviction, and absorb other essential elements of the appropriate performance style. Fortunately there are some songs from both the East and Africa which are simple enough in structure and idiom to be learnt easily. A number of pentatonic Chinese songs come into this category, and they have satisfactory translations available. Other songs have choruses in which all can join, even if the verses prove less accessible. If we do decide to use printed notation for a specific purpose let us remember that some of the ethnic minorities have their own pitch symbols which are equivalent to our tonic solfa (e.g. the sa, re, ga, ma, pa, dha, ni, of India).

It is valuable for pupils to acquire instrumental skills which will enable them to join in the ensembles of their local communities. Opportunities for this will depend on the instrumental teachers available, but where teachers of non-Western instruments exist in any area it will be advantageous to include the teaching of those instruments side by side and on equal terms with Western instruments. It may be considered presumptuous to ask pupils to reproduce music of another culture – without access to disciplined study over a long period within an appropriate cultural context. In this connection it is important to stress that the primary purpose of learning non-Western instruments is to gain a deeper understanding of the process rather than the achievement of a polished end product. The pupils are embarking on an exploration not only of the instrument and its culture, but also of themselves.

What about the use of the steel band in schools? The steel band has particular relevance to contemporary society, since its music grew out of the needs of a people in a multiracial society. Its enjoyment is not confined to pupils of West Indian origin. It develops aural awareness, memory, a harmonic sense, the instinctive modification of melodies, rhythmic skills, and physical control and coordination. If a band is formed, let us make sure that it is fully integrated into the school's musical life through, for example, accompanying the school choir and playing for assemblies.

The studies of other cultures

Although the approach in the lower forms will be conceptual, there will be a place later for the detailed study of particular cultures if this is demanded by pupils whose interests have been stimulated by their aural and performance experiences. This may lead them into project work for CSE or GCE, for which there must be sufficient resources of books, tapes, cassettes and films. Better still, if they can experience live the music they are studying through visits to the school of bearers of the relevant tradition, by going to concerts and festivals, and by performing the music, as far as possible, themselves. This is an area of work where schools may have to cooperate, since each of them may have very few pupils who wish to pursue a study in depth. It is very important, too, that there should be appropriate courses in higher education to which such students can proceed.

Integrated studies

One of the things that will strike pupils about music in non-Western cultures is that it has to be understood in relation to other arts, and to its own social and cultural context. In some African societies music is so closely linked to poetry, dancing, chanting and oral literature that there is no separate word for it. Music, movement and the visual arts are all essential parts of the whole event, forming a complete entity and serving a recognizable societal function. So when we introduce music from other cultures into our schools we must try not to abstract it completely from the other activities with which it is associated. That is not easy in secondary schools, but as we look at the way music and the other arts belong together in many other societies we may get some hints as to how we can adapt our own school society to enable this to happen there. Outside the school, movement, bodily decoration, visual effects and theatrical presentation are all essential parts of the pop scene, with music central but not all-important.

Music is not only associated with other arts. It must be seen as part of a wider social and cultural pattern, not just as a discrete body of skills. Shanties sung by a shantyman and his sailors to ease the work of hauling in sails lose some of their significance when sung by boys seated in rows and accompanied by a piano, as does the church cantata performed in the concert hall, or the Eskimo rain chant played in an Appreciation class. Should our pupils then be denied the opportunity for these aural experiences, because the situations in which they are re-created are different from those in which they originated? For the purist there is only one reply. But most of us would consider this a loss for the pupils. Let us create situations as realistically as possible and then use our imaginations: for this purpose books, pictures, films and visits are all helpful. The shanty can at least be accompanied by appropriate movements and employ the solo-chorus method, with less attention paid to the quality of voice production than to the improvisation of verses appropriate to contemporary events and people. This improvisation can then be compared with the West Indian calypso. The singing of calypsos and shanties may help pupils glimpse a different mode of living, just as listening to the Gagaku may give them some feeling for the Japanese feudal court.

It may appear more difficult to enter imaginatively into the context of a non-Western culture. But this need not always be so. There are no windjammers now where we can hear shanties, but there are temples where unfamiliar chants are sung and the religion which gave rise to them is practised, halls where music is performed to audiences from the tradition which created it, festivals where the music is heard in conjunction with dancing, symbolic acts and family get-togethers – and almost everywhere there are restaurants and food with its smells and tastes providing another entry into the lives of other people. There are so many new experiences around us if we will only open ourselves to them. We may not be as isolated from them, even in country areas, as we think. Numbers of European groups – Poles, Lithuanians, Cypriots etc. – all around the country have singing and dance groups which sometimes remain unknown to other people in their locality. Arts societies can draw our attention to them, and we must persuade television and radio companies to bring into our homes and schools those experiences we cannot get live.

The multicultural school

The approach that has been described so far is as appropriate in multicultural schools as in those with few pupils of minority origin. In all schools every pupil must be helped to feel at home and needed – to know that they have something to contribute – for frightened, bewildered pupils cannot learn. If their own culture is ignored and undervalued a sense of inferiority is likely to be generated. So an environment and situations must be created in which all pupils feel free to make a positive contribution to the life of the school.

This is quite a delicate matter, and we must tread carefully. The well-meaning teacher who plays a record of North Indian classical singing because of the small group of girls of Indian origin in her class may only succeed in making them feel embarrassed and alienated from the rest of the pupils, who are finding the sounds rather funny. But to ignore the presence of the girls altogether would be equally disastrous.

In creative music-making all the pupils have an equal part to play and to contribute from their own backgrounds. As they become absorbed in the music of other cultures they discover aspects of these cultures within themselves of which they had been unaware. Such festivals as Diwali, Christmas and the Chinese New Year are obviously times for sharing each other's songs, dancing and theatrical performances in a relaxed atmosphere. Underlying the different methods of celebration they will find activities common to all – sending cards, giving gifts, preparing of special foods and decorations, the coming together of families and friends. The festivals can involve the whole school and spread out beyond to its community, so that families can celebrate together, with local musicians joining in the teaching and performance.

Another area of school life where themes from the festivals can unite the pupils is the morning assembly. In a multicultural, multifaith school an exclusively Christian act of worship is inappropriate; but through the exploration of concepts pupils may gain an insight into each other's faiths and perhaps find a meeting place. If we take the concept of light, for example, there are available the candle songs of Diwali, the carols of Christmas, and the lantern songs for the Chinese New Year. Into the assembly too, can be introduced a musical exploration of the concept of 'light' through the performance of pupils' own compositions and those of other composers. It may also be related to local folk traditions (e.g. carrying flaming tar barrels during the darkest days of winter).

The activities that have been described can bring together all children, whatever their background. We must also remember that music is a crucial force in maintaining the cohesion of a group, and that there is a continuing need for young people to learn more about the cultural heritage of their own and other ethnic groups. What was said about vocal and instrumental performance in schools is even more important in the multi-cultural school. We must make sure that teachers are appointed, wherever possible, to teach the instruments from the pupils' own traditions and that any teaching given outside the school is integrated into the life of the school. If all instruments receive equal treatment, and introductory courses are provided in both Western and non-Western instruments, the pupils can suggest which instrument they would like to learn. Some pupils may wish to concentrate on the development of their vocal technique, and they too should receive lessons in their particular style of singing wherever possible. They should be encouraged to teach songs from their own country of origin to their fellow pupils. Perhaps an appropriate accompaniment can be devised with the instruments available, but in most cases the piano should be kept well out of the way.

Whilst wishing to emphasize opportunities rather than problems, we must not be unrealistic. There *are* problems. In any class there will be pupils from quite different backgrounds who cannot just be treated as one category labelled, for example, 'ethnic minority'. Their antecedents, social, religious and cultural, and consequently the idioms with which they identify vary enormously. All teachers will be faced, too, with many different types of music – religious, secular, popular, folk, tribal, hybrid, high-art. Are they all equally important? And we must remember that our efforts to encourage creativity and self-expression may be misunderstood by those parents who were brought up to learn by rote and repetition.

Resources

In all this we must draw heavily on the resources of the local community, so that the school can be seen to be both a reflection of its life and a focus for its aspirations. From the leaders of its ethnic groups we must learn what to avoid, as well as how to act, what susceptibilities and religious sensibilities to watch, where embarrassment or resentment may be caused. We must learn, too, at what stage our attempt to increase racial understanding may produce just the opposite effect – and why.

Goodwill, tolerance and understanding are not enough: they must be supported by knowledge, materials and practical experience. As yet we are not sufficiently well resourced in this country for our work to be really effective. Things are gradually improving, however, and some of the resource sources needed to follow through the suggestions made earlier in this chapter are given at the end, together with two examples of projects which have been used in schools. Much can be done by teachers themselves to collect resources from their schools, to encourage pupils to go out and record members of the community (whatever their ethnic background), and to invite members of the community into the school. The Cultural Sections of the embassies are helpful in providing information, as are tourist bureaux and local libraries. Some museums have collections of non-Western instruments, and there are shops where such instruments can now be bought easily and cheaply. The Minority Arts Advisory Service (MAAS) acts as an agency for ethnic artists, and there are several festivals where music is performed in association with other arts. More in-service courses are badly needed at local, regional and national level, and more centres where an experience in depth of the music of different cultures and a rudimentary practical involvement are accompanied by relevant background information. Regular links between teachers, advisers, community leaders and ethnomusicologists are essential.

Above all, the primary requisite is an attitude which respects music in its various manifestations just as music, and which explores ways in which the rich diversity of music can contribute to the multicultural education of all pupils in our classrooms.

Two classroom projects

The projects described below illustrate ways in which elements of musics from other cultures may be incorporated into the classroom teaching and give pupils skills that will enable them to understand better musical performances from those cultures.

Project 1

Aim – to use a well-known Western tune to develop perception for varying tensions of notes relative to the tonic and to improvise melodic units devised from the notes of that tune. This will help pupils to understand the meaning of Indian rāg.

Stage 1:   Sing the tune with chords I, IV and V.

Stage 2:   Sing the tune with a continuous drone, preferably sung, made up of (a) the tonic triad, and (b) the tonic in octaves.

Stage 3:   Compare and discuss the differences in singing the tune when harmonized and with the different drones. Also the effect of the tune on the sung drones.

Stage 4:   Practise singing the notes on which the tune is based:

Stage 5:   Extend the singing of these notes into the adjacent octaves, each pupil exploring in free time, and within her/his own range, the relationships of the notes to each other and to the drone.

Stage 6: Use the notes of the tune for improvisation of melodic units free from a regular pulse. The drone is to be sounded continuously.

Discuss the relative success of melodic units improvised by pupils keeping to the melodic character of the tune as defined in Stage 4.

The following examples show:

(a) an uncharacteristic interval introduced without changing the fundamental character of the tune:

(b) Notes and intervals introduced that are alien to the character of the tune:

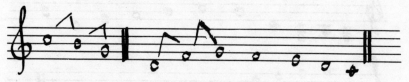

Stage 7: Listen to:

1. Ustad Ali Akbar Khan: Melodisc Records Ltd, ML14, side 1 (alap).
2. Himangshu Biswas and Dulal Roy: EMI ECSO 2361, side 1 (alap).

Project 2

Aim – to develop an ability to maintian a steady pulse and to group beats accurately in a variety of ways around this pulse. This will help pupils experience the complex rhythmic patterns inherent in Indian, African and Indonesian music.

Stage 1:   All pupils practise clapping or tapping on a drum a steady pulse at a medium tempo.

Stage 2:   One group of pupils to maintain a steady pulse while the other group practises alternating between the steady pulse and one of the following beats (a) to (g) which follow:

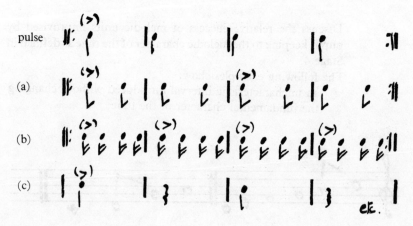

(d)

(e)

(f)

(g)

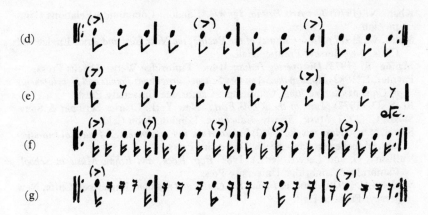

Stage 3:   Group the claps into four by a louder clap (or a beat on a drum
head vibrating freely) followed by three softer claps (or damped
drum sounds). To the original relationship of the claps to the
pulse is now added a pattern set up by the new groups formed by
the accents (shown in brackets). This exercise can be developed
much further by using other rhythmic groupings and distribu-
tions of accents.

Stage 4: Listen to:

1. Rhythms of India: Ustad Ahmad Jan Thirawata, EMI EASO
1335, side 1.
2. Master Drummer from Ghana: Mustapha Tettey Addy
Tangent TGF 113, side 1, band 1.
3. Music of Africa Series (Tanzania): Hugh Tracey, Taleido-
phone TMA 9, side 2, track 5.

General reading list

Anderson, W. (1975) *Teaching Asian Music in Elementary and Secondary Schools.*
Michigan: Leland Press.

Bebey, F. (1975) *African Music: A People's Art*. London: Harrap.

Elder, J.D. (1969) *From Congo Drum to Steel Band*. University of West Indies.

Farmer, P. (1981) *Steel Bands and Reggae: An Introduction to the Development of
Caribbean Music*. London: Longman.

Grove's Dictionary of Music and Musicians (1980) London: Macmillan (for articles
about the individual cultures).

Hebdige, D. (1982) *Reggae and Caribbean Music*. London: Routledge and Kegan
Paul.

Khan, N. (1976) *The Arts Britain Ignores*. London: Community Relations Commission.

Malm, W. (1977) *Music Cultures of the Pacific, the Near East and Asia*. Englewood Cliffs, New Jersey: Prentice Hall.

Manon, R. (1973) *Discovering Indian Music*. Tunbridge Wells: Abacus Press.

Paynter, J. (1982) *Music in the Secondary School Curriculum: Trends and Developments in Class Music Teaching*. Cambridge: Cambridge University Press.

Rech, D. (1977) *Music of the Whole Earth*. New York: Charles Scribner & Sons.

Small, C. (1977) *Music, Society, Education*. London: John Calder.

Sorrel, N. and Narayan, R. (1980) *Indian Music in Performance: A Practical Introduction*. Manchester: Manchester University Press.

Vulliamy, G. and Lee, E. (eds.) (1982) *Pop, Rock, and Ethnic Music in School*. Cambridge: Cambridge University Press.

Wade, B.C. (1979) *Music in India: The Classical Tradition*. Englewood Cliffs, New Jersey: Prentice Hall.

Resources for the classroom

Bartholomew, J. (1980) *The Steel Band*. London: Oxford University Press.

Brocklehurst, B. (1968) *The Pentatonic Song Book*. London: Schott.

Connolly, Y., Cameron, G. and Singham, S. (1981) *Mango Spice*. London: A & C Black.

Floyd, L. (1980) *Indian Music*. London: Oxford University Press.

Lewis, O. (1974) *Brown Gal in de Ring*. London: Oxford University Press.

Paynter, E. and J. (1974) *The Dance and the Drum*. London: Universal Edition.

Sephula, M. (1970a) *Sing Africa*. Great Yarmouth: Galliard.

Sephula, M. (1970b) *Sing Again Africa*. Great Yarmouth: Galliard.

Walke, O. (1976) *Folk Songs of Trinidad and Tobago*. London: Boosey and Hawkes.

'World Around Songs' (RT. 5, Box 398, Burnsville, North Carolina 28714, USA) produces a useful series of pocket songbooks of international songs, with separate books for Africa, the Philippines, Hawaii, China, Japan, Guiana, Trinidad, Tobago and India, and a good representation of songs from the Near East in the general collection.

Recordings

Recordings of ethnic music may be found on the following labels:

Afrotone, Anthology, Bahrenreiter – Musicaphon, Boîte à Musique, Capitol, EMI (including the UNESCO Collection – Musical Atlas), Folkways, Harmonia Mundi, Le Chant du Monde, Lyrichord, Nonesuch (Explorer Series), Ocora, Odeon, Philips (including the UNESCO Collection – Musical Sources), Tangent, Vogue, World Pacific.

Suppliers

Record shops

ABC Music Shop, 7 The Broadway, Southall, Middx. Tel. 01–574–1319

Collets Record Shop, 180 Shaftesbury Avenue, London WC2. Tel. 01–240–3969

Discuria International Record Store, 9 Shepherd Street, London W1. Tel. 01–493–6939

HMV Record Shop, 363 Oxford Street, London W1. Tel. 01–629–1240

Hitman Records, 13 Beadon Road, Hammersmith, London W6. Tel. 01–748–5355

The Gramophone Company of India, Unit 8, Boeing Way, International Trading Estate, Southall, Middx. UB2 5LB. Tel. 01–843–0650/0670

Virdee Bros., 26 South Road, Southall, Middx. Tel. 01–571–4870

Instrument shops

Aklowa Centre, Takeley House, Brewers End, Takeley, Bishops Stortford, Herts. Tel. 0279–871062

Bina Musicals, 31–33 The Green, Southall, Middx. Tel. 01–843–1411

Global Village Crafts, Roundwell Street, South Petherton, Somerset. Tel. 0460–40194

Book shops

Africa Centre, 38 King Street, London WC2. Tel. 01–836–1976

Independent Publishing Company (S. Asian, African and Caribbean), 38 Kennington Lane, London SE11. Tel. 01–735–2101

Sabarr Books (Afro–Caribbean), 378 Cold Harbour Lane, Brixton, London SW9. Tel. 01–274–6785

Shakti Bookhouse (Indian), 46 High Street, Southall, Middx. Tel. 01–574–1325

Soma Books Ltd. (S. Asian, African and Caribbean), The Commonwealth Institute, Kensington High Street, London W8. Tel. 01–603–4535 or 603–0754

Walter Rodney Publications Ltd. (African and Caribbean), 5A Chigwell Place, Ealing, London W13. Tel. 01–579–4920.

Other useful addresses

Bharatiya Vidya Bhawan (Indian Cultural Centre), 4 Castletown Road, London W14. Tel. 01–381–3086

British Institute of Recorded Sound, 29 Exhibition Road, London SW7. Tel. 01–589–6603/4.

Commission for Racial Equality, Elliot House, 10–12 Allington Street, London SW1. Tel. 01–828–7022

The Commonwealth Institute (Education Department), Kensington High Street, London W8. Tel. 01–603–4535

Dartington College of Arts (Multicultural Music Section), Totnes, Devon. Tel. 0803–862224

Horniman Museum, London Road, Forest Hill, London SE23. Tel. 01–699–2339

MAAS (Minority Arts Advisory Service), Beauchamp Lodge, 2 Warwick Crescent, London W2. Tel. 01–286–1854 or 286–1858

Museum of Mankind (British Museum Dept of Ethnography), 6 Burlington Gardens, London W1. Tel. 01–437–2224

The School of Oriental and African Studies, (Extra-Mural Department), Malet Street, London WC1. Tel. 01–637–2388

The Steelband Organisation of Great Britain, 10 Gainsborough Gardens, Greenford, Middx.

Chapter 12*

ART AND DESIGN

Allan Leary

'[There is] confusion, even conflict over the function [of arts subjects] in a programme of general education' (Ross 1975).[1]

This 'predicament of arts education' referred to by Ross, has encouraged a considerable polarization of attitudes. While many art teachers continue to 'insist upon the personal and expressive impulse of art', with self-realization through creative art as a fundamental goal, a considerable dissenting group seeks a 'functional utilitarian role', primarily through design-based approaches, and cognitive rather than affective in style. Malcolm Ross's own position, in common with a number of other influential writers during the last decade, is that 'the prime concern of the arts curriculum should be with the emotional development of the child through creative self expression'. He concurs with Witkin's warning that 'so-called creative work . . . can suffer radical distortion in the interests of . . . functionalism'.[2] In this context, the issue of multiculturalism and of the possible role of arts curricula (especially in the visual arts) in catering for the specific needs of ethnic minority pupils or in endeavouring to expand and enrich the cultural and artistic experience of all pupils, may well attract (and deserve) criticism; for it may be seen to be overtly pedagogic rather than expressive, and failing to keep 'the emotional development of the child through creative self-expression' as its primary goal.

Concern for a multicultural dimension in art education need not, however, run counter to that aim. As Ross reminds us, 'the arts have an important social role, not just as the leisure interest of a privileged élite, but

---

* Some of the ideas in this chapter are an extension of those in *Assessment in a Multicultural Society: Art and Design at 16+* by Allen Leary, Schools Council Programme 5 Pamphlet Series. Longman, York, 1984.

as an essential element of lifelong education', while more recently Maurice Barrett has drawn attention to the 'strong social and cultural overtones' of much art teaching practice, despite the great emphasis on individual creativity and development.[3] Barrett does not regard the social and cultural aspects of art as incompatible with good art teaching, although he is concerned to ensure that they serve expressive ends. The social and cultural aspects of art may therefore 'be used to reinforce the process through which the pupil is educated, but they should be part of the means towards an end which is located essentially within the individual reality of the pupil. Eventually within the complete and continuing education of the individual, it will be up to him to decide how he wishes to relate his own reality to social reality and during the process of art education he should be given the opportunity to discover the nature and form of social and cultural reality.' The concepts of individual and social reality are closely linked to the whole issue of teaching and practising art in the ethnically mixed society which is Britain today. Social and individual reality is also ethnic reality.

The social role of the arts has certain other implications for arts educators – not only is there 'a restlessness among artists who have become dissatisfied with traditional forms and predictable responses', but there has been a 'resurgence of artistic creativity of the grassroots of our society throughout Europe and America' and 'dramatic demands for live contact' which mark 'a strongly felt need by artists and audience for direct involvement, for engagement with experience which is immediate and personal'.[4] A fundamental characteristic of many of these newer art forms is that they are no longer socially uncomitted and therefore they have an obvious relevance to our multicultural society with all its inequalities.

Denis Lawton has pointed out that 'problems of knowledge and meaning become particularly acute in pluralistic societies where a multiplicity of groups have different perspectives and theories of the world and of knowledge'. 'Separate development based on the existence of different perceptions of reality is however socially undesirable' – unless some communality is preserved there is a danger that society will tend to break down completely.[5] How then is such a communality to be achieved? Not, in the opinion of the author, by any sort of cultural *pax britannica*, which may seek to impose majority cultural values on ethinic minority groups. As George Steiner perceived nearly 20 years ago – in the not unrelated context of English literature and literary criticism – a shifting of 'the centre of creative and linguistic gravity' away from Britain was already a well-established, if largely unrecognized, phenomenon.[6] Steiner suggested that 'there may be other coordinates of cultural reference that touch more urgently on the present contours of our lives, on the way we now think and feel and try to find our way', in the undoubtedly 'polycentric field' now impinging more and more on the visual arts in Britain. Those 'other coordinates of cultural reference' must be seen as important agents for change, challenging in certain contexts the dominance of European and Anglo–American culture. As Steiner went on to note, 'the almost total lack of comparative studies in English academic circles . . . may also be a symptom of a more general withdrawal, of the fist closing tight against an altered, uncomfortable world – in culture, no less than in politics, chauvinism and isolation are suicidal options'.

The influence of examinations

During the last two decades, approaches to art and design teaching and examining have undergone considerable change, to take account of the constantly developing and innovative nature of the visual arts. There has been an increasing emphasis on personal expression and the communication of ideas and emotions as well as information. Terms such as sensitivity, receptivity, awareness, perception and judgement, are now typical of many school syllabuses. Choice of media and themes is generally wider and craft-specific categories have tended to merge. However the author's recent review of 16+ syllabuses and examinations in art and design (Leary, 1984) reveals little which might reflect or stimulate multicultural initiatives.[7] Although syllabuses emphasize personal expression and 'universal' aesthetic values (the latter giving an impression of cultural neutrality), examination papers in Art and Design tend to be Eurocentric, making few concessions to the understanding and valuing of the rich fabric of art, craft and design traditions in non-European societies. As a consequence, although there is a developing concern for multicultural approaches to art education in schools with large ethnic minority populations, this is far less true of schools with smaller numbers of such pupils. Art and design courses which reflect only the values and interests of the dominant culture tend to devalue, however subtly, the cultural and artistic heritage of the not inconsiderable proportion of British society whose origins lie outside Europe. To the extent that this cultural parochialism prevails, wider educational opportunities have been neglected – not only in extending and deepening the artistic experience of all pupils, but also in contributing towards a greater measure of cross-cultural understanding.

It is nevertheless heartening to find that despite the fairly widespread lack of multicultural examination provision there are indications that a quite substantial group of teachers have for some time regarded multicultural approaches to art and design education as important. The Schools Council Working Paper No 50 showed that even in the early 1970s 54 per cent of heads of art departments in a cross-section of multiracial schools (based on 65 per cent response from 150 schools) believed that 'preparation of pupils for life in a multiracial society' should be one of their aims, 34 per cent of them indicating that their syllabuses took account of this to some extent.[8]

It was less encouraging to note the contrary views of some teachers, summarized in Working Paper No 50 as follows: 'The problem of race does not present a barrier in Art since children of all races generally enjoy the language of colour and pattern etc . . . the concepts, values and conceptual judgements that are fostered and attained in this area of the curriculum are to a degree constant within different societies – for this reason no major changes [to syllabuses] are necessary or envisaged'. There is no experimental evidence to support such a statement – rather the contrary. The variety of symbolic meanings attributed to particular colours within different cultures, for instance, is well documented and serves to remind us that notions about the universal 'enjoyment' of colour and pattern tend to obscure the diversity of culturally determined 'iconic' meanings capable of being expressed through an artistic 'language'. As Barbara Lloyd has pointed out: 'Scepticism about the exotic – the feeling that cultural differences in today's world are often contrived – is nurtured by a belief that with universal education, jet travel, communication satellites and the other marvels of an advanced technical age, men are becoming the same in their thoughts . . . cultural differences are expected to vanish as soon as science is taught in schools, as television becomes universal and as literacy replaces illiteracy. The knowledge and national thought process of Western man are expected to become universal and any barriers to the diffusion of Western knowledge are expected to be differences of time and attitude, rather than question of basic differences in perception, thinking and learning.'[9] Theories about the 'universality' of artistic expression are based on similar assumptions.

Some 10 years after the publication of the Schools Council Working Paper No 50, Little and Willey in their survey of heads of art departments in a cross-section of 124 multiracial schools found that many of them believed that 'the nature of the art curriculum naturally catered for cultural differences, [and] that [as] the subject was concerned with individual personal expression no particular action or emphasis was necessary to make the curriculum relevant to a multi-ethnic society'.[10]

However, the findings gave some support to the view that art did have an important role in multicultural schools. Some of the implications of cultural difference for art and design education have been discussed by Ann Taber.[11] For many of her secondary-aged pupils at a language centre, coming as they did from East Africa or India, art in a Western sense was quite a new experience with 'a very different meaning from that which it has for an English child'. The 'Western' concept of art – 'involved with notions of innovation, creativity and originality: all essentially concerned with change' – was often alien to them. In many non-Western societies, she points out, 'the artist works within hallowed tradition, keeping to rules and set forms which . . . are learned gradually from a master and skill . . . achieved through constant study and practice. Personal feelings are subordinated to the traditional art learnt. The artist's individual expression merges with that of others and becomes the manifestation of the group's philosophy. For this reason the individual's identity as an artist is unimportant.'

These are particularly important points to bear in mind in the assessment of group work, or of work conceived in terms of non-Western chromatic or spatial convention.

At the same time we must not oversimplify the nature of innovation and the role and status of the artist in some non-Western cultures – there is much evidence, for instance, of informed critical differentiation between individual artists in certain African societies, despite the apparent constraints of particular artistic traditions. Franz Boas reminds us in *Primitive Art* (1975) that 'the impression that primitive culture is almost stable and has remained what it is for centuries . . . does not correspond to the facts. Wherever we have detailed information we see forms of objects and customs in constant flux, sometimes stable for a period, then undergoing rapid changes.'[12] Frequently such changes arise from contacts between cultures. 'Hybrid' and innovative art forms resulting from such contacts are common in the history of art, often bringing a new vitality to older and well-established art forms. In the interests of greater cultural 'fairness', different art and design modes and conventions should, as has been suggested above, be judged as far as possible in culturally relative terms, but it is equally important that 'hybrid' art is not undervalued or simply dismissed as an 'impure' version of a more established tradition, or of 'received' modes of artistic expression. Nor should it be assumed that cultural borrowing is necessarily a one-way process – Picasso, Braque and Modigliani certainly prove the contrary. Cultural and artistic pluralism is a likely outcome of multicultural approaches to art and design education.

Attitudes to art and design are often closely linked with religious beliefs, as are particular forms of artistic expression, and these can pose challenges for pupils, teachers and examiners. Again Ann Taber has noted that 'to embrace the concept of art which we have adopted in the Western world is impossible [for many pupils] as aspects of it run contrary to religious ideas and make "art" as we see it, in some ways incompatible with religion'.[13] Much of Islamic art has, for example, been described as 'aniconic' and Muslim attitudes to figurative art may involve rejection of human imagery. Although the avoidance of representation is not wholly consistent through-out Islam – differences of exegesis or emphasis having always typified the orthodox Muslim legal schools as well as Shi'ite Islam – culturally fairer courses and examinations in art and design, in taking account of possible constraints on Muslim pupils, should also seek to encourage wider access to the rich alternative modes of expression within the Islamic tradition. These are but some of the considerations which may constrain or inform art and design teaching in our multicultural society.

There seems to have been little external comment from those involved in art and design education on this whole area, though one exception is Brian Allison. In an unpublished paper (1982) commenting on the Draft National Criteria for 16+ examining in Creative Arts (produced by a Working Party of the GCE and CSE Boards' Joint Council) he noted that 'in the last few decades, art and design educators in this country and abroad have done much to clarify the individual as well as social values of art and design education. They have also established realistic and substantiated views on what contributes to the understanding of the role, purposes, function and practices of art and design in contemporary cultures. Further, recognition has been given to the value of acquiring some genuine understanding of the art and design of cultures other than one's own and to the fact that, in this multicultural society, the Western European art and design forms are the equivalent of a foreign language to a substantial proportion of the school's population.'

Some current changes in examining board policies are beginning to both reflect and influence the development of art teaching appropriate for a multicultural society. For example, the London GCE Board has stated that 'every effort is made to set questions which would appeal to children with various backgrounds, and the marking of work from pupils with non-English origins is dealt with sympathetically, and indigenous cultural attitudes encouraged'. The Interim Report of the Midlands Examining Group's 16+ Subject Working Party for Art and Design, published in amended form in July 1982, took some account of the opportunities inherent in the recognition and acceptance of cultural diversity. It is significant that this report reflected the views of teachers. Subject 'aims and objectives' included the following: 'through direct experience of practical skills and theoretical studies, art and design leads to a fuller understanding of the part played by visual arts . . . and the varied history of mankind's development and successive civilisations. In doing so it widens cultural horizons and enriches the individual's personal resources . . . It is hoped that courses will to some extent reflect this view of the subject.'

The following three sections consider the multicultural opportunities in two-dimensional art, in two- and three-dimensional design and craft, and in art appreciation and art history.

Two-dimensional art

Secondary school work, especially in Years 4 and 5, in the area of two-dimensional art consists of two main groups: work from the imagination or memory and work from observation, although these distinctions are not always clear cut. Further subdivisions are common – figure/genre, environment/landscape, etc. – and these often merge into each other. Formal qualities of line, colour, tone, texture and the sensitive choice and handling of media are frequently emphasized. It is useful to consider two-dimensional art education in the light of two fundamental questions: to what extent does it take account of the need to encourage, first, culturally diverse approaches to art and design studies and, secondly, a concern for cultural fairness? The nature and extent of cultural bias thus revealed has considerable implications for curriculum planning. Many topics and themes which involve working from memory or imagination are capable of interpretation in the light of personal and more immediate experience; environmental themes, such as Urban Skyline or Derelict Cars, are often emphasized. These and other fairly generalized topics, such as The Meal, The Gossips, Dangerous Work, Hot and Cold, Food, Musicians or Smoke, all relate to most pupils' experience, irrespective of ethnic background. As such they may be interpreted in personal terms by most art students. More exotic starting points based on fantasy or science fiction (also fairly common) are similarly capable of quite personal interpretation. The comparative absence of overt cultural bias of much art teaching in classrooms is largely due to the prevalence of such short-title topics and themes. To the extent however that the latter become more specific, the risk of cultural unfairness increases.

Drawing and painting from observation is generally intended to develop pupils' ability to analyse and explicate form and structure, and work from observation is often one of a number of possible 'starting points' for an expressive personal response. However, insofar as many non-European art traditions place no emphasis on analytical objective drawing as a separate discipline, and given that expressive values in the visual arts do not necessarily depend on competence in this field, teachers need to be aware that stressing an analytical cognitive approach may put otherwise quite gifted pupils at a disadvantage.

Two- and three-dimensional design and craft

Similar observations may be made with regard to the area of two- and three-dimensional design and craft. There is little risk of cultural bias in topics and themes which draw on common experiences in the life of a school or the local community, but where more emphasis is placed on specific aspects of British life, opportunities may be restricted for many pupils from non-British backgrounds (as indeed for pupils from particular social backgrounds). Literary themes are common in graphics and the problem of cultural balance is a delicate one.

It is in the area of lettering and calligraphy that a more obvious failure to take account of the cultural background of many pupils is especially apparent. Virtually all work in this area is located directly or by implication, within the European tradition. Thus lettering and calligraphy is still concerned with skills based on a knowledge of Roman letter forms or their mediaeval and renaissance derivatives. However there are many pupils who are familiar with other writing systems; calligraphy is central to the Islamic tradition and Muslim pupils usually have some knowledge of Arabic and related scripts. Despite apparent difficulties it would seem essential, if greater comparability of opportunity is to be achieved, to establish more choice and certainly to include the area of Arabic/Urdu calligraphy and possibly other Asian scripts. Here expert advice and teaching is needed. The study of basic Arabic pen hands – *kūfī*, *naskhī* or *thuluth*, for example – and the gaining of an understanding of their history and development could provide a fascinating and rigorous course of work. The disciplines imposed by the pen are fundamental to both European and Arabic calligraphy and while it is hardly practicable that all art teachers should learn Arabic, the comparative study and understanding of letter-forms and of simpler approaches to Arabic calligraphy can be fairly readily acquired by those outside the culture.[14] The bridging of cultural gaps should, where possible, be a two-way process.

Despite the essentially cross-cultural nature of the craft, textile design and fabric printing also exhibit many of the above tendencies. Although batik, block-printing and tie-and-dye are included in classwork within the range of possible techniques, historical, cultural and technical studies often deal predominantly with the development and contemporary practice of the craft in Europe. The importance of non-European design in this as in other fields is usually presented not so much for its own qualities as for its contribution to European design. To this extent it is often effectively devalued.

Broadly similar comments apply to sculpture and ceramics. Greater emphasis is given to European examples and practice, with little concern, except peripherally, for the rich sculptural and ceramic traditions of Africa or Asia for example.

Art appreciation and art history

Courses in the history and appreciation of art and design are still predominantly Eurocentric and take little account of the arts of societies outside Europe, except where these may have influenced the West. Japanese art, for instance, is acknowledged only insofar as it has influenced European artists – the same is true of, say, African, Oceanic or pre-Columbian American art. The reason for this neglect is not entirely clear, but is probably attributable in part to an historical division between the disciplines of art history and anthropology. Attitudes are, however, gradually changing. Frank Willett, an archaeologist and historian of African art, has written that 'anthropologists are paying increasing attention to the cultural background of African art'.[15] And as Robert Goldwater (writing a little earlier) has pointed out, 'We are . . . today at a point where the anthropologist and the art historian can come together and look at these arts with some objectivity. But to do this they must also be conscious of, examine, and evaluate all those ways of "seeing" that the artists have been teaching them throughout the indispensible interim period.'[16] The arts of

Africa and the East and of early America are no longer the sole preserve of the ethnologist and the archaeologist – nor to be interpreted solely through the subjective eyes of European artists; a sufficient body of art-historical scholarship now exists for the development of art and design history and appreciation courses which may encourage a broader multicultural approach to understanding and appreciation of historical, cultural and environmental aspects of art and design.

Resources

In the context of integrated approaches to cultural diversity in visual arts curricula, reference should be made to the Ethnographic Resources for Art Education project developed by Birmingham Polytechnic's Department of Art Education, which since 1979 has devised and published a series of well-researched resource packs dealing with particular craft themes.[17] The packs published so far cover various ceramic traditions (including those of the Hausa and Ashanti cultures of West Africa, peasant potters of North-West Pakistan and the pottery of pre-Columbian Peru), as well as starch and wax-resist dyed textiles from West Africa and South-East Asia, and a composite pack dealing with Playthings as Objects (including kites, dolls and sound-making objects) drawn from a number of cultures throughout the world. They have been used experimentally with success in a number of Birmingham schools. Various approaches and 'starting points' for personal and expressive work have proved possible – through materials, techniques, functions or social contexts. There seem to be considerable educational and expressive possibilities in the integration of practical activity with all elements of contextual information. Enhanced respect for apparently 'primitive' technologies and societies is proving to be a valuable subsidiary outcome.

Art and Design in a Multicultural Society (AIMS) is a project which has recently been established at Leicester Polytechnic. AIMS explores the significance and meaning of the distinctive forms of art and design, and the attitudes towards visual imagery among different cultures. Working with local schools, the project hopes to draw upon and develop ways in which art and design courses can reflect and respond to cultural diversity. Although locally based and locally funded, this project seems likely to play an important national role in translating into practice the theoretical support for culturally diverse and culturally fairer art and design curricula outlined in this chapter.

Notes and references

1 Ross, M. (1975) *Arts and the adolescent*, Schools Council Working Paper No. 54. London: Evans/Methuen Educational.

2 Witkin, R. (1974) *The Intelligence of Feeling*. Eastbourne: Holt, Rinehart and Winston.

3 Barrett, M. (1979) *Art Education: a strategy for course design*. London: Heinemann.

4 Ross, M. (1975) *op. cit.*

5 Lawton, D. (1973) *Social Change, Educational Theory and Curriculum Planning*. Unibooks, University of London Press.

6 Steiner, George (1979) *Language and Silence*. Peregrine Books.

7 Leary, A. (1984) *Assessment in a Multicultural Society: Art and Design at 16+*, Schools Council Programme 5 Pamphlet Series. York: Longman.

8 Schools Council (1973) *Multiracial Education: need and innovation*, Working Paper No 50. London: Evans/Methuen Educational, pp. 34–37.

9 Lloyd, B. (1972) *Perception and Cognition: a cross-cultural perspective*. Harmondsworth: Penguin, p. 15.

10 Little, A. and Willey, R. (1983) *Studies in the Multi-Ethnic Curriculum*. London, Schools Council.

11 Taber, A. (1978) Art in a multicultural school. *New Approaches in Multiracial Education* Vol 7, No 1, Autumn.

12 Boas, F. (1975) *Primitive Art*. Dover Press, p. 7 (published originally in 1927).

13 Taber, A. (1978) *op. cit.*

14 A great deal of calligraphic work by Muslim pupils may be religious in emphasis – a few basic religious inscriptions such as the *basmallah* 'in the name of God, the compassionate, the merciful' or the Muslim's simple declaration of faith, the *Khalimah* 'there is no god but Allah; Muhammad is the messenger of Allah', will tend to recur. Good examples of these are to be found for instance in Safadi's *Islamic Calligraphy* (Thames and Hudson 1978). There are also many modern variants of Arabic scripts which may be suitable for secular inscriptions and graphic work. Some of these – contemporary versions of *kūfī* – have considerable design potential in a modern context. Examples of these may be found in newspapers such as *al-'Arab* and quite a selection appears in the Letraset catalogue. Steel calligraphic pens (and to a lesser extent those of reed or bamboo) may prove discouraging for beginners at first. Larger-format inscriptions written with a double pencil (as originally advocated by Edward Johnston for practising English round-hand scripts) offer considerable advantages initially, especially as letter-forms constructed in this way are ideal for larger-scale graphic work in which traditional and contemporary design modes may come together.

15 Willett, F. (1971) *African Art*. London: Thames and Hudson, p. 34.

16 Goldwater, R. (1969) Judgements of primitive art, 1905–1965. *In* Biebuyck, D. (ed.) *Tradition and Creativity in Tribal Art*. Berkeley: University of California Press.

17 For further information about the availability and cost of the packs, write to The Ethnographic Resources for Art Education Project, Department of Education, Birmingham Polytechnic, Margaret Street, Birmingham.

Chapter 13

PHYSICAL EDUCATION, DANCE AND OUTDOOR PURSUITS

Oliver Leaman

It has been well established than many teachers tend to have stereotypes of the mental and social abilities of their pupils, which are heavily affected by their ethnicity. Pupils of Asian origin are widely supposed to be intelligent and quiet, while those of Afro-Caribbean origin (sometimes referred to within this chapter as 'blacks') are often regarded as unacademic and noisy. Attached to these stereotypes is the risk that pupils, depending on their particular ethnic origin, may be encouraged to, or discouraged from, pursuing the well-established routes to the attainment of credentials and the 'glittering prizes' which our society sometimes offers as a reward. As one might expect, these assumptions concerning the academic and behavioural characteristics of the pupils are supplemented by additional assumptions about their physical abilities. Physical education teachers frequently talk in terms of there being a continuum of abilities, with pupils of Afro-Caribbean origin clearly most physically able, pupils of Asian origin least physically capable and other pupils somewhere in the middle.

This chapter considers the ways in which schools often channel pupils into physical activities in different ways dependent upon their ethnic origins; whether these methods are objectionable; what physical education, dance and outdoor pursuits have to offer to the effective implementation of a genuine multicultural curriculum; and what steps are already being taken in British schools to adapt these areas of the curriculum to take account of the interests and abilities of different ethnic groups.

Let us look first in more detail at the involvement in physical education of pupils of Afro-Caribbean and Asian origin, always recognizing that to talk in terms of such broad groups is to run the serious risk of dangerous overgeneralization.

Pupils of Afro-Caribbean origin and physical education

There is a good deal of evidence (Carrington and Wood 1982, Cashmore 1982) to suggest that black pupils are heavily overrepresented in school sports teams. During and preceding adolescence young people frequently adopt an attitude of hostility towards school sport, a hostility which is particularly marked among girls, yet it appears that in general pupils of Afro-Caribbean origin reject school sport less completely than their peers. A particularly marked distinction is between girls of Afro-Caribbean origin and other girls; the former do not in general appear to regard sport as unfeminine, childish, or as an activity inconsistent with the cultivation of the social role of a woman (Leaman 1983). Pupils of Afro-Caribbean origin are usually more enthusiastic about participation in the traditional team games which schools offer, and are often vigorously encouraged in those activities by the physical education staff. After all, in many schools the status of the physical education department is dependent upon the success of the leading school teams – teams which are without many good players due to many pupils' hostility to school-based activities and organized events.

There is no obvious explanation as to why pupils of Afro-Caribbean origin are generally more enthusiastic about school sport, yet there are certainly many multiethnic schools where they predominate in some school teams. Of course, there are a number of well-established black sportsmen and women – Bruno, Conteh, Thompson, Sanderson, Fashanu and so on – who contrast strongly with the relative absence of successful blacks in other areas of life. It is often pointed out that it is only on the sports pages of our newspapers that a positive image of British blacks is presented; an image which contrasts strongly with that often presented on other pages of unemployed, sullen, potentially aggressive and dangerous black youth, heavily involved in street crime and civil disturbances. While the vast majority of black youth do not expect to achieve the sorts of outstanding success that these role models have accomplished, it may be that many of them are motivated to succeed in a desire to participate in the positive image which British society is prepared to allow to blacks who are skilled in sport.

On the whole the physical education profession has not been slow to take advantage of this sporting potential. Physical education teachers are interested in different qualities in pupils from those considered important by other teachers. They are obviously more concerned with those abilities which are relevant to their performance in the physical activities which the school has to offer. A school in which pupils of Afro-Caribbean origin dominate in sport, and where by contrast the other pupils concentrate on acquiring academic credentials, may seem a very satisfactory way to employ the different talents of pupils from different ethnic groups. Yet there is a real danger that such a division discourages many black pupils from the pursuit of academic qualifications in favour of the more immediate gratification to be attained through success in sporting competitions. There is a tendency for many teachers to regard black pupils as *naturally* better at physical activities while pupils from other ethnic groups are considered as *naturally* better at mental skills. Thus many teachers attempt to cope with difficult black pupils by directing them, explicitly or implicitly, to replace academic with non-academic activities. This may have the result of disabling blacks in competition with their peers in activities which are more closely related to success in the employment market and the prospect of higher income and status when adult. Paradoxically, then, the relative success of black pupils in physical education may work against their chances of success in the wider world when they leave school.

This is not a criticism of the physical education profession but rather of the organization of the school as such. It is quite understandable why PE teachers often put so much time and effort into the training and skill development of their black pupils. The school may well be insistent upon competitive success and its black pupils may be seen as one means by which some success is achieved in sport. When one sees the great care that the PE teachers often give to the development of black pupils, one can only wonder what results would accrue if similar attention were always given to them in other areas of the curriculum. Black pupils frequently report the considerable efforts made on their behalf by their PE teacher, often involving work after school and during weekends, and sometimes continuing even after the pupils have finally left school. This sort of teaching will generally be highly individualized, designed to bring out the talents of the particular pupil and help him or her to work towards the greatest possible success in the chosen activity. Links will often be established with clubs and teams which exist outside the school and the pupil may well be introduced to expert trainers and other enthusiasts in the activity.

In the physical education lessons there is usually a good rapport between the teacher and black pupils, with the teacher clearly trying hard to communicate with these pupils who respond so readily to the teacher's own enthusiasm for physical activities. Indeed, in many ways the structure of the physical education lesson, where black pupils find encouragement and optimism concerning their abilities, is in marked contrast to other lessons where the teachers may expect their black pupils either to misbehave or to fail to benefit from their teaching.

It is ironic that this desire on the part of many PE teachers to communicate successfully with their black pupils may not be entirely in the interests of those pupils themselves, since in some schools it results in their being provided with an enhanced physical education programme along with a diminished academic curriculum. There are many instances of the school curriculum being 'watered down' to take account of the 'specific needs' of black pupils, with their absence being accepted in many lessons provided they are training or otherwise involved in physical education. It should be clearly acknowledged that this detracts from the provision of a balanced curriculum for all children in school, whatever it might do for the school's sporting image. Interestingly, black parents are often suspicious of schools that channel their children into physical rather than academic activities, and are very much in favour of their children receiving as academic a curriculum as any other child. It is a shame that the skill, hard work and enthusiasm of so many PE teachers should in some situations unwittingly conspire with the low opinion that some of the teaching profession has of the academic abilities of black pupils, and thus reduce the life chances of those pupils relative to their peers.

Pupils of Asian origin and physical education

The parents of pupils of Asian origin are usually concerned that their children should spend their time in school acquiring academic qualifications so that they can compete on relatively equal terms with others for employment on leaving the education system. Many Asian parents may also have a negative view of the educational potential of physical activities, given their own experience in school of a very limiting form of physical training – a negative view which they might well share with a large number of other parents. The notion that play has educational significance may be difficult to communicate to those Asian parents who do not provide their children with many toys or spend much time with them in specifically differentiated activities labelled as 'play' activities. There are also religious and cultural factors that may relate to out of school activities, especially those on Saturdays and religious festivals. Lastly, the physical education of girls of Asian origin is often regarded as problematic by their parents once puberty is reached, and this can be a frequent cause of strife between parents and schools. Muslim parents in particular object in some cases to their daughters wearing 'revealing' physical education kit, especially when they might be seen by men. Such dress is classified as 'shameless' in some Asian cultures.

In the classroom, pupils of Asian origin are often stereotyped as quiet, hardworking and intelligent, and this stereotype is often reinforced by the physical education context where they may be regarded as unenthusiastic about non-academic pursuits, physically puny and unadventurous. For these 'reasons' the PE teacher may fail to put as much effort into their physical education as one might expect. Teachers often have rather exaggerated views of the weakness of pupils of Asian origin and may be reluctant to attack directly what they see as powerful religious and cultural factors which stand in the way of these pupils' enthusiastic participation in physical education. They will tend to concentrate upon stimulating the already existing interest in physical activities of other pupils, allowing the sometimes reluctant and relatively unskilled pupils of Asian origin to drop out of physical education in all but presence.

Schools which for the first time had large numbers of pupils of Asian origin often found that they were offering an inappropriate physical education curriculum. Sometimes, for example, they were placing a great deal of emphasis upon team games for boys such as rugby, a game which is less suited to pupils of generally smaller stature and slighter physique (Wills 1980). Some schools ignored the change in their pupil composition, and continued to insist on everyone following the traditional curriculum with the goal, increasingly unrealized, of producing successful sports teams. Other schools decided to think through the new situation and redesign the curriculum to stimulate the interest of pupils of Asian origin, along with those from other ethnic groups, in physical education. Games such as rugby, which involve muscular strength and in which weight is sometimes an advantage, have been reduced in emphasis, and greater stress given to skills which are common to a number of different games, sometimes involving the use of smaller and softer balls and bats. Team games like hockey, which are in any case popular with pupils of Asian origin, can be employed in the place of games like rugby in interschool competitions. A gradual construction of a repertoire of physical skills can play a large part in increasing confidence along with interest in a wide variety of sports which many pupils of Asian origin might at first have thought were not seriously open to them at all.

Similar flexibility is required when dealing with girls' games. It is still the case in most schools that mixed physical education is not available – the separation of the sexes being one of the few aspects of girls' physical education of which many Asian parents approve! Trying to teach the traditional girls' games in schools with a significant proportion of pupils of Asian origin can be a very unrewarding activity, and similar changes in the activities offered to the girls to those offered to the boys may usefully be made, with a stress upon the acquisition of basic skills built up in small-game situations.

It may be necessary to abandon the operation of school teams altogether, given the restrictions which parents sometimes place upon their daughters' attendance at games run after school hours or at weekends. This can come as a terrible shock to PE teachers who expect to establish their skill as teachers by the success of their teams in competition with other teams, yet the impossibility of such competitions may be seen in some contexts as an advantage. For instance, a move away from the selection of and concentration upon élite squads may well lead to more pupils being enthusiastically involved in physical activities at all levels, with a stress upon recreational activities which are often more relevant to postschool leisure than the highly competitive traditional sports. For example, an activity popular with many girls of Asian origin, badminton, is popular among young people as a whole, and can be played successfully in mixed groups. Badminton is more likely to be played by adults, both men and women, than many of the staple activities which many within the physical education profession are still trying to promote. Indeed cultural differences between ethnic groups which make team games less viable may result not in a narrower but rather in a wider physical education curriculum, one which makes greater efforts at involving *all* pupils in physical activities, and thus benefits the physical education of all rather than just those deemed more skilled.

Dance

One of the purposes of offering a multicultural curriculum in the area of movement skills is to make all pupils more aware of the vast variety of ways of moving that are related to cultural background. Thus pupils should know about the different kinds of sport and gymnastics and the variety of forms of dance practised throughout the world. Some schools have tried to spend time on developing games and physical activities which originally come from Africa, the Caribbean or Asia as part of the physical education curriculum, but these have not generally been very successful. Despite the enthusiasm and skill of the teachers involved, there seem to be two reasons for this relative failure. One is that the physical activities which tend to be offered in British schools have a well-defined position in the majority culture which give those activities their social meaning, and the implantation of different activities from other cultures may fail to get a grip. The other reason is that teachers and pupils often suspect that the use of such distinct physical activities can be simply an exercise in the 'exoticizing' of them unless they are placed within the appropriate cultural context, something which it is difficult to do without a great deal of additional work across the curriculum. This is an issue which is considered again later in the chapter.

The position of dance in schools has changed a great deal recently, largely due to the influence of television programmes such as *Fame*, films such as *Saturday Night Fever*, and the popularity of dance as recreation for adults. As with physical education, there is a marked tendency in some schools for pupils of Afro-Caribbean origin to be encouraged to develop dancing skills at the expense of academic skills, and there is once again a plentiful supply of successful black role models in modern dance. Thinking of black pupils as especially skilful at dance is to stereotype them not only as physically strong but also as more expressive and emotional than pupils from different ethnic groups. This may motivate them to achieve success in dance, but will not be of much use in the development of their academic potential. It is worth pointing out that the career prospects for dancers are as irregular and limited as those for sportspersons, and that success is very much dependent upon a continuation of physical skills and stamina – very few blacks will enter the more managerial or choreographic levels of dance and sport administration. The worlds of sport and dance are hierarchies, and blacks have as role models people who are clearly at the bottom of those hierarchies, a point which is frequently forgotten by those who think that the presence of successful role models will of itself increase the self-esteem and reduce the underachievement of blacks as a whole.

The introduction of ethnic dance into the curriculum can be immensely rewarding in any school. For one thing, it provides an interesting link with different kinds of world music which can considerably broaden pupils' knowledge (see also Chapter 11). Most significant, perhaps, is the fact that the basic principles of ethnic dance are so dissimilar that they lead to the exercise of a very varied series of movement skills. West African dance, for instance, emphasizes the use of the bulk of the body with a very low centre of gravity, while some kinds of Asian dance place a great deal of emphasis upon the hands and neck, with a staggering expressiveness based upon different symbols which these parts of the body can represent. Both forms of dance contrast sharply with aspects of most European dance, with its high centre of gravity, rigid body bulk and emphasis upon uprightness. It is not surprising that dissimilar cultures should express themselves differently through the medium of dance, and this diversity can be used by the dance teacher to increase both pupils' movement vocabulary and their understanding of different lifestyles and countries. The teacher may be able to learn from ethnic minority pupils for whom traditional dance might still play an important part in recreational activities, and work with those pupils to develop movement phrases which can be shared with the whole class; the class could be led to discuss why ethnic dance forms have the form they do, how they are connected with religious and social attitudes and so on. This would be to use different dance forms not just to increase pupils' repertoire of movements but also to increase understanding of ethnic cultures in a valuable way.

Of course, it is often difficult to tap this kind of source. A school may have no ethnic minority pupils, or those there are may not be forthcoming about dance. Fortunately there are in existence a small number of dance in education groups which are concerned with a broad range of ethnic dances, including European and Far Eastern, and which are prepared to travel to schools and explore with pupils and teachers the possibilities of using dance to aid understanding of different cultures. One such example is the Ludus group. There are also centres such as the National Academy of Indian Dance, Felix Cobbson's Aklowa and the DRUM Arts Centre which make available tuition in West African and West Indian dance. On a small scale in different schools there is encouragement of ethnic minority activities in the curriculum, but much more progress could be made. In the first place, only a very small number of teachers in our schools are trained to teach dance. Those who are dance teachers may not have the requisite flexibility to use their skills to make sense of and adapt ethnic dance for their pupils. They may quite justifiably be nervous about the dangers and difficulties involved. Very little if anything in their training will have prepared them for this sort of work. It is worth mentioning too that there are considerable practical difficulties involved in using ethnic dance. For example, some pupils of Afro-Caribbean origin are not keen to try out traditional African dances, seeing this as an attempt to deny their status as Britons. Black pupils may not have a positive image of their roots in Africa and may regard the efforts of dance teachers to use aspects of African dance with all their pupils as at best patronizing and at worst insulting. One of the problems in involving black boys in dance in the quite recent past was that many of them saw dance as effeminate and no part of the persona of masculinity which they were trying to construct, although, indeed, one of the interesting aspects of African dance is that it uses as many male as female dancers. However, now boys as well as girls have been swept up in the new enthusiasm for dance, more boys may well feel that being macho and being a dancer go hand in hand! Yet the teacher has to be sensitive to the particular individuals in the class and should be wary of innovations which might provoke hostility and resentment when applied all at once.

One of the advantages of having an ethnically varied class is that the pupils may learn different ways of moving by observing and learning from each other. When such lessons are successful they can be very exciting for all concerned. An important aspect of modern educational dance is the notion that pupils will think about and develop their own movement ideas, working together and comparing their performance with those of others. Pupils who are accustomed to dancing in just one sort of way are often stimulated by trying out new techniques based on different cultures, especially when those techniques are very dissimilar from their own. Yet it is important to emphasize yet again that it is far from easy to bring about this desirable state of affairs. It is not difficult to produce what can only be called a pastiche of a different culture's dance forms which, due to its apparent simplicity and lack of interest, may fail to motivate pupils either to learn how to dance in that way or to enquire into the culture which produced that sort of dance. Unfortunately, quite a bit of this crude misrepresentation goes on in schools, and it is often due to limitations in the training of the dance teacher. A large number of the dance teachers in British schools have comparatively little training even in the techniques current in the majority culture, and it is unrealistic to expect them to master, or at least feel comfortable with, a variety of different forms of dance which are very distinct from each other. Yet teachers who do not use the different forms of movement which exist in a multicultural class as a resource are limiting the learning of their pupils.

Right across the movement spectrum *all* pupils should be given the opportunity and encouraged to experience the full range of movement qualities and not just those with which they immediately feel familiar. Ethnic diversity in the dance lesson gives pupils the chance to observe and work with others who do not display the same movement characteristics as themselves, and this can only be of educational value.

Outdoor pursuits

The very varied activities which are offered in many schools under the label of outdoor pursuits can be very useful in bringing pupils of different ethnic groups together. Many of the activities involved, such as canoeing, climbing, camping, orienteering and sailing, have as important constituents the cooperation of pupils in circumstances of some degree of danger, with perhaps also the experience of living and working together intensively for a period. As far as social education is concerned, outdoor pursuits can be very effective. Yet there is some evidence that pupils of Afro-Caribbean origin do not take part in such activities in the numbers one would expect, sometimes for financial reasons. It is perhaps worth suggesting that no pupil should be prevented from participating in outdoor pursuits solely due to lack of financial support, and any sensible multicultural policy should seek to ensure that no one is excluded on economic grounds from any activity which the school regards as educationally important. Asian parents often regard outdoor pursuits as frivolous activities not relevant to their children's education, and so are reluctant to release them for weekends. Girls of Asian origin often come up against strong opposition from their families should they wish to go on these trips, which in effect is often to deny them any opportunity while young to acquire outdoor skills, and experience of living for a short period with their peers in a structured yet enjoyable manner. The question of girls of Asian origin will be discussed again shortly.

Conclusion

In this last section I would like to draw some general implications from the previous discussion. Physical education teachers should be critical of their frequent practice of explaining differences in performance between pupils from different ethnic groups as though they reflected natural characteristics which inevitably differ along ethnic lines. It certainly is the case that most PE teachers report that their pupils of Asian origin tend to be of small stature and slight physique, with less strength and stamina than pupils of Afro-Caribbean origin, who appear to mature earlier than their peers and so have an advantage when it comes to employing speed, strength and jumping ability. Teachers often say that black girls are better at activities which involve muscular power, endurance and strength, while other pupils excel at some activities like swimming where flexibility, rhythm and coordination are important. Girls of Asian origin are sometimes assumed to be so physically frail that they can hardly be expected to bring themselves to do anything physical at all! Yet these stereotypes can be very misleading. There is often more variety within an ethnic group than between groups as far as physical characteristics are concerned, and many of the so-called 'natural' differences seem heavily affected by cultural factors. For example, black pupils are supposed by many to be naturally better at activities which involve strength and stamina, yet they do not tend to perform so well in swimming, which actually does require both strength and stamina.

Thinking of pupils from different ethnic groups as having certain naturally defined physical characteristics can be very limiting, and indeed may form a self-fulfilling prophecy. A pupil who is regarded by the PE teacher as naturally gifted in athletics will tend to act as if he or she *is* thus gifted, and vice versa. It is not uncommon to see pupils in physical education classes who appear to have similar physical characteristics, but who perform quite differently because their teachers have different attitudes towards them. Physical education teachers should think very carefully about the distinctions they may make between the 'natural' abilities of pupils from different ethnic groups. They should consider whether they are excluding some pupils from meaningful participation in physical activities by their negative views of their 'natural' abilities. One of the criteria in adopting a multicultural curriculum is sensitivity to the opinions and attitudes of the communities from which the pupils themselves come. The PE teacher needs to develop contact with these communities to explain to parents the educational purposes of physical activities and why it is important for their children, both boys and girls, to participate in those activities. It is certainly true that as much flexibility as possible should be applied to rules concerning dress, showers and the physical activities themselves in order to reflect the sensibilities of the parents. Yet there comes a point at which the PE teacher has to try to explain that it is not necessarily flirtatious for a Muslim girl to dance or take part in gymnastics and athletics before others, and that restrictive clothing may well hide much of her body but it will also prevent her from performing adequately in many areas of the physical education curriculum. If teachers seriously believe that physical education is an important part of the curriculum, and that some ethnic minority girls are prevented from playing their full part in that aspect of the curriculum, then they and the school must argue on behalf of those girls with their parents. It may be that such an approach would be labelled as 'cultural imperialism' because it assumes that other conceptions of the role of women are inferior to Western ideas, yet there is surely a need for serious debate when such conceptions stand in the way of equal opportunities. One of the features of liberal education is the desire to widen the opportunities and ideas available to all pupils, thereby presenting them with alternative lifestyles as options to be accepted or rejected. In this context, girls of Asian origin undoubtedly should be presented with the opportunity of participating fully in physical education, dance and outdoor pursuits – this should represent a right available to all pupils in the British education system. We should not allow parents from whatever ethnic group to deny this right to their children without protest and persuasion.

The burden of the argument in this chapter has been to suggest that a mixed-ability approach to the teaching of physical education and dance is the method which fits in best with the notion of a multicultural curriculum. Such an approach is best equipped to provide all pupils with the means of gaining access to, and the enthusiasm to use, the recreational and sporting facilities and opportunities which exist. Attitudes to leisure are important constituents of a person's lifestyle and personality, and they are capable of making a sizeable contribution to the value and enjoyment of an individual life. Physical education teachers are certainly not the only people in schools who have a responsibility for preparing children to make worthwhile use of their present and future leisure, yet they are surely among the most important. Far from making this preparatory task more difficult, the introduction of multicultural considerations makes it easier, since these considerations involve designing a curriculum which will enable all pupils to benefit from physical education regardless of their abilities. We saw when discussing the different levels of performance in physical education and the different styles of performance in dance how important it is to rearrange the curriculum so that every pupil will gain from these physical activities. If the stress is on cooperation and closely observing and learning from the performance of one's peers, then we shall have a curriculum which genuinely encourages the participation of every single pupil. What this requires is teachers who are well trained and flexible enough to take account of different teaching situations so as to maximize the physical and expressive potential of all their pupils.

It should be stressed that physical education, dance and outdoor pursuits from only one area of the school's curriculum and that this area cannot be expected to work miracles by itself. A teacher who is trying to get pupils in a physical education class to work together by encouraging interethnic groups will find life difficult if in the rest of the school there is a poor atmosphere of racial harmony. Similarly, a dance teacher who is concerned to use ethnic dance to put forward ideas about different cultures and societies will be working in a vacuum if other parts of the curriculum either ignore completely or fail to consider seriously those cultures. In any multicultural strategy physical education, dance and outdoor pursuits must be integrated with the rest of the curriculum. It is unfortunate that at the moment physical activities are regarded as rather marginal to the central concerns of many schools, and PE teachers are not usually drawn into discussions about multicultural policies in education which are thought to relate more immediately to the academic aspects of the curriculum. This is particularly unfortunate since the physical education and dance teachers have arguably had considerable success in integrating pupils from different ethnic groups in their lessons while at the same time using their cultural differences to educational advantage.

References

Carrington, B. (1982) Sport as a sidetrack. *In* L. Barton and S. Walker (eds.) *Race, Class and Education*. London: Croom Helm.

Carrington, B. and Wood, E. (1982) School, sport and the black athlete, *Physical Education Review* Vol 5, pp. 131–7.

Cashmore, E. (1982) *Black Sportsmen*. London: Routledge and Kegan Paul.

Leaman, O. (1983) *Sit on the sidelines and watch the boys play*, Schools Council Programme 3 Pamphlet Series. York: Longman.

Wills, M. (1980) *Physical Education in a multicultural society*. Coventry: Elm Bank Teachers' Centre.

AUTHOR INDEX

SUBJECT INDEX